THE HISTORY OF STARVED ROCK

THE HISTORY OF STARVED ROCK

MARK WALCZYNSKI

NORTHERN ILLINOIS UNIVERSITY PRESS
AN IMPRINT OF
CORNELL UNIVERSITY PRESS
ITHACA AND LONDON

First published 2020 by Cornell University Press

Printed in the United States of America

Library of Congress Cataloging-in-Publication Data

Names: Walczynski, Mark, author.
Title: The history of Starved Rock/Mark Walczynski.
Description: DeKalb, IL : NIU Press, 2020. | Includes bibliographical
   references and index.
Identifiers: LCCN 2019026063 (print) | LCCN 2019026064 (ebook) |
   ISBN 9781501748240 (paperback) | ISBN 9781501748264 (pdf) |
   ISBN 9781501748257 (ebook)
Subjects: LCSH: Illinois Indians—Illinois—Starved Rock State
   Park—History. | Kaskaskia Indians—History. | Indians of North
   America—Illinois—Illinois River Valley—History. | Starved Rock
   State Park (Ill.)—History. | Illinois River Valley (Ill.)—History.
Classification: LCC F547.L3 W35 2020 (print) | LCC F547.L3 (ebook) |
   DDC 977.3/5—dc23
LC record available at https://lccn.loc.gov/2019026063
LC ebook record available at https://lccn.loc.gov/2019026064

CONTENTS

THE HISTORY OF STARVED ROCK

INTRODUCTION

Throughout its long history, Starved Rock has been known by many names. Lost to time, today we can only know some of these, and only those that come to us from the relatively recent past since the last quarter of the seventeenth century. Names such as "Le Rocher" (the Rock) and "Rockfort" have been used to describe Starved Rock's formidability. During the last one hundred fifty years, titles such as "the Gibraltar of the West" boasted of the site as a place of strategic defense, ironically during times of general peace and prosperity that earlier occupants of the Starved Rock area never enjoyed. Despite the colorful characterizations that these names conjure up, very little is known about the history of the famous rock.

While archaeologists, historians, and students of the French period in the upper Illinois Valley are familiar with the names of Marquette, Jolliet, La Salle, Tonti, and Charlevoix, it has been my experience that few know much about the wonderful eighteenth-, nineteenth-, and early twentieth-century history of Starved Rock. When surveying people with some knowledge of it, the most common narrative recounted is one of an Indian tribe taking refuge atop Starved Rock while the tribe's Indian enemies took up the watch below. Unable to hunt for food, the people atop the rock starved, thus providing the name for that place. In fact, this is simply a legend—a tale of carnage, bloodshed, and revenge that became enhanced and altered in each retelling, at a time when communications over long distances were unreliable. The legend has become part of the fabric of the place called Starved Rock and still provides an interesting footnote. More interesting and exciting is the real history of the site. It is one that resides in the deep recesses of both public and private historical collections, in archival libraries of Canada and France, and in the archaeological record. Unlike the word-of-mouth legend, the factual history of this place has not been easily or eagerly passed down through generations. The history of Starved Rock relies not on tales of bloodshed and revenge but on the unique strategic and international significance of Starved Rock, from the first days of the French in the Illinois Country.

The forces of nature exemplified by warming, cooling, and flooding carved and scraped Starved Rock into what it is today. Glaciers that had once spread across the North American continent had acted like huge, mile-high snowplows pushing debris, rocks, and other material from the north and into Illinois. We can see evidence of the glaciers' thrust southward in glacial debris—formed "C-shaped" hills called moraines, where today on their summits, wind turbines harness another force of nature. About 18,000 years ago, the land that was to become Starved Rock lay beneath the massive weight of the glaciers. Back and forth these mountains of ice had moved, flowing south when the Earth's temperatures cooled, and conversely melting and withdrawing when temperatures warmed. Eventually, the climate warmed and the glaciers began to melt, trapping water behind the moraines. When these glacially made dams could no longer hold the ever-increasing volume of water behind them, they gave way. Water poured over the landscape and eventually carved out the Illinois Valley. The powerful torrents, however, could not raze the sandstone at all places in the valley. Instead, massive flows of meltwater cut channels around the sandstone, forming islands that include what is now Buffalo Rock and Starved Rock. When the ice disappeared and the waters subsided, plants and animals again populated the valley and eventually people began moving into the Starved Rock area. Since that time, land that today comprises Starved Rock State Park and the adjacent countryside was nearly continuously occupied by Native Americans until the early nineteenth century. Items manufactured and used by the Archaic, Woodland, and Mississippian cultures have been found throughout the Starved Rock area. Although the Rock itself was not an occupied Native American site *per se*, like a semi-permanent village, it was a place where, for millennia, Native Americans camped, sojourned, and in a few instances had their earthly remains interred. With the advent of agriculture, small-scale villages were established nearby and grew over time. West and north of Starved Rock, along the ancient river channels that once crisscrossed the Illinois Valley, aboriginal people hunted, fished, and farmed. Most researchers believe that these adaptive and industrious people, living in a culture in which iron and steel had yet to be introduced—from approximately 10,000 years ago until about the mid-1600s,—made the best technology out of what nature provided, continually adapting and improving methods and tools they employed to kill fish and game, cook and store food, construct dwellings, and manufacture watercraft. Oblivious to the movement of Europeans from the Old World to the New, the Indians in the Starved Rock area established a village named Kaskaskia, after the Illinois subtribe that lived there, just upstream from the Rock. European trade goods that made the chores of killing, cleaning, and cooking easier, reached the Kaskaskia a decade or so before French missionaries and traders made their debut at Starved Rock. To facilitate trade with the Illinois and other tribes who lived in the Starved Rock area, men working under the direction of René-Robert Cavelier, sieur de La Salle, built Fort St. Louis on the summit of the Rock during the winter of 1682–1683. In 1691, the Kaskaskia Indians and the other Illinois subtribes that lived near the fort moved away when the area's natural resources could no longer sustain their growing population. With both religious and financial interests bound to the Indians, the French followed. Two decades later, the Peoria Indians—another Illinois subtribe—and a few Frenchmen would return to the upper Illinois Valley to live in relative obscurity. By the early nineteenth century, American frontier settlers would arrive and change the entire dynamic of the Starved Rock area. Their attitudes concerning the use of lands and waterways, and their exploitation of natural resources, embodied values that would have seemed utterly foreign to the Indians who proceeded them.

Starved Rock became Illinois' second state park in 1911 and first opened to the public under state management in 1912. The purchase of Starved Rock was in itself a remarkable bit of foresightedness by the State of Illinois, one which may have saved the site from ultimate destruction. As a state park, Starved Rock has been visited by millions of people, many of whom have come to see the bald eagles, view the beautiful Illinois Valley, or simply to relax. The Starved Rock Hotel, built in 1891, was an important place for visitors to stay and get a good meal. Over Labor Day weekend, in 1923, Starved Rock State Park hosted over 50,000 visitors, many of whom drove to the site in simple automobiles—10,000 of them— over narrow country roads.

Today visitors come from all over the world—places such as India, China, Poland, Mexico, Nigeria, and Australia. Although fishermen, hunters, birders, hikers, photographers, picnickers, and artists can be seen throughout the park on any given day, every now and then a few curious individuals come to the park to learn about the Rock's past. They view the site through the eyes of inquisitive historians. For them, the Starved Rock Visitor Center has displays such as the Newell Fort exhibit, historical videos, and a bookstore that sells several well-written and scholarly books on the Rock's past. The Starved Rock Foundation conducts guided hikes that give park visitors insightful and informative tours of the cliffs and canyons.

This is a unique book about Starved Rock. Rather than reference Starved Rock in the larger context of historical events that occurred in Canada, Louisiana, the Illinois Country, the Northwest Territory, and the state of Illinois, this book instead views historical events from the perspective of Starved Rock, tracing history as it unfolds on and around the famous site. This book is not a detailed biography of the French explorer La Salle or an assessment of his enterprise at Le Rocher, as Starved Rock was known between 1680 and 1683.[1] Nor does this book attempt to refute any of the many versions of the legend of Starved Rock, a fictional account of the alleged destruction of the Illinois Indians at the site in 1769 that gained considerable notoriety during the late nineteenth and early twentieth centuries.[2] It is my sincere hope that in this book I have provided insight into some of the little-known historical events that occurred in this special place we call Starved Rock. Although some people might be disappointed that park legends have been exposed as tall-tales or myths, the real story of real people who did real things should more than compensate for any disillusionment.

Part 1

STARVED ROCK IN THE SEVENTEENTH CENTURY

1673–1679:
THE BLACK ROBE ARRIVES AT KASKASKIA

(Kaaskaaskinki waahpiiwa mahkateehkoreya)

On a late August-early September day in 1673, two bark canoes carrying seven Frenchmen and an Indian boy ascended the Illinois River near today's Utica, Illinois. In the party were Louis Jolliet, a Canadian fur trader, and Jacques Marquette, a Jesuit missionary. They were returning north from their voyage of discovery, a journey that took them from the Jesuit mission located at Michilimackinac—today's St. Ignace, Michigan—to an Indian village presumably located near the mouth of the Arkansas River. These men were the first *known* Europeans to have navigated the Illinois River. Paddling up the shallow and rock-strewn Illinois, the men observed several tall and steep sandstone bluffs along the river's south bank. One of them was today's Starved Rock.

Paddling another mile Jolliet, Marquette, and the crew disembarked at a place the Indians called *kaaskaaskinki* or *kaaskaaskingi* and the French called Kaskaskia, a large Illinois Indian village named for the Illinois sub-tribe that lived at the site.[1] Marquette, seeking demographic information about the village to better report on his hopes of converting the Indians to Catholicism, carefully recorded that there were seventy-four "cabins," or a population of about 1,450 people. Religious conversion, trade, and building alliances with the Illinois Indians who lived at Kaskaskia would become the primary reason for French interest in the Starved Rock area.

At the time of first contact between Native Americans and Europeans in the Illinois Country, the predominant Indian tribe of the region was the Illinois. The Illinois were not a single ethnic group but were an association of subtribes including the Kaskaskia, Peoria, Cahokia, Tamaroa, Coiracoentanon, Chinko, Chepoussa, Espeminkia, and Tapouaro, and others who shared a common culture, customs, and language. Linguistically, the Illinois spoke a language in the Eastern Great Lakes group of Algonquian that is known today as Miami-Illinois.[2] Seventeenth-century French missionaries in the Illinois Country noted that the Illinois called their intertribal alliance "In8ca" (Inoca), the names "Illiniwek" and "Illini" being corruptions of the Illinois name.[3]

The Illinois maintained a seasonal cyclical subsistence pattern. Every spring, the Illinois subtribes gathered at large semi-permanent agricultural villages where they planted staple crops such as maize (*miinčipi*) and squash (*eemihkwaani*). To till the soil and sow their seeds, Illinois women utilized farming tools fashioned from antlers, mussel shells, and stone. After the fields had been planted and the crops had been established, or "hilled up," the Illinois village civil chief would lead the entire Illinois group into the vast upland prairies for a three-to five-week-long communal bison hunt.[4] Everyone in the village contributed in one way or another to the hunt's success: men hunted: women prepared the meat, hides, and bones: and children did menial chores such as gathering wood for fires that were essential for drying meat into jerky. After the hunt was completed, the Illinois packed their bounty and returned to their village. In late summer, they harvested their crops; the women removed the dry maize kernels from the cob using mussel shells, a process we still call "shelling" today. The Indians then placed the shelled maize in underground pits where it remained until the following spring, when it would be either eaten or used as seed for that year's crop. By mid-September, the Illinois would begin to leave the village for their assigned winter hunting camps, dispersing by family or clan group to smaller camps. From autumn until their return to their village in the spring, Illinois men sought game mammals such as deer (*moonswa*) and elk (*mihšiiweewa*) for meat and used their by-products of antlers and hides for clothing, tools, and adornment. The men also hunted and trapped fur-bearing mammals such as beaver (*amehkwaki*), mink (*šinkosaki*), and otter (*kinohšameewa*), whose thick pelts were fashioned into warm clothing that was necessary for wintering in the region. During historic times, 1673 and later, these furs were bartered for European knives, hatchets, kettles, and other trade goods that later became essential to the Illinois. With the approach of spring, the scattered Illinois groups would return to their village where the annual cycle of planting, hunting, harvesting, and dispersing would begin anew.

Not only did the Illinois subsist on what they grew and what they killed, they also gathered nuts and berries, dug assorted roots, and caught fish. A seventeenth-century missionary at an Illinois village reported that the Illinois people ate "14 kinds of roots, which they find in the prairies" and "gather from trees and plants 42 different kinds of fruits, all of which are excellent; and catch 25 sorts of fish—among them, the eel."[5] The Illinois maintained this seasonal cyclical subsistence pattern until the natural resources they depended upon for survival became depleted. When this occurred, the tribe would move their village to a different site where resources were abundant.

The Illinois Indians lived in semi-permanent villages along major Illinois Country rivers for most of the year. At times, other Illinois groups lived near the Des Moines River in Missouri while one native group that would become an Illinois subtribe, the Michigamea, lived as far south as the Arkansas River. They also sojourned at Chequamegon Bay, Green Bay, and on the Fox River in Wisconsin. The Indians had an intimate knowledge of the interconnectedness of the waterways, flowages, and associated portages and used them as highways for trade, travel, and migration.

The Frenchmen, especially Marquette, were well received, so well that the Kaskaskia headmen reportedly "obliged" the missionary to return to their village to teach the people about Marquette's faith and God.[6] While Marquette sincerely believed that the elders had an interest in learning about Roman Catholicism, the Indians already had their own spiritual beliefs. The Kaskaskia Indians may have had a more practical purpose in maintaining a relationship with the Jesuits—one that facilitated access to European trade goods.

After their visit with the Indians, the explorers continued their journey north under the escort of Illinois guides. Entering Lake Michigan, the party paddled the coastlines of Illinois and Wisconsin, and eventually arrived at the St. Francis Xavier mission, near Green Bay, Wisconsin. Since the Jesuit order required missionaries to submit an annual report of their activities, Marquette entrusted Jolliet with his report which, included his journal and map. Jolliet was to deliver the documents to the missionary's superior, Claude Dablon, in Quebec.[7] Leaving the Des Pères mission, Jolliet and the others raced to get to his, Jolliet's, trade post at Sault St. Marie before autumn weather made travel difficult.

Marquette never mentioned Starved Rock in his report. While we can only speculate, there are several reasons for this omission. First, the two explorers saw many rock outcrops and bluffs during their wilderness trek along the rivers of Wisconsin, Iowa, Illinois, Missouri, Kentucky, Tennessee, and Arkansas. A single rocky outcropping would not have more significance than any other. Second and more importantly, Marquette, the author of the journal of the expedition, was primarily interested in locating villages where potential converts lived, not landforms, to record the location of Indian villages. On his 1673 map, Marquette documented the locations of Indian villages, including latitude readings, and recorded

Figure 1.1 A depiction of Jesuit missionary Jacques Marquette meeting the Ilinois Indians at Kaskaskia in 1673. Photo: Mark Walczynski, taken at the Starved Rock State Park Visitor Center, Utica, Illinois.

the names of the tribes who lived in them. Such was the case of the Indians who lived at Kaskaskia. While the Rock would take on later significance as the site of an easily defendable fort, Marquette performed the duties of Jesuit scout, ambassador, and cartographer.

The Kaskaskia Indians had a number of reasons to locate their village site just upriver from Starved Rock. First, the village was situated on or near several important rivers including the Illinois, *Aramoni* (Vermilion) and *Pestek*ouy (Fox). These streams were interconnected, providing access to hunting areas, trade with other tribes, and if necessary, an escape route in case of attack. These waterways were also sources of food and water. North and west of Kaskaskia lay a series of shallow paleo-channels, remnants of the ancient Illinois River where large fish (*kiihkoneehsaki*) such as redhorse carp (*kinoontepeewa*), snapping turtles (*eečipoonkweeyaki*), and other aquatic life could be caught. The channels also provided easy access to beaver (*amehkwaki*), mink (*šinkosaki*), raccoon (*eehsípanaki*), and muskrat (*ahsahkwaki*) that the Indians trapped or hunted with bow and arrow. Large cottonwood trees that grew along the riverbank were ideal for hollowing-out dugout canoes, known as *mihsoori* by the Illinois. Across the river, on land that is now part of Starved Rock State Park, were forested hills where deer (*moonswa*), bear (*mahkwa*), and elk (*mihšiiweewa*) lived, and where fresh clear streams flowed through the piney canyons. West of Kaskaskia roamed herds of bison (*irenanswa*), essential for food, clothing, and other necessities.

Another important factor in the Illinois' choice of Kaskaskia for their village was that the site is located on a sandy terrace, one that was formed by residual sand that remained from the erosion caused by glacial meltwater that carved out the Illinois Valley. Kaskaskia's sandy-loam soil could be easily cultivated with primitive tools such as hoes fashioned from mussel shell, bone, and stone. Archaeological investigations at the site have uncovered the remains of two ceramic vessels that date from Early Woodland times (600–300 BCE), items that are typically associated with agriculture.[8] What is interesting is that Early Woodland occupation of the Kaskaskia site predates that of the Illinois by roughly 1,800 years. The site has also been occupied intermittently by Late Woodland and Mississippian cultures. Considering the archaeological evidence, it appears that the Illinois may have been the last in a long series of groups who occupied the site and who, like their predecessors, relied heavily on agriculture.

Although the Indians used Starved Rock as a campsite and for an occasional burial, nothing in the historical record seems to indicate that the Rock itself had spiritual significance for the Indians. Nonetheless, the Indians probably had a name for the Rock since it was one of the two largest geological features in the vicinity of Kaskaskia. According to Michael McCafferty, a linguist who specializes in the Miami-Illinois language at Indiana University in Bloomington, *aahshipehkwa* meaning "stone cliff, rock formation, bluff" and *kihchi-aahshipehbkwa* "big stone cliff, big rock formation, big bluff" are the terms that the Illinois would have used for a rock face such as Starved Rock. The locative form meaning "on" and "at" would be *aašipehkonki*.[9]

Remaining for a year at the St. Francis Xavier mission recuperating from a serious illness, Marquette left the mission in late October 1674 with two companions, Pierre Porteret and Jacques Largillier, and headed back to Kaskaskia and the Starved Rock area, arriving at the village in April 1675. Marquette was reportedly received "as an angel from heaven" by the Illinois tribesmen.[10] During this visit, he established the Mission of the Immaculate Conception, the first Catholic mission in Illinois. Although he was very ill at the time, Marquette found the strength to personally visit many Illinois cabins and to say Mass on Good Friday and Easter Sunday. Marquette saw that the village population of about 1,450 less than two years prior, had grown to 1,500 men alone. Besides access to European trade goods, the Illinois subtribes had also gathered at Kaskaskia to defend themselves against the Iroquois (Haudenosaunee), also known as the Five Nations, long-time enemies of the Illinois who, rumor held, were planning to raid Illinois villages.

Marquette remained at Kaskaskia only a short time; suffering from a condition that would soon take his life, he hastily left the village, hoping to get to the St. Ignace mission at Michilimackinac to receive medical care, or at least some desperately needed rest. Marquette never reached Michilimackinac; the missionary died, presumably somewhere near today's Ludington, Michigan, on May 19, 1675.

The next European to visit the Starved Rock area was Jesuit Claude-Jean Allouez. Allouez was well-known among the tribesmen of the Great Lakes and North Country, having established missions and worked among the tribes at the St. Esprit mission near Chequamegon Bay, at St. Marc's along the Wolf River in Wisconsin, and at Sault St. Marie at the

Michigan-Ontario border. Allouez had been assigned by Claude Dablon, Jesuit Superior of Canada, to continue Marquette's work among the Illinois at Kaskaskia. Arriving at the village on April 27, 1677, the Indians welcomed the priest and escorted him to his cabin, where, according to his hosts, Marquette had dwelt two years earlier.[11]

Shortly after arriving at Kaskaskia, Allouez began gathering demographic information about the village and its residents. The priest counted 351 cabins at the site, or an approximate population of between 7,000 to 8,000 people. He also noted that besides the crops that the Illinois grew at Kaskaskia and animals that they hunted in the Starved Rock area, the Illinois also ate an assortment of roots, fruits, and nuts and they caught and ate aquatic life such as fish and eels.[12]

On one side of Kaskaskia, Allouez wrote, "is a long stretch of prairie, and on the other a multitude of swamps, which *are* [render the atmosphere] unhealthy and often Covered with fog." These swamps, ancient paleo-channels that course along this stretch of Illinois River, according to the priest, gave rise "to much sickness, and to loud and frequent Peals of thunder." He also wrote that the Illinois "delight, however, in this location [Starved Rock and adjacent bluffs], as they can easily espy from it their enemies."[13]

Allouez wrote that his primary purpose for coming to Kaskaskia was to "acquire the information necessary for the establishment of a complete mission."[14] He also wrote that he baptized at least thirty-five people and taught the Indians how to recite prayers. On the day of the Festival of the Holy Cross, Allouez watched his enthusiastic Indians erect a thirty-five-foot-high cross in the village.

Allouez was pleased with the spiritual progress of his Indians. Even though many tribesmen did not confess Catholicism, most of them still respected Allouez personally. However, notwithstanding the hopeful prognosis for an enduring Christian presence at the site, lurking deep in the minds of the Indians and the missionary were rumors circulating at the time that the Iroquois were planning to attack the Illinois, something that could destroy the priest's hard work and scatter his converts. Concerned, Allouez left Kaskaskia.

Change would come to Kaskaskia and to the Starved Rock area. No longer would the Jesuits be sole envoys of the King and Cross to the Illinois tribes. A new group of men would arrive who, in the eyes of the missionaries, would undercut the inroads they had made into the hearts and minds of the Indians. Leading these men was René-Robert Cavelier, sieur de La Salle.

Cavelier was born in 1643 on an estate near Rouen, France. Young Cavelier received a Jesuit education. He studied logic, physics, metaphysics, and mathematics, the latter an umbrella term that included geography, astronomy, and hydrography. He was a polyglot, reportedly having an exceptional aptitude for languages including Spanish, Arabic, Hebrew, Greek, and Latin.[15] Cavelier, restless and outgoing by nature, felt smothered by Jesuit university life, a regime where conformity, strict discipline, and obedience to a rigid hierarchy were central to the order's *modus vivendi*. No longer able to cope with what he felt were undue restrictions that limited his talents, and finding that his aspirations and those of the order were mutually exclusive, Cavelier left the Jesuits to embark on a new path for his life. Although he was ambitious and well educated, Cavelier had little money. His vow of poverty as a Jesuit forbade him to share in his familial inheritance and French law decreed that this tenet remained even after Cavelier had left the order. Cavelier, however, was not without resources; his brother Jean was a Sulpician priest in Canada and his uncle Henri had been associated with the Company of One Hundred Associates—a private consortium of investors, merchants, government officials, and clerics—organized to develop Canada's trade and establish settlement.[16] With the assistance of his brother, Cavelier hoped to begin anew in New France where his ambitions could be realized. In 1667, he left his native France and sailed to Canada.[17]

Cavelier arrived in Canada and eventually made his way to Montreal where he obtained a piece of land from the Sulpicians. In 1669 and 1670, Cavelier led two expeditions from Montreal, south and west into the wilderness, intending to locate a water route that led to the sea and ultimately Mexico. Although speculation abounds, no one knows for certain how far La Salle had traveled during the two expeditions.[18]

Cavelier's adventures did not go unnoticed. In 1673 Canada governor Louis de Buade, Comte de Frontenac et de Palluau sent Cavelier west to arrange a council between the governor and Iroquois leaders to persuade the Iroquois to allow the French to erect a fort/trading post at Katarakoüi, present-day Kingston, Ontario. Both Cavelier and Frontenac were successful in their undertakings and shortly after the council had ended, the French erected Fort Frontenac.[19] The next year, Cavelier sailed to France. There, Cavelier presented letters of recommendation from the governor to the French Court that requested that Cavelier be granted seigniorial rights to the negotiated property, and also be granted a patent of nobility. The Court approved both of the governor's petitions and Cavelier, now a nobleman, could be called La Salle.

In 1677, La Salle returned to France where he petitioned French finance minister Jean-Baptiste Colbert for permission to explore the western lands of New France where Jolliet and Marquette had reported seeing large herds of bison, as many as four hundred of them in a single herd, ambling in the tall grass prairies. La Salle reasoned that bison hides were "capable of building up a great commerce and of supporting powerful colonies." La Salle further explained that buffalo hides were bulky and cumbersome, which made them difficult to haul in canoes. Because of this, he requested permission to locate a fort near the mouth of the Mississippi, where the hides could be loaded on to ships sailing to France.[20] La Salle was granted a five-year patent; in that term, La Salle was to discover the western part of New France. He was permitted to build forts wherever necessary, but he was permitted to trade only in buffalo hides and he was strictly forbidden to acquire peltry destined for Montreal.[21]

While he was still in France, La Salle sought investors to help fund his enterprise. He also recruited carpenters, sawyers, blacksmiths, and other tradesmen, men whose skills would be needed to build ships, boats, and forts, and who knew how to fashion tools from a few bits of scrap metal and keep the muskets firing. Signing on with La Salle was Henri Tonti, a military man who had served in both the French army and navy. Tonti would eventually become La Salle's most trusted lieutenant, and would also play an important role in the French occupation at Starved Rock.[22] With a crew hired and arrangements apparently in good order, La Salle and company sailed to Canada.

La Salle planned to navigate the Great Lakes and western rivers to reach the Gulf of Mexico where he would build a fort. Along his route, he intended to construct forts to secure strategic points, establish trade alliances with regional tribes, and build sailing vessels to carry hides, men, and materiel to the Gulf. La Salle was sure that his new enterprise would be a success. He had studied at least one of Jean-Baptiste-Louis Franquelin's maps of the western waterways, a chart based on information Franquelin had received from Jolliet when he and Marquette had paddled the central portion of the Mississippi. Moreover, La Salle knew that Jolliet had also met with Claude Dablon, and reported to him that except for a single portage near today's Chicago, a bark (a large sailing vessel) could easily sail from Niagara to the Gulf.[23] Considering that Franquelin's map and Jolliet's report were the best sources available for information on the western lands and waters at the time, La Salle was confident that his expedition would be a success.

After La Salle arrived in Quebec, he instructed a number of his men to proceed to Fort Frontenac, the expedition's embarkation point. A few months later he dispatched a group of men that included carpenters to a site located above Niagara Falls, near present-day Buffalo, New York. La Salle directed this second group to build a palisaded enclosure to shelter the men and store supplies. It was at this location that the men would build a vessel known to history as the *Griffon*, a ship to carry trade goods and supplies west and heavy bison hides back east. This vessel was vital to the success of La Salle's enterprise.

La Salle also sent two advance parties west to trade with bison hunting tribes such as the Otoe, the Iowa, and the Illinois. Leading one of the parties was Michael Accault, an experienced bison hide trader who had signed on with La Salle prior to the explorer's second voyage to France. La Salle wrote that Accault was familiar with the "ways" of these tribes and was also acquainted with some of their dialects including Chiwere, the language of the Siouan speaking Otoe and Iowa. After collecting a load of bison hides, Accault and his men were to transport the commodities to a designated location on an island in Lake Michigan. There the hides would be loaded onto La Salle's ship and carried east.

After leaving Niagara, La Salle's ship sailed to Michilimackinac to deliver goods and to pick up a load of hides that one of the advance parties should have acquired. However, rather than proceed to the Illinois as instructed by La Salle, several members of the advanced party deserted and took with them trade goods valued at 5,300 *livres*. Four other deserters remained at Michilimackinac, where they were arrested by La Salle. These four men told the explorer that they deserted because from the beginning of the expedition there had been talk among the crew members that the voyage would end in disaster, that the *Griffon* would never reach Michilimackinac, and that the entire enterprise was "chimerical," or delusory and unrealistic.[24] La Salle was furious at the men's duplicity as he trusted them and even loaned some of them money, on generous terms, to pay off their creditors so they could join his expedition. La Salle directed Tonti and six men to find and arrest two other deserters who were reported to have fled to Sault St. Marie. La Salle's ship then left Michilimackinac and sailed to the island where Accault was waiting with a shipment of bison hides. There the hides, worth more than twelve thousand *livres*—a substantial amount—were loaded onto the ship. La Salle instructed the captain to deliver the cargo to Niagara, to pick up a load of goods waiting there, and then return to Michilimackinac where he would receive further instruction.[25] It appears that the captain would have been instructed by La Salle to next sail south and to the mouth of the St. Joseph River in Michigan's Lower Peninsula.

La Salle and his party left Michilimackinac and paddled down the western and southern shores of Lake Michigan. Edging the shorelines of Wisconsin, Illinois, and Indiana, they eventually reached Michigan's St. Joseph River. There La Salle's men built a small unimposing structure called Fort Miami. In late November, La Salle was joined there by Tonti and his party, along with several captured deserters. Responding to La Salle's inquiry about whether or not he had seen the *Griffon* during his trek to the St. Joseph, Tonti reported that he had neither seen the vessel nor had he learned of its whereabouts. Concerned about the status of his missing ship, La Salle dispatched two men to return north to find the vessel, or at least learn where it had been last seen, and report their findings. The explorer and the French group left the Miami fort and began their trek to the Illinois Country, hoping to arrive at Kaskaskia before the onset of winter.

The French paddled up the St. Joseph, trudged through the marshy portage that led to the Kankakee River, and then followed that stream to the Forks, where the Kankakee converges with the Des Plaines to form the Illinois River. The stoic La Salle prodded his men along. Suffering cold, hardship, and likely hunger, La Salle's men, mostly urbanites, skilled tradesmen from France, fully realized just how far from civilization they had strayed. They found themselves in an alien territory, an expanse of land that seemed to stretch to the ends of the earth, where a simple mishap or Indian ambush could take their lives. Fear and anxiety were surely omnipresent. Travel was dreadfully slow, and tempers likely flared. The men in La Salle's party were led to believe that they would find food and shelter at Kaskaskia, the Illinois village near Starved Rock.

2

1680–1682: EVERYTHING IS DIFFICULT

(Čeeki kiikoo aarimatwi)

On January 1, 1680, La Salle's party passed the mouth of the river *Pestek-ouy*, the Fox River of Illinois, and soon afterward saw the immense sandstone bluff known today as Buffalo Rock. After gaining another mile, they at last viewed their destination, Kaskaskia. Approaching the village, the men saw no signs of life as Indians had left the site several months earlier for winter hunting camps downstream. After pulling their canoes ashore, the men searched the deserted village for food, eventually locating the Indian's buried maize cache.[1] Likely following La Salle's instructions, the men loaded about forty bushels of the grain into their canoes.

While the men rummaged for food, Father Zénobe Membré, one of three Recollect missionaries attached to La Salle's group, began surveying the village, hoping to learn what he could about the Indians who lived at Kaskaskia. La Salle wrote that Membré counted 460 Indian cabins at the site, a number representing over 9,000 people. It is likely that La Salle understood the correlation between the number of people who lived at Kaskaskia and the number of Illinois hunters who could provide him with bison hides.

La Salle and his men continue their trek down the Illinois River. Paddling their canoes through the knee-deep and rocky waters, La Salle's party saw two, tall sandstone features, today's Eagle Cliff and Lover's Leap bluff, and Starved Rock. Winding their way through a series of islands, the group eventually passed the mouth of the Vermilion River, where the Illinois' current slowed and the waters deepened. They continued their slow and deliberate journey downstream, arriving at Lake Pimiteoui, or Lake Peoria, four days later.

The next morning La Salle and his men left camp and stopped at a winter village of Illinois Indians consisting of eighty cabins located along the shore of the lake. There La Salle, likely with the aid of an interpreter who could speak the Miami-Illinois language, addressed the chiefs and elders of the village at a council.[2] He first presented the Illinois headmen with gifts. After some coaxing, La Salle was able to induce the Illinois to accept his offer of payment for the maize he and his men had taken from Kaskaskia. The council ended amicably. However, that night a Miami chief named Moonswa, the Deer, mysteriously appeared at the Illinois camp. Moonswa had been sent by Father Allouez, who was then living in Wisconsin, to turn the Illinois—the priest's Indian friends and Catholic converts—against La Salle. Moonswa claimed that La Salle was reviled by the Jesuits, proven friends of the Illinois, and that the explorer had collaborated with their Iroquois enemies. Moonswa also claimed that the explorer possessed a potion that could kill everyone in the village. After delivering his message and a few obligatory gifts to the Illinois, Moonswa and his companions disappeared quietly into the night.

Not only had Allouez sent Moonswa to turn the Illinois against La Salle, it also appears that the missionary attempted to turn some Miami and Mascouten bands against the Illinois in order to destabilize the region, making it difficult for the Illinois to hunt and to trade with La Salle.[3] Furthermore, evidence suggests that Allouez may have also colluded with the Iroquois to convince them to "carry on war against the Illinois."[4] It is in this uneasy and troubled environment of intrigue and influence that La Salle found himself fully immersed.

The next morning, an Illinois chief named Omoahoha met with La Salle in confidence and informed the explorer about Moonswa's late night visit to the village. The explorer was incensed by the news and he planned to counter Moonswa's falsehoods at a feast and council planned for later that day.

At the council, La Salle sat uneasily through a lengthy and meaningless harangue delivered by a principal village chief named Nicanapé, who attempted to dissuade the explorer from continuing his voyage to the Mississippi. Eventually, La Salle had his opportunity to speak. Likely through an interpreter, the explorer first addressed Nicanapé's concerns for his safety and those of his men. He then lashed out at the Illinois for their gullibility, for believing Moonswa's lies. La Salle demanded that they answer to him why Moonswa came in secret and at night. He also told the chiefs that if he wanted his Illinois hosts dead, his men could kill them now, if they chose to do so. Although La Salle had ably defended himself, some Illinois tribesmen still remained suspicious of the French group. Several Frenchmen became fearful of the Indians and deserted that night, returning to the Great Lakes by the same route they took to get to Lake Peoria. La Salle decided to leave the Illinois village and establish a base a short distance downstream where his men would build Fort de Crèvecoeur.

Of the Roman Catholic religious orders that labored in New France during the time of La Salle, the Jesuits were the most influential. Arriving in Canada first in 1611 and then again in 1625, the Jesuits set out to instruct the tribes in "the way into heaven."[5] Having limited success converting the indigenous people of eastern Canada to Catholicism, the Jesuits took aim at tribes such as the Wendat (Huron) who lived in large semi-permanent summer agricultural villages in Huronia, southern Ontario, for much of the year. After the destruction of Wendat villages and those of the regional Erie and Neutral by the Iroquois during the late 1640s and early 1650s, the Jesuits next focused on other native groups who gathered in large numbers at places such as Sault St. Marie and at La Pointe, the latter located near today's Ashland, Wisconsin.

Not only did the Jesuits attempt to convert and instruct the tribes in the ways of Catholicism, they also sought information about the region's lands, waterways, and inhabitants. Allouez learned of the large Illinois Indian tribe and the Mississippi River that traversed Illinois lands during his time among the La Pointe tribes. Marquette planned to visit the Illinois villages during the fall of 1671.[6] Unfortunately for the priest, intertribal conflict that erupted between the La Pointe tribes and the Sioux who lived west of La Pointe, and the consequent relocation of the La Pointe tribes to today's St. Ignace, Michigan and Manitoulin Island, delayed Marquette's visit until 1673. During the mid-1670s, both religious and secular interests sought to establish themselves in the Illinois Country: the Jesuits to build missions and convert the Indians to Catholicism and secular interests, including those of Jolliet, to establish trade ties with the Illinois Indians and to start a colony.

The Jesuits won the first round of this rivalry. Marquette returned to Kaskaskia in 1675 and Allouez arrived at the village in 1677 to continue Marquette's work. In 1676 Jolliet petitioned the French Court to establish a colony in the Illinois Country. His request was denied as French authorities hoped to consolidate Canada's population along the Lower St. Lawrence Valley rather than have it spread across twelve hundred miles of sparsely inhabited country.

The Jesuits were well aware of the disruptive behavior that some traders and voyageurs, legal and otherwise, exhibited in Indian villages, since hardline missionaries such as Allouez had been summoned by tribal leaders to control the antics of rowdy Frenchmen.[7] With the Jesuits now situated as sole representative to King and Cross at Kaskaskia, and by extension the Illinois Country, Allouez and his Jesuit associates were prepared to do whatever was necessary to keep secular influences away from the lands and the people whose souls the order worked so diligently to save. This included turning the Illinois against La Salle. Without the support of the Illinois, there was little chance that La Salle's enterprise could succeed, because the explorer's royal patent permitted him to trade only in bison hides, and the Illinois were bison hunters. In addition, it appears that Allouez was prepared to turn Native American against Native American. If the Jesuits could set the Miami against their close linguistic and cultural cousins the Illinois, Illinois villages would be vulnerable to Miami attacks, which would cause Illinois hunters to remain at their villages instead of hunting and providing La Salle the buffalo hides he needed to fund his enterprise and his creditors. And with the threat of an Iroquois invasion of the Illinois Country looming in the minds of the Illinois people, the timing of Moonswa's visit and his attempt to convince the tribe that La Salle was an Iroquois agent, could not have been better. It will be seen in chapter 5 that Allouez communicated Jesuit intent to destroy La Salle to Frenchman Henri Joutel, who wintered at Starved Rock in 1687–1688.[8] In fact, the practice of pitting one tribe against another seems to have been standard French policy during this time.[9] The goal of Moonswa's secret visit to the Illinois village was intended to disrupt a relationship that La Salle hoped to form with the Illinois. Without the Illinois as trade partners and hunters, La Salle would likely fail.

Fort de Crèvecoeur was a palisaded fortification located about a mile and a half downstream from the Illinois village at Lake Peoria. Surrounding the fort were natural defenses such as ravines and a marsh, features that were supplemented by a hand-dug trench. The purpose of Fort de Crèvecoeur was not only to protect La Salle, his men, and supplies from enemies, it was also where his sawyers, carpenters, and shipbuilders began construction of a forty-two-foot long vessel weighing forty tons that the explorer hoped to use to complete his voyage to the Gulf. The bark would also be used to transport large quantities of bison hides obtained in the Illinois Country to his proposed fort on the Gulf. The Illinois River at Fort de Crèvecoeur was wide and deep, located far below the rapids of the upper Illinois River. From there, La Salle's bark would have a clear and unobstructed pathway to the Gulf.[10]

It was late February and La Salle had heard nothing about his missing *Griffon*. The vessel was essential for the success of his enterprise. In addition, La Salle's men had run out of rigging, tackle, iron, canvas, and other materials needed to finish the new bark at de Crèvecoeur. Without these items his expedition could go no farther. La Salle needed to travel to his Fort Frontenac seigniory to fetch the materials needed to complete his unfinished bark, and to recruit men to replace those who had deserted. La Salle also had to find out what had become of his ship.

Before leaving Fort de Crèvecoeur, La Salle dispatched three Frenchmen to explore the Mississippi River: Louis Hennepin, a Recollect missionary; Michael Accault; and Antoine Aguel. The best evidence indicates that Accault's mission was to reestablish trade ties with the trans-Mississippi tribes, people with whom he had previously traded, while Hennepin was to introduce Catholicism to them,[11] Before leaving for Fort Frontenac, La Salle gathered his men and beseeched them to obey Tonti, the new commandant. He instructed them to disregard any rumors or gossip told to them by the Indians. He also directed Tonti to keep the men busy, and he likely encouraged him to learn what he could about Illinois Indian language, customs, or anything else that might contribute to the success of La Salle's expedition. Leaving Tonti in command of fifteen men at Fort de Crèvecoeur, La Salle, Jacques d'Autray, La Violette, Collin, and an Indian hunter began the long, miserable, and wet late-winter trek east.[12]

Slogging their way back up the Illinois River, La Salle's group eventually reached Starved Rock. There the explorer likely took a second and closer look at the bluff. He saw that the rock's steep sides, towering heights, and level surface made it the most defensible site he had yet seen in the Illinois Country, an ideal place to build a fort. The rapids in front of the bluff would provide an added layer of protection from enemies, and Kaskaskia, home to approximately 1,800 Illinois bison hunting warriors, was located only about a mile upstream.[13] These considerations, it will be seen, would soon figure into La Salle's decision to construct a fort on the summit of Starved Rock.

La Salle and his group continued their trek up the Illinois. Somewhere near Kaskaskia the explorer had a chance encounter with three Illinois hunters, one of whom was Chassagoac, the primary chief of the Illinois village at Peoria. After presenting him a few gifts of friendship, La Salle, likely through his Indian interpreter, pleaded with Chassagoac to bring provisions to Tonti and the others at Fort de Crèvecoeur, promising to repay him for his generosity when he returned to the Illinois Country. The chief understood that by helping the explorer, he was cultivating relations that would eventually benefit his own people. He knew that La Salle and his men represented access to trade goods and perhaps protection from the Iroquois. It was in his people's best interest to do what he could to assist La Salle. The chief assured La Salle that he would bring maize to Tonti and the others at de Crèvecoeur.

La Salle also communicated to Chassagoac that he planned to broker peace between the Iroquois and the Illinois, deliver guns and other goods to the Illinois, and that he hoped to establish a colony in the Illinois Country. The news resonated with the chief, who promised that he would do whatever he could to help the explorer. Confident that an alliance between himself and Chassagoac would be forthcoming, the explorer continued his trek.

Before reaching his fort on the St. Joseph River, La Salle's party met the two men he had previously dispatched to search for his missing ship. The men told La Salle that although they had traveled around Lake

Michigan, they had not seen the ship nor learned of its whereabouts. La Salle instructed the two men to join Tonti and the others at Fort de Crèvecoeur, and to direct Tonti to return to the bluffs near the Kaskaskia village "to visit a high rock, and to build a strong fort upon it."[14] This directive is the first *known* direct written reference to Starved Rock.

Arriving at de Crèvecoeur the men relayed La Salle's orders to Tonti. Sometime later, Tonti left the fort and traveled to Starved Rock. While he was away, most of the men at de Crèvecoeur deserted and took with them anything of value, leaving only a few items that were too heavy or too cumbersome to carry away. For reasons unknown, the deserters also tore down the fort's wooden palisades. Only six men remained of the thirty-three who were with La Salle in January. Furthermore, Tonti and the men with him were not skilled woodsmen who, even if equipped with firearms and knives, would have a difficult time surviving in the wilderness. Their only hope was to live at the mercy of the Illinois, who had since returned to Kaskaskia, and wait for La Salle to return.

The men who deserted from de Crèvecoeur had experienced pangs of hunger, shivering cold, dread, and calamity. They were in an unforgiving land, stuck in a ramshackle wooden enclosure hundreds of miles from the nearest sign of civilization, where Indian attacks were, in their minds, not only possible, but likely. They were tasked with building a vessel to sail to the Gulf but were without the necessary components to complete it. The stern hand of La Salle was gone; he had left for Fort Frontenac. When he would return to de Crèvecoeur was anyone's guess; maybe never. Perhaps too, they were haunted by fond memories of their former lives in France, recounting happier days with family and friends. They had had enough of La Salle, his expedition, and the wilderness. They were going home.

While La Salle was away at Fort Frontenac, he learned that at least twenty deserters from his expedition had been seen on Lake Ontario, some of them along the north shore of the lake en route to Quebec while others along the south shore hoped to reach British-claimed territory in today's New York state. Both groups were headed east, to ports where they hoped to board vessels on which they would to return to France. La Salle also learned that the deserters had destroyed his Miami post, had stolen pelts he had stored at Michilimackinac, and had pillaged the storehouse at his Niagara fort, all likely done to gather funds to pay for their voyage to France. La Salle with a cadre of loyal men set out to find and arrest the deserters. They eventually captured ten men who were jailed at Fort Frontenac, and they killed two others who resisted arrest. The remaining deserters managed to elude the explorer in the rough waters of Lake Ontario and eventually reached British-claimed territory.[15]

Tonti and the men with him arrived at Kaskaskia in April. Despite Illinois suspicions, they were allowed to stay at their village. With La Salle away, the Illinois likely suspected that, as Moonswa had warned, the explorer was negotiating with the Iroquois, formulating a plan to destroy the Illinois. Conversely, if the Illinois did not help Tonti, and the explorer was not among the Iroquois, La Salle might shun the Illinois and establish trade alliances with other tribes. Tonti and the others would remain at Kaskaskia, but the Indians would keep a watchful eye on them.

It is uncertain exactly what Tonti and the others did at Kaskaskia during the summer of 1680. The group surely learned important Miami-Illinois words and phrases, was introduced to Illinois customs, and accompanied the tribe during the summer bison hunt. In addition, Fathers Membré and Ribourde likely ministered to and attempted to instruct the Illinois tribesmen in Catholic teachings. By September, the Illinois had harvested the village crop and placed the grain in underground caches for storage. Illinois clans and family groups began leaving for winter hunting camps. It was at this time that alarming news reached Kaskaskia.

A Shawnee guest, who may have been living at the village, left Kaskaskia and began the long journey to his Ohio Valley homelands. Paddling up the Vermilion River, he stumbled upon a large Iroquois war party camped along its banks. Undetected, the Shawnee returned to Kaskaskia and spread the alarm. The Illinois immediately dispatched scouts to verify the Shawnee's report. The scouts returned with horrific news: approximately six hundred Iroquois and some Miami were within striking distance of Kaskaskia. Making matters worse, the scouts erroneously reported that La Salle was among the Iroquois.[16] The long-anticipated Iroquois invasion of the Illinois Country was at hand.

Illinois suspicions regarding La Salle and the Iroquois seemed justified, and they lashed out at Tonti, accusing him of complicity with the Iroquois. Tonti made it known to the angry tribesmen that he was not a friend of the Iroquois, that he will "die tomorrow" with them and he will fight the Iroquois with the men who are with him.[17] Tonti's words, for the moment, placated the Illinois. To defend themselves and their families, the Illinois leaders were forced by circumstances to make a tough decision: since most of the Illinois had left the village to participate in the winter hunt, only about two thousand Illinois remained at Kaskaskia, and most of these were noncombatants.[18] From this number, the Illinois could muster roughly four hundred warriors to fight at least six hundred Iroquois. To their advantage, the Illinois were intimately familiar with the local terrain, the hills, bluffs, and valleys along the Vermilion River, while the Iroquois probably were not. If the Illinois struck the Iroquois before the Iroquois force arrived at Kaskaskia, the Illinois would gain the psychological advantage. Furthermore, the Iroquois war party was a long way from its logistical support, far from sources to procure arms, ammunition, and other supplies. The Iroquois war captains hoped that some of these items, and food such as maize, would be available to them after they captured Kaskaskia. However, if the Illinois chose to flee downstream, their escape would be hampered by the slowness of the children, elderly, and handicapped in the group. It is also unlikely that the Illinois group would be able to out-paddle well-conditioned warriors who would surely pursue them downstream.

Considering their circumstances, the Illinois knew they had only two options: secure the safety of their families by sending them downstream to hide in the river's backwater swamps while they then attacked the unsuspecting Iroquois, or flee before the Iroquois arrived at Kaskaskia. The Illinois decided to strike the Iroquois.

The Illinois noncombatants boarded *mihsoora* and set off for a designated site in which to hide, a place located about eighteen miles downstream from Kaskaskia. Tonti and the Illinois next threw into the river anything that the Iroquois might find useful including some tools and several scraps of iron. The Illinois men then spent the rest of the night feasting and dancing to boost their courage.

When morning arrived, Tonti led the Illinois warriors across the shallow river and through parts of today's Starved Rock State Park. Gaining the uplands above the timberline, Tonti cautiously guided the Illinois group south through the prairie toward the Iroquois encampment, a site that was likely located somewhere near today's Vermilion Day Use Area in Matthiessen State Park. Somewhere on the plain between the Illinois and Vermilion Rivers, Iroquois scouts spotted the Illinois party headed

Figure 2.1 An illustration of Illinois Indians making a *mihsoori*, a wooden dugout canoe. Photo: Mark Walczynski, taken at the Starved Rock State Park Visitor Center, Utica, Illinois.

toward them and opened fire. At the head of the party, Tonti was tackled and stabbed by a charging Iroquois. Dazed but still very much alive, he was carried to the Iroquois camp. There the Iroquois commanders, speaking through a Sauk interpreter, questioned Tonti, wanting to know what business he had with the Illinois. Tonti informed the Iroquois that the Illinois were under both the king's and the governor's protection. Tonti also communicated to the war captains that he led twelve hundred Illinois and sixty French.[19] The news must have surprised the chiefs. Believing that they had arrived at Kaskaskia while the Illinois were leaving the village for their winter camps, the Iroquois likely hoped to strike a much smaller Illinois force. However, if Tonti was telling the truth, the Illinois and French would outnumber the Iroquois by two to one. The Iroquois next debated what to do with Tonti: should they keep him alive and by doing so preserve the tenuous truce between the French and the Iroquois that both sides had agreed to in 1666, or should they consider Tonti an enemy combatant and ally of the Illinois, and kill him? After a brief but intense debate, the chiefs decided to release Tonti. Tonti was instructed to deliver to the Illinois a necklace, an overture of peace that was intended to bide time in order to determine if Tonti was telling the truth about the size of the Franco-Illinois force. He was also instructed to fetch maize for the hungry Iroquois.

Soon after his release, Tonti reunited with Fathers Membré, and Ribourde, and his Illinois companions. He made it known to the Illinois chiefs that even though the Iroquois had offered them peace, the Iroquois were not to be trusted.

Tonti and his group began the hike back to Kaskaskia. Looming menacingly behind were the Iroquois. Arriving at the village, the Illinois decided that instead of remaining at the site, they would join their families downstream. Tonti and the five French now sat uneasily at Kaskaskia among over six hundred warriors who could claim the village as their own.

Two days later the Illinois returned to Kaskaskia, arriving at the outskirts of the village where they and their Iroquois counterparts exchanged hostages to secure each other's good behavior. Later, the Illinois attempted in good faith to negotiate a peace agreement with their enemies, while the Iroquois feigned interest. It was inevitable that the Iroquois would learn that Tonti had lied to them. An Illinois tribesman, for whatever reason, told the Iroquois the truth—that there was no Franco-Illinois force numbering over twelve hundred men. What the Iroquois had encountered during their skirmish with the Illinois was all that the tribe could muster. The Iroquois chiefs were furious that they had been duped and they ordered Tonti and his men to leave Kaskaskia. Boarding a leaky canoe the next morning, Tonti's group paddled about fifteen miles upstream where they disembarked to dry their wet clothes and cargo. There Father Ribourde entered the timber to pray. He was never seen alive again. Tonti later learned that a Kickapoo war party passing through the area stumbled upon the priest and killed him. A marker at St. Patrick's Catholic Church in Seneca, Illinois, commemorates Ribourde's slaying. The name of two nearby streams, both named Kickapoo Creek, also recall this unfortunate incident.

After a harrowing journey north, the French party reached today's Door County, Wisconsin. Tonti took up residence with a band of Potawatomi while Father Membré headed southwest to the St. Xavier mission located along the Fox River where he found a temporary abode among the Jesuits.

After completing his business in Canada and learning that his ship lay somewhere on the floor of Lake Michigan, La Salle returned to the Starved Rock area, arriving on December 1, 1680. It is probable that from a distance, and before the explorer and his party had reached Kaskaskia, they saw that no fort had been built on the summit of Starved Rock, a sure sign that something was amiss. Upon reaching Kaskaskia, the explorer and his men witnessed with shock and horror a village that had been destroyed by the Iroquois. He saw that the victors had burned, plundered, and sacked most of Kaskaskia; the bodies of the dead lay on the ground, ripped from their mortuary scaffolds; and scavengers had gathered to feast on their remains. Everywhere was devastation and destruction. No living Illinois remained at the site. To where they had fled, La Salle had no idea. Also missing were Tonti and his men.

Why did the Iroquois attack the Illinois at Kaskaskia, and what were the implications for La Salle and French policy in the West?

Relations between the Iroquois and the French since the days of Samuel de Champlain's first confrontation with the tribe in 1609 had been strained. Trading with and participating in Wendat and Algonkin war parties against their long-standing enemies, the Iroquois, set the stage for conflicts that would occur between the French in Canada and the Iroquois, and the Iroquois and French native allies for the next ninety-plus years. What had been in earlier times small-scale conflicts between the Iroquois and their Algonkin neighbors, fights that employed simple hit-and-run tactics, by the 1640s had evolved to become brutal, large-scale affairs that seem to center around a new motivation, economics.

Fur-bearing animals were the trade currency of the Iroquois. With their increasing dependency on European trade goods, the Iroquois sought to replace the now devastated fur-bearing animal population of their upstate New York territories with control of the fur pipeline that flowed between the upper country and Montreal. The Iroquois took full advantage of their ability to procure firearms and ammunition from Dutch traders to attack Wendat, Erie, and Neutral villages in Huronia and around the shores of Lakes Erie and Ontario. Making matters worse for the Wendat was the devastation to their population brought on by the ravages of smallpox several years earlier. Some Wendat escaped and fled west and into Wisconsin and Michigan where they lived in camps next to the Odawa and Ojibwe, others took refuge near the French at Quebec, while some were captured and adopted into the Iroquois tribe, making an already formidable fighting force even stronger.[20]

The Iroquois also menaced French settlements, ambushed French trade convoys, and killed French missionaries. Canada during this time was administered by private interests, concessionaires who were obligated to provide for, among many other things, the colony's defense, financed by funds acquired through the fur trade. But when the conveyance of furs was disrupted due to intertribal warfare, the concessionaires were unable to meet their financial obligations and provide for the basic security of the colony. Under these circumstances, the Iroquois took full advantage of the perceived weakness of the French administration to protect its citizens. Iroquois attacks all but curtailed French trade, exploration, and missionary endeavors above Montreal: these were trying years for the French in Canada.

Not until 1663, two years into the reign of Louis XIV, did the French Crown begin to take decisive action to prevent Iroquois attacks against French interests. First, the king took authority away from the Company of One Hundred Associates and declared Canada a royal colony. Next, Louis, through his minister, Colbert, reorganized the colony's government, creating a Sovereign Council, appointing a new governor, and sometime later appointing an intendant, or chief financial officer. With a new governmental structure in place Colbert then dispatched twelve hundred soldiers of the Carignan-Salières Regiment to Canada to protect the beleaguered colonists. In September 1666, these troops—supplemented by Canadian militiamen and Indians led by Sieur de Montigny de La Fresnaye et de Courcelle—marched into Iroquois territory to confront the tribe. Although no pitched battles were fought between the two sides because the Iroquois fled their villages ahead of the approaching army, the French incursion into Iroquois lands proved to the tribe that their territory could be penetrated and their villages sacked if the French military chose to do so. This realization led the Five Nations to seek terms with their French adversaries. An agreement was reached between the two sides and a tenuous truce was established. French trade, exploration, and evangelization among the Great Lakes tribes could resume.[21]

But while warfare between the Iroquois and the French had abated, the Iroquois did not remain idle. During the 1660s, the westernmost Iroquois group, the Seneca, sparred repeatedly with the Andaste tribe who lived to their west, while the easternmost Iroquois group, the Mohawk, skirmished with the Mohegan tribe who lived to their east. By 1676, the Seneca ended their conflict with the Andaste, many of whom moved to Seneca villages. At about the same time, the Mohawks came to terms with the Mohegan. Free from fighting a war on two fronts and having their numbers bolstered by the addition of the Andaste and Mohegan, the Iroquois could now focus their attention on other enemies, such as the Illinois.[22]

Making matters worse for the relationship between the French and the Iroquois was La Salle, who was not only trying to establish a trade alliance with the Illinois, but who sought to provide them with weapons, ammunition, and other goods. This potential Franco-Illinois alliance clearly agitated the Iroquois: it not only created a barrier to Iroquois influence in the West, it made a formidable enemy even more powerful. Since La Salle needed the cooperation of the Illinois Indians, the Iroquois must have realized that if they attacked the Illinois before La Salle was fully ensconced in the Illinois Country, and before La Salle had sufficiently armed the tribe, they would be indirectly striking the French. In the eyes of the Iroquois, Kaskaskia was the de facto capital of the Illinois Indian tribe.

Leaving Kaskaskia, it appears that La Salle and his men continued down the Illinois River, beaching their canoes at a large rock formation about four miles downstream from the village, a site known today as Little Rock. Flowing next to Little Rock is a stream that emanates from a canyon south of the river. La Salle's men located a difficult-to-access "rock hollow" where the group hid their goods and supplies to disencumber themselves of the weight.[23] They set up camp and stationed sentries to guard against any Iroquois warriors who might still be in the area. The next morning La Salle posted three men on the eastern point of a "neighboring island" where they were instructed to keep a watchful eye on the hidden merchandise. La Salle and the others headed down the Illinois to search for Tonti and what remained of his crew. The location of the rock hollow at the Little Rock site will be discussed in the next chapter.

It appears that the Illinois bands who had fled Kaskaskia ahead of the Iroquois encountered other Illinois clans and groups who had previously left the village for the winter hunt before the Iroquois had arrived. The retreating Illinois group, in time, grew too large for the Iroquois to strike.

When the Illinois reached the Mississippi River, some Illinois reportedly fled down the stream, others up the stream, while a third group, the Peoria, returned to their old village located near the Des Moines River in Missouri, today's Illiniwek State Historic Village.[24]

After making several stops and without having found any trace of Tonti and the other Frenchmen, La Salle's party eventually arrived at the confluence of the Illinois and Mississippi Rivers. There the La Salle's party beheld a gruesome sight: the bodies of about 350 Tamaroa, Tapouaro and Espeminkia (Illinois subtribes) women and children lay dead, scattered on the ground, many of them mutilated. It is likely that these victims were not among the Illinois group who fled Kaskaskia ahead of the Iroquois, but instead, had been living along the Mississippi River in Southern Illinois at the time the Iroquois arrived.[25] La Salle and his men picked through the corpses in a desperate search for Tonti and the others but found no trace of the missing Frenchmen. The Iroquois could boast of their success: they had chased the Illinois Indians from their lands and by doing so, denied La Salle any opportunity to establish an alliance with the Illinois, a partnership that the explorer needed if his enterprise were to succeed.

La Salle and his group boarded their canoes and paddled back up the Illinois River to Little Rock. Temperatures were falling rapidly and the river was beginning to freeze.[26] Consequently, La Salle's men spent the next eighteen days building wooden sleds to haul their cache of merchandise up the soon-to-be ice-bound river. While some men built sleds, others paddled to Kaskaskia where they gathered maize that had somehow survived the Iroquois pillage. After construction of the sleds was complete, the men loaded their cargo and headed up the frozen river. Reaching the forks of the Des Plaines and Kankakee Rivers, La Salle's men struggled to move their bulky and weighty sleds up the semi-frozen Des Plaines River. At an island believed to be near today's Romeoville, Illinois, the Frenchmen unloaded their sleds and hid the goods in the brush. Two men, d'Autray and a man known only as "the surgeon," agreed to stay behind to guard the merchandise while La Salle and the others journeyed to the St. Joseph River post. The island where the goods were stored is believed to be today's Isle à la Cache (Island with the Hiding Place).[27]

By early 1681, time had become La Salle's enemy. In three years he had accomplished very little. He had lost ships, merchandise, and men; the

Iroquois had driven the Illinois from their lands; and he had not yet reached the Gulf. Juxtaposed with these losses were La Salle's creditors, who were demanding to be repaid. It was imperative that La Salle quickly revitalize his enterprise. To do this, he had to establish a base from which to operate in the West and he had to convince the Illinois to return to Kaskaskia. To bring stability and peace to the region, La Salle also had to convince the Miami to end their wars with the Illinois. But first, he had to reach the Gulf. La Salle had much to do and little time to do it.

Arriving at his Miami post, the explorer was met by a mixed group of Indians from New England who had come to Miami country to hunt. La Salle communicated to the tribesmen through an Indian interpreter in his employ named Nanangoucy that he would meet with them to convince them to become part of an intertribal alliance he hoped to establish, but only after he had first located the scattered Illinois bands and convinced them to return to Kaskaskia. He also had to retrieve d'Autray and the surgeon, and the goods they were guarding back on the Des Plaines. Just before leaving for the Illinois, a large group of Shawnee also appeared at the fort. They had come to meet La Salle and to seek French protection from the Iroquois. La Salle made it known to the Shawnee chiefs that he would place them under the protection of the king if they accompanied him to the Gulf. The Shawnee agreed to make the long trek to the Gulf with the explorer and planned to rendezvous with him at his St. Joseph River post that autumn.

On March 1, La Salle and fifteen men, one of whom was an Indian named Ouiouilamet who according to the explorer, "had acquired a wide knowledge of the languages of the neighboring nations," left Michigan's Lower Peninsula and began the cold winter trek back to Illinois. After suffering a bout of snow blindness and having learned from a wintering band of Mesquakie Indians that Tonti was alive and living among some Potawatomi Indians in Wisconsin, La Salle lucked upon a group of Illinois hunters near Kaskaskia. He conveyed to them the importance of ending their wars with the Miami and the benefits of allying with him. The Illinois hunters listened to La Salle's plea and made it known to him that they would relay his message to their chiefs. Leaving the Illinois, the explorer's party traveled up the Des Plaines where they found d'Autray and the surgeon. There, La Salle dispatched several men north to the Potawatomi to find Tonti, while La Salle would return to his St. Joseph fort.[28]

Back at the St. Joseph, La Salle met with the New England chiefs and later with the Miami. During both councils the explorer communicated to the Indians the advantages of an alliance with him, a partnership that would include protection from Iroquois war parties, and in the case of the New England tribes, the British. Both parties, La Salle insisted, had to work to mend the rift between the Illinois and the Miami. Additionally, the explorer made the tribesmen understand that he had to first locate the mouth of the Mississippi in order to deliver to them inexpensive trade goods and other items. La Salle's proposals were accepted by both Indian groups.

La Salle spent the summer and part of autumn making arrangements to travel to the Gulf. By January 1682, he, his crew of Frenchmen, and his Indian allies were ready to set out. Accompanying La Salle during this expedition was Tonti, his second-in-command, with whom he had reunited at Michilimackinac earlier that summer.

La Salle's group entered the Illinois Country at the Chicago River. Following that stream to the Chicago-Des Plaines portage, they descended the Des Plaines and then the Illinois, following that waterway to its confluence with the Mississippi. They then paddled their canoes south, reaching the Gulf on April 6. Three days later, at a ceremony held on the shore of the Gulf, La Salle claimed the entire Mississippi River basin for France, an area that comprises all or part of thirty-two US states.

La Salle and his canoes then retraced their route north. However, falling gravely ill, the explorer sent Tonti ahead to tend to his affairs at Michilimackinac. La Salle would rendezvous with Tonti after he had recuperated from his malady later that September.

While La Salle struggled in the West, a change of colonial administration occurred in Canada. No longer protected by his ally and supporter Frontenac, La Salle would soon be forced to contend with a man so vengeful that he wanted the explorer dead.[29] This man was the new governor, Joseph-Antoine Le Fèbvre de La Barre.

The contrasts between Frontenac and La Barre are stark. Frontenac was a controversial figure, at times bombastic, petty, and vindictive, especially to those he believed owed him proper and due respect that his office demanded. The governor had gone so far as to have arrested prominent politicians, the son of a Canadian intendant, and even a priest. Frontenac was also deep in debt, the lavish lifestyle he enjoyed but could nary afford among the exclusive social circles in France left him all but financially bankrupt. He hoped to improve his pecuniary standing by promoting western expansion and western trade, something that both he and La Salle would attempt to exploit to their benefit.[30]

For reasons unknown, Frontenac did little to curb Iroquois attacks on tribes allied with the French, even when the tribes sought French aid and support. Bolstered by Frontenac's inaction, Iroquois war parties began attacking French canoes and other French interests. Making matters worse was Frontenac's tacit approval of La Salle's alliances with the Illinois and other western tribes and his promise to supply them with arms and other goods, which ultimately contributed to the attack at Kaskaskia in 1680. By 1682, the consternation that Frontenac had sown among Canadian authorities—such as the intendant, the colony's chief financial officer, the colony's Sovereign Council, and the colony's governing assembly—combined with his inability to effectively deal with an escalating Iroquois threat and his failure to address British intrusion into French trade turf led to his recall to France.[31]

Frontenac's successor La Barre had been instructed by the king to right the wayward direction of the colony. He was ordered to prevent Iroquois attacks on the French and on France's Indian allies. La Barre was also tasked with restricting Canada's French population to the settlements of the lower St. Lawrence. To protect Canada's fur trade, an enterprise that was regulated by the Crown and that also was the colony's primary source of wealth, La Barre had been instructed to prevent men from leaving the lower settlements to travel to and to trade with the western tribes. La Salle's activities in the Illinois Country and beyond violated everything La Barre had been sent to correct.

When La Salle had learned of Frontenac's recall and La Barre's appointment to governor, he wrote the new governor to advise him, among several things, that the Miami and Illinois would be moving to new camps near a fort that he, La Salle, was preparing to build in the Illinois Country. He also relayed to the official that he planned to apportion land to settlers. In case La Barre was unaware that La Salle had the authority to do these things, the explorer included in his letter a copy of his royal license.

Perhaps rankled by the haughty tone of La Salle's letter, or simply because La Salle's operations ran contrary to what he had been sent to Canada to correct, La Barre began a campaign to destroy the explorer's

name and disparage his discoveries. The governor seized La Salle's seigniory at Fort Frontenac, claiming that the explorer had failed to maintain
the fort's defenses, thus leaving the fort "to confusion."[32] Siding with the
governor was Canada's intendant, Jacques Duchesneau who accused the
explorer of violating his royal patent, abusing the Iroquois, and inciting
the Illinois against the Iroquois.[33] To pry La Salle from his western hide-
out and force him to appear at Quebec, La Barre dispatched two officers, Olivier Morel, Sieur de La Durantaye, and Chevalier Louis-Henri
de Baugy, to take command of French forts at Michilimackinac and at
Starved Rock.

Realizing that his patent would soon expire, the explorer hoped to
travel to France sometime during the next year to ask the king for an
extension. Until then, La Salle chose to remain in the West and avoid the
vengeful governor. The explorer ordered Tonti to "go and collect together
the French who were on the St. Joseph River to construct the Fort of St.
Louis in the Illinois."[34] Complying with La Salle's orders, Tonti and his
Frenchmen traveled to the abandoned Kaskaskia village and set up camp.
Surprisingly, they soon were joined by La Salle who instead of sailing to
France, returned to the Illinois Country. The explorer then ordered his
men to relocate their camp to the south side of the river and to begin con-
struction of a fort atop Starved Rock.

1683: THE FRENCH BUILD A FORT

(maamistikoošiwa wešihtooka niimihki)

Located along the south shore of the Illinois River in LaSalle County, Illinois, the 125-foot-tall bluff known today as Starved Rock, or *Le Rocher* to the French, is the tallest and best-known geological feature in the upper Illinois Valley. The summit of this isolated sandstone crag occupies approximately 32,000 square feet, or about two-thirds of an acre. The strategic advantages of the site, especially during times of Iroquois unrest, were many.

Fort St. Louis

La Salle described the site of his fort: it was located "on the top of a rock steep on almost every side, the foot of which is bathed by the stream so that water can be drawn from the top of the rock, which is about 600 feet in circumference. It is accessible on one side only, where the ascent is still rather steep."[1] He wrote:

The rocks near are all lower than that one, and the nearest is two hundred paces off [Lover's Leap bluff], and the others further still [Eagle Cliff] and between them and Fort St. Louis a great valley extends on both sides, with a brook dividing it about the middle and flooding it when it rains [French Canyon creek]. On the other side there is a meadow bordering the river [the park's Lower Area and parking lot] in which, at the foot of the fort, there is a fine island formerly cleared by the Ilinois [sic], in which I and my settlers have sown our seed within musket shot of the fort [Plum Island].[2]

The summit of Starved Rock is relatively level when compared to all other sandstone bluffs in the vicinity. It was easily defended by a handful of men, and lookouts could monitor both upstream and downstream approaches to the bluff.

The explorer also described his fort:

This side [the south side] is enclosed with a palisade of white oak stakes eight to ten inches in diameter and twenty-two feet high, flanked by three redoubts made of squared beams set one above another to the same height, so placed that they all protect one another. The rest of the inclosure [sic] of the rock is surrounded by a similar palisade, only fifteen feet high because it is not accessible, flanked by four other redoubts, like the others behind the palisade. There is a parapet of great trees laid lengthwise one upon another to the height of two men, with the whole filled up with earth; and the top of the palisade is a sort of cheval-de-frise, with the points tipped with iron, to prevent escalade.[3]

The fort's palisades corresponded to the configuration of the edge of the Rock. A parapet—logs piled horizontally on top of each other and augmented with earth—was constructed along the south edge of Starved Rock to protect La Salle and his men from enemy gunfire emanating from what is today's Devil's Nose bluff. Three blockhouses (redoubts) were located at the approximate locations of today's walkway overlooks.[4]

Small buildings including huts, a chapel, and living quarters were located inside the fort. As a gesture of respect to the Indians, the bones of an important Illinois chief were interred in a "corn loft" located in a structure inside the fort.[5] The men may have constructed other buildings and sheds along the base of the Rock.[6]

Figure 3.1 A model of La Salle's Fort St. Louis on the summit of Starved Rock (1683–1691). Photo: Mark Walczynski, taken at the Starved Rock State Park Visitor Center, Utica, Illinois.

Natural resources were abundant in the Starved Rock area. Coal, hemp, timber, and slate were plentiful and copper nuggets had allegedly been found in the Illinois Valley. Timber at and around Starved Rock provided carpenters with the material needed to build the fort and outlying structures. Moisture-resistant red and white cedars were used for shingles and for roofing; logs cut from pines were used for structural support and palisades; and dense hardwoods such as hackberry, oak, and elm were used for parapets and fuel. During the construction of the fort, the area immediately around the base of Starved Rock was probably cleared of trees and shrubs to eliminate cover for enemies approaching the fort on foot.

Because Fort St. Louis was located far from other French outposts, La Salle's men had to be able to make, fix, or invent items that they needed such as gun parts, tools, and clothes. Blacksmiths, armorers, carpenters, sawyers, and other tradesmen were important members of the French group. For example, their ability to fashion a piece of scrap into a useful tool was an essential skill needed to survive in the Illinois wilderness.

The Illinois River was an important water route. Tributaries of the Illinois such as the Des Plaines connected the Illinois Country to the Great Lakes: the Fox River linked Starved Rock with Wisconsin: and the Vermilion and Kankakee connected the Illinois to Indiana. When low water prevented travel by canoe, the shorelines of these streams could be used as foot paths.

La Salle's Fort St. Louis, like the river below it, a stream La Salle and other Frenchmen called the River St. Louis, was named in honor of Louis IX (1214–1270), King of France, who died while leading the Eighth Crusade. According to the *Catholic Encyclopedia*, Louis:

> Was renowned for his charity. The peace and blessings of the realm come to us through the poor he would say. Beggars were fed from his table, he ate their leavings, washed their feet, ministered to the wants of the lepers, and daily fed over one hundred poor. He founded many hospitals and houses: the House of the Felles-Dieu for reformed prostitutes; the Quinze-Vingt for 300 blind men (1254), hospitals at Pontoise, Vernon, Compiégne.

While La Salle's men were busy building the Starved Rock fort, the explorer returned to the St. Joseph to meet with the Miami headmen. La Salle hoped to make official the overtures to which the Miami had informally agreed in 1681. La Salle had to convince the Miami groups to leave their villages and settle in the Illinois Country, where they and the Illinois would be safe from Iroquois attacks and influence. He would also promise the Miami easy access to French trade goods. After hearing La Salle's pitch and debating the advantages and disadvantages of remaining in their St. Joseph villages, the Miami leaders agreed that it would be in the best interest of the Miami people to move to the Illinois Country.

It appears that the Iroquois learned that the Miami, like the Illinois and Shawnee, were preparing to ally with La Salle. Likely angered at losing an ally against the Illinois as well as the annual ransom paid by the Miami to the Iroquois to prevent an Iroquois attack, the Five Nations sent war parties into northwestern Indiana.[7] Swiftly fleeing their villages ahead of their Iroquois enemies, the Miami arrived in the Illinois Country in the spring of 1683. There they established new villages: one on the Iroquois

River: another near what is today's Hennepin, Illinois: one at the forks of the Des Plaines and Kankakee Rivers: and two others near Starved Rock.

Just as builders were completing the final work on the fort, Tonti traveled west to find the scattered Illinois bands and to convince them to return to Kaskaskia. After he had located at least one Illinois camp, Tonti convinced the group to return to Kaskaskia. Safety in numbers among other tribes such as the Miami and easy access to French trade goods were two primary inducements for the tribe's return. The Illinois groups who returned to Kaskaskia arrived later that summer.

The tribes that had made alliances with La Salle or those that had sought French protection from the Iroquois began relocating to the Illinois Country. Not only had the Miami, Illinois, and Shawnee moved to the Illinois Country, so had one trans-Mississippian group, the "Ouabona," the Otoe, or as La Salle referred to them, the "Missouri." Historians sometimes refer to this collection of tribes who lived in northern Illinois during this time as "La Salle's Colony": a smattering of villages, large and small, spread across a wide swath of land extending from the Iroquois River on the east to east-central Bureau County on the west.

It is difficult to determine how many Indians relocated to villages in what is now northern Illinois in 1683. The principal source of information for the Indian population of northern Illinois during this time is a nineteenth-century copy of Jean-Baptiste Franquelin's 1684 *Carte de la Louisiane*, a map that Franquelin drew from information provided by La Salle. Franquelin's original map went missing sometime after the nineteenth-century map had been produced in Paris by a copyist in the employ of American historian Francis Parkman, an ardent admirer of La Salle. Without the original map to evaluate accuracy, it is impossible to determine if copying errors, omissions, or information not included in Franquelin's original map had been added to Parkman's map.

Next to each Indian village illustrated on Parkman's map is a number that represents the population of the corresponding village. However, some of these numbers include an *h* such as one village of the Tohatchaking "Miamy" (1,300h), one of the "Oiatenon" (500h), a "Kilatica" village (300h), and the "Pepikokia (160h)," all Miami subtribes, numbers that denote other village populations do not include the *h*. The seventeenth-century Jesuits developed a simple formula to estimate the population of Indian villages: each cabin or hut consisted of about twenty people, inside each cabin or hut were two fires, at each fire lived two families, and each family consisted of one warrior and four non-warriors. To estimate the population of a village, missionaries (and later, secular French officials) would multiply the number of cabins or huts by twenty. Using this method and assuming, for example, that 1,300h meant 1,300 warriors, the Tohatchaking "Miamy" village population was about 6,500 people. However, 6,500 people living at one Miami village seems disproportionately high, because this village alone, consisting of only one Miami subtribe, would have had a larger population than that of all the Illinois subtribes gathered together at Kaskaskia, a village that numbered 6,000.[8] The populous bison hunting Illinois tribe were fundamental to La Salle's success while the Miami played a secondary role, that of providing security, a shield against Iroquois war parties, to the Illinois. Although the majority of researchers assume that the *h* represents men, or hunter-warriors, we ask if it is not possible that the *h* could mean *habitants*, the total village population, or possibly something else.

Tribal affiliations and group populations depicted on Parkman's map differ wildly from those mentioned in La Salle's own reports and correspondences. For example, in one correspondence La Salle claimed 6,000 Tamaroa (300 cabins) alone had returned to Kaskaskia. This is an incredible number as, according the information illustrated on Parkman's map, a number that is corroborated by Tonti, only 6,000 Illinois in total lived at the site, and this number does not take into account the other Illinois subtribes that had, according to La Salle, relocated there.[9] Furthermore, Parkman's map depicts the Tapouaro, Coiracoentanon, Moingwena, all Illinois subtribes, and perhaps the largest Illinois group, the Peoria, living in villages west of the Mississippi in Iowa. The map also shows the Tamaroa living in southern Illinois, more than 220 miles from Kaskaskia during this same time. The question is: Did these five Illinois subtribes relocate to Kaskaskia as La Salle had claimed, or did they live elsewhere as they are depicted on Parkman's map?[10] Whether or not these Illinois groups returned to Kaskaskia at this time would affect the Native American population of the Illinois Valley by thousands of people. Information illustrated on Parkman's map and La Salle's own statements cannot be reconciled. These are only a few of the many problems associated with an honest attempt to determine the number of Indians living in northern Illinois in 1683.[11]

Most if not all of these tribes established large summer agricultural villages where maize, squash, and other crops were grown and where adjacent lands provided enough meat, fish, nuts, roots, and other assorted foods to supplement the domestic crop-based diet. Like the Illinois, the other tribes left their summer villages in autumn to participate in the winter hunt and returned to their villages in spring.

With the fort on Starved Rock completed and alliance with the tribes established, La Salle hoped to provide the Indians much-needed trade goods. Having promised the tribes that trade goods would be available at his fort, La Salle was now tasked with procuring those goods and transporting them to Starved Rock.

Land Grants

Among the powers and responsibilities specified in La Salle's royal patent was the authority to award grants of land to settlers. La Salle recognized that these grants would likely make it difficult for Governor La Barre to extricate the explorer, his men, and his operations from Starved Rock and the Illinois Country because La Salle's settlers could claim the right to remain on their legally acquired property. La Salle also likely determined that if he remained in the Illinois Country even after his patent expired, he would be available to help guide his fledgling group of Indian settlements, to ensure their viability and purpose. This would strengthen his case when he returned to France to negotiate for an extension of his patent. La Salle was not leaving the Starved Rock area until either he had been served official papers that required him to do so or circumstances dictated otherwise.

The first land grant issued by La Salle was to Jacques Bourdon d'Autray, son of the first *procureur général* of Quebec and a trusted member of the explorer's inner circle. The property was awarded "in recognition of his [d'Autray's] service which he has performed as well in the discovery of Louisiana as in the construction of Fort St. Louis where he has served well and has done his duty and honor."[12]

According to La Salle's handwritten deed, d'Autray's grant extended from the "brook besides which we wintered," approximately 4.57 miles

Figure 3.2 The Little Rock and adjacent creek. The site is the likely location where La Salle and d'Autray wintered in December 1680. The creek marks the boundary of the first land grant in today's state of Illinois. Photo: Mark Walczynski.

up the south shore of the Illinois River, "together with the island which is in the middle of the aforesaid river of the Illinois above the beginning of the great rock [possibly Starved Rock] which the river bathes on the north side about one league above the aforesaid brook." The grant was also about 1.525 miles deep.[13] It is probable that the brook where La Salle and d'Autray wintered is the Little Rock site, the likely place where the explorer and his men spent eighteen days building sleds to carry their merchandise up the frozen Illinois River in December 1680. Little Rock is located in today's Starved Rock State Park nature preserve. The Little Rock site is the only location within the boundaries of the grant where a brook, a *ruisseau*, flows directly into the Illinois River and not into one of the paleo-channels located between the river and the nearby bluffs. At the north end of Little Rock and facing the river is a cavern and a large rock shelter that could have been used to shelter La Salle's men and store his merchandise. Nineteenth-century Army Corps of Engineers maps reveal that an island was once located a short distance downstream from the Little Rock site, precisely where La Salle would have stationed his three men while he descended the river in search of Tonti. The large Little Rock promontory is also the only obtrusive geological feature located along the south shore of the river within the boundaries of the grant and below Starved Rock. Much of Starved Rock State Park including the main parking lot, picnic area, Lover's Leap, Visitor Center, and the adjacent nature preserve are located on d'Autray's land grant.

La Salle awarded a second land grant to Pierre Prudhomme, the explorer's gunsmith. According to the deed, Prudhomme's land commenced about 256 yards west of today's Little Vermilion River, along the north side of the Illinois River, extending about 1.6 miles in length. The grant was also 1.6 miles in width. Part of Prudhomme's land is within the city limits of La Salle, Illinois. La Salle, as we will see in a later chapter, also awarded land grants to other Frenchmen near Starved Rock.

La Salle hoped to remain at his Starved Rock fort until he was forced to leave. Having told the tribes that they would have access to French goods, La Salle sought to deliver to them what he had promised. Guns, powder, and ammunition needed to defend themselves against Iroquois attack were of singular importance to the tribes. The explorer dispatched two "settlers" to Canada to get guns and ammunition. La Salle gave the men a letter that was addressed to La Barre requesting that the governor allow the men to procure the necessary items and return to Starved Rock. Aware that La Salle's patent had expired, the governor detained the settlers and by doing so, denied La Salle goods that he desperately needed. With promises of access to trade goods to the tribes, having few items to trade to the tribes, and with no opportunity to acquire more, there was little more that La Salle could accomplish at Starved Rock. He had no choice but to sail to France.

La Salle and a small group of French and Indians left Starved Rock in late August 1683. Before leaving, the explorer again placed his trusted associate Tonti in command of the fort and, by extension, in command of his western enterprise. Somewhere along their voyage, possibly near the forks of the Des Plaines and Kankakee River, La Salle's group encountered several canoes of Frenchmen. Leading the group was the Chevalier Baugy who had been sent by La Barre to take command of Fort St. Louis. Baugy was also ordered to arrest illegal traders and to seize any or all of La Salle's property if he, Baugy, believed that the goods were obtained contrary to the provisions of the explorer's patent. Baugy served La Salle with papers, orders from La Barre that instructed him to report at once to Quebec. It was either at this time or perhaps when the explorer reached the Chicago Portage that La Salle scribbled a quick letter to his "settlers" at Fort St. Louis, beseeching them to gather as many bison hides as possible and to accept Baugy as the fort's new commandant.[14]

Historians have assumed wrongly that Baugy's party was large, consisting of as many as thirty canoes.[15] This number is based on La Salle's 1684 letter to French minister Jean-Baptiste Antoine Colbert, Marquis de Seignelay, in reference to La Barre's seizure of the explorer's Fort Frontenac. In the letter La Salle claims that La Barre had sent west in 1683 "more than thirty canoes loaded with goods" to Fort Saint Louis.[16] Leading the canoes, La Salle wrote, were Baugy, Olivier Morel La Durantaye, and Daniel Greysolon Du Lhut (Duluth). However, the historical record is clear: of the thirty canoes mentioned by La Salle, most were either under the command of La Durantaye, who took most of the vessels with him when he took command at Michilimackinac, or were led by Du Lhut, who after confronting a village of Potawatomi on the Fox River of Wisconsin who had been actively propagating anti-French sentiment among the regional tribes, led his canoes to Sioux country to trade with Indians there. The few canoes remaining, those led by Baugy, traveled to Starved Rock.[17]

La Salle continued to Quebec where he boarded a ship and sailed to France. There he met with Minister Seignelay, son of the late minister Colbert, to petition the French Court to extend his expired patent. The king granted La Salle's request. The new expedition, one that included soldiers, settlers, and missionaries, sailed to the Gulf in four ships. Missing the mouth of the Mississippi by four hundred miles, they landed at Matagorda Bay, Texas. There the expedition ended in complete disaster. Many disgruntled settlers and soldiers who refused to remain in Texas with the explorer boarded the expedition's escort battleship and returned to France. The other three vessels were either seized by privateers or had wrecked along the Texas coast. For three years the French colonists suffered Indian attacks while they eked out a miserable existence in an unforgiving and alien environment. The colonists lived in near constant fear, uncertain and pessimistic about their fate as there was little chance of French support. They knew that the only hope to survive lay at the closest French outpost in the West, at La Salle's Starved Rock fort. La Salle and a group of Frenchmen left the Texas fort, also named Fort St. Louis, and began the long trek to Illinois. Along their route, in March 1687, La Salle was lured into an ambush and was murdered by several of his own men, shot near today's Navasota, Texas.

The name La Salle will forever be associated with Starved Rock. From his hand we read the first historical reference to the famous bluff, a site he passed while attempting to establish a viable waterway route that connected the Great Lakes with the Gulf of Mexico. It was where he united regional tribes such as the Illinois and Miami with tribes from the Ohio Valley including the Shawnee, with New England tribesmen such as the Mohegan, and with the trans-Mississippi Otoe. Although it was not realized during his lifetime, La Salle laid the foundation for the Illinois fur trade that traders during the French, British, and American period would build upon. It was under his authority and through his vision that the Illinois Country came into actual historical significance and it could be said that La Salle's influence brought the European dream of wealth and colonization to what is now Illinois, and this more than three centuries ago.

4

1684:
THE IROQUOIS LAY SIEGE TO THE FORT

(Niimihki wiiyostamwa pahsiikania)

In the Illinois Country, Baugy continued his journey to Starved Rock. When he arrived at the fort, he removed Tonti from command and undertook that authority himself. Tonti and his sixteen men (La Salle had left the fort with three men) were now under the command of Baugy. In time Baugy's scheme became manifest as he, according to Tonti, "was doing all he could to debauch our people, and as the Sieur La Durantayes, when he came did not refrain from efforts directed to the same end" (La Durantaye arrived at the fort in May 1684).[1] During the next seven months, Tonti and Baugy lived uneasily in the fort as each man served a different master—one, La Salle, and the other, La Barre. Tensions likely ran high between the two French captains as Tonti saw his hard work commandeered by Baugy and witnessed La Salle's enterprise unraveling. Baugy may have assumed that Tonti was nothing more than a co-conspirator in La Salle's make-believe empire. In addition to Tonti, Baugy had to contend with other men who remained loyal to Tonti. To shift the balance of power, Baugy attempted to entice Tonti's men to change their allegiance and to put their efforts to work for the governor. Tonti countered Baugy's proposals by promising the men higher wages and future land grants.[2]

While the two leaders bickered and likely tried to sabotage each other's efforts, a more disturbing and serious enemy was approaching Starved Rock. A large Iroquois war party was first detected on March 5, 1684, when two hundred of their warriors from the Seneca and Cayuga tribes captured fourteen Frenchmen in seven canoes that had been bound for the fort. The incident occurred on the River Teakiky (Kankakee River), about six leagues or seventeen miles from the river's mouth.[3] Lost in the assault were fifteen or sixteen thousand pounds of badly needed supplies and merchandise.[4] The Iroquois warned the captured voyageurs of other Iroquois war parties that were en route to attack Fort St. Louis, including five hundred warriors that were allegedly traveling up the Mississippi and an additional one hundred on the shore of Lake Michigan. The captured Frenchmen were marched north for nine days. At the river "Chicagou," they were released without canoes, provisions, or operable firearms. The Iroquois then headed back south to continue their advance to Starved Rock. Four days later, the cold and hungry voyageurs were found by a group of Mascouten Indians. The miserable Frenchmen begged for help and the Indians obliged them by taking them to a Mesquakie (Fox) Indian village where they were fed and protected.[5] Soon after the Frenchmen arrived at the Mesquakie camp, a young Mascouten raced to Fort St. Louis to warn the garrison of the approaching Iroquois army.

The French at the fort were low on supplies and ammunition because La Barre's embargo on La Salle's business had drained most of the post's resources. This was not cause for concern though, even in the remote Illinois Country, as Baugy and the others were anticipating the arrival of a canoe convoy bearing supplies for the fort and trade goods to be traded when the local tribes would return from the winter hunt in a few weeks. A document written in March 1684 reveals that Baugy expected the return of an advance party of Peoria Indians who would, they hoped, have furs to trade. Anticipating the arrival of the convoy, French traders possessing most of the remaining supplies and ammunition left the fort, planning to meet the Peoria downstream from Starved Rock.[6] What the French command at the fort did not know was that the convoy that they had been expecting had been sacked and seized by the Iroquois on the

Kankakee. Baugy learned of this attack and the loss of their trade goods to the Iroquois when the Mascouten youth arrived at the fort.

Responding to the terrible news, the few local Indians who had been wintering near Starved Rock gathered their families and hastened inside the fort. The French and their Indian allies reportedly secured a supply of water by filling a large dugout canoe with water and strengthened the post's outer defenses. Prepared to defend the post and possessing only a limited supply of ammunition were twenty-four Frenchmen, nine Loups (Mohegan), eight Miami, and five Shawnee warriors who were, according to Baugy, "very much resolved to defend us to the death."

Nearly all of the Illinois, Miami, and Shawnee Indians were still away. Baugy wrote, "All the aforementioned tribes were about to arrive here to do their planting." He expected that their "youth will come with the wherewithal to kill many Iroquois because we on our side would not fail to make [them] leave." Baugy knew that their Indian allies would return to their camps near the fort, but exactly when was unknown.

Tonti reported that on March 21, the Iroquois war party "greeted" the fort's defenders. In response, a volley of musketry was returned that killed several enemy warriors which, as Baugy remarked, "keeps them from getting too close." Hearing the exchange of musketry, the French traders who were still downstream with the Peoria Indians hid the ammunition and supplies and returned to the fort. The Peoria apparently hurried back downstream to expedite the return of the others.

Although some local Indians who had wintered near Starved Rock were fortunate to get inside the fort, others were not so lucky. About fifteen Shawnee men, women, and children were captured by the Iroquois and were paraded in front of the fort in full view of their families inside. Their captors made them, as Baugy wrote, "sing to our beard[s], to make fun of us."[7] The exhibition was an obvious attempt to draw the defenders from inside the fort, but the attempt to prey on the emotions of these Indian failed; stoically, they watched the anguish of their kin and friends from their vantage point atop Starved Rock.

On the fourth day of the siege Baugy, seeking assistance, penned a letter to La Durantaye, the French captain at Michilimackinac, describing the events that had occurred before the Iroquois had arrived. He also described conditions in and around the fort, including its small number of defenders, and his resulting concern about the anticipated large number of Iroquois reinforcements. The correspondence included instructions regarding caching and dumping ammunition in Lake Michigan should La Durantaye encounter Iroquois. In preparation for what could be a prolonged siege, Baugy requested that supplies and ammunition be brought to Starved Rock.

Sometime during the incident, about twenty Iroquois asked to enter the fort, most likely to find out who and what were inside and to determine weaknesses in the fort's defenses. The defenders allowed the Iroquois to enter under the condition that they did so unarmed. The Iroquois agreed to the conditions and made their way up the south side of the bluff to the gate. Soon after the Iroquois had entered the fort, the Indians inside ordered the Iroquois to sit down. Only minutes after the Iroquois complied, they were killed, most likely in retaliation for parading the pitiful captive Shawnee family in front of the fort, a deplorable taunt and mocking display of Iroquois power. The bodies of the victims were then dismembered, and their heads and arms were thrown over the fort's palisades.

On the sixth day of the siege, the first groups of returning Indians arrived. The Iroquois, determining that they would soon lose the advantage of numbers and be overwhelmed, appear to have made one last assault on the fort. Tonti later wrote that they "retired with loss." Outnumbered and far from their upstate New York home, the Iroquois fled Starved Rock, taking with them their Shawnee prisoners. With a large party of Illinois and other regional tribesmen in pursuit of the Iroquois, the two sides exchanged musket volleys. Although the Iroquois defended themselves bravely, they were unable to maintain control of their captives, several of whom escaped.[8] The exact number of casualties during the siege at Starved Rock and in the skirmish that followed is unknown. Father Nouvel, a Jesuit missionary in the West at the time, was later told by Indians that twenty Iroquois had been killed and four had been wounded.[9]

When this immediate threat was gone, Fort St. Louis still held sway on the summit of Starved Rock. The anticipated six hundred Iroquois reinforcements, of whom Baugy had been warned, never arrived. In May, La Durantaye's relief party arrived at Starved Rock with reinforcements and supplies. With La Durantaye were about sixty men including Father Allouez, a known adversary of La Salle. It is almost certain that the party delivered some supplies and other goods, and they may have brought a few soldiers or other men to supplement the meager garrison at the fort. For Tonti, La Durantaye carried orders to report to Quebec.

The sixty Frenchmen with La Durantaye likely represented the largest group of Frenchmen ever to arrive at any one time at Starved Rock. There were only twenty-four French defenders in the fort during the six-day Iroquois siege, and this at the busiest time of year for traders there, when the tribes returned from their winter hunt with fur to trade. Some historians have concluded that during the time of Baugy's command at the fort, while under the auspices of La Barre, the number of illegal traders and other French based at Starved Rock and in the Illinois Country was quite large, perhaps even as many as two hundred. However, documents demonstrate that there were substantially fewer French there, only a small number in 1684, even with the addition of La Durantaye's party.[10] With the Indians back at their summer villages near Starved Rock and the Iroquois threat diminished, it is likely that La Durantaye and his men left to return to Fort Michilimackinac not long after they had arrived at Fort St. Louis.[11]

This little-known pillage of canoes and the attack on Fort St. Louis are important events in French history in the West because, in the eyes of the Illinois Indians, they diminished the power of the French, both as protector and trade partner—the very reasons that the tribes had been drawn to the upper Illinois River Valley. The siege, which underscored French weaknesses, occurred during a time of social and commercial instability in the region. The near-success of the Iroquois validated their strength and encouraged their arrogance. It was clear that if the Iroquois could wrest the Canadian fur market from the French and control it themselves, then the Western tribes would trade with the Iroquois. The Iroquois would then trade those furs to the English. Had the outcome been reversed and Fort St. Louis had fallen to the Iroquois, the English would have achieved a major victory by gaining a greater role as a supplier of goods to the Western Indians.

Another interesting point concerns the seven canoes that had been captured by the Iroquois on the Kankakee. It is possible that they carried merchandise that belonged to La Barre's associates or to someone intimately affiliated with La Barre himself. The pillage cost a few well-connected investors a great deal of money and cost La Barre credibility with his king. About this event, the king wrote to La Barre, "in a word, you have in all this done just the opposite to all that you have been ordered." He continued, "The course which you have pursued gives rise to the belief on the greater part of the people of the country that you have an interest in the trade carried on by these individuals [illegal trade]; and, though I am persuaded by the contrary, it is necessary that you avoid even the suspicion."[12]

In the end, the repulse of the Iroquois at Starved Rock kept the important Franco-Native American trade alliance intact, and securely maintained French control of the gateway to the Mississippi through the Illinois Country. Even though the incident occurred in the distant Illinois Country, the Iroquois attack on a French fort flying the French flag was viewed by those in France as an unprovoked act of war. In July 1684, in Quebec, in a move designed to impress the Iroquois with French might, La Barre responded to the siege on Fort St. Louis by leading approximately eighteen hundred French soldiers, militia, and Indians to Anse de la Famine, near today's Oswego, New York, where the Iroquois were meeting at council. Nevertheless, this show of strength was completely overturned by a combination of supply mishandling and a fever that struck and overcame La Barre's men. Without soldiers to enforce any demands, the governor approved a cowardly treaty with the Iroquois, one which included an agreement that allowed the Iroquois to make war upon and destroy the Illinois Indians.[13] This concession so "displeased" the king that La Barre was recalled to France in 1685; in his stead, Marquis de Denonville was appointed governor of Canada.[14]

Complying with the orders brought to him by La Durantaye, Tonti journeyed to Quebec.[15] While there, Tonti met François de La Forest, a loyal partisan and faithful employee of La Salle who had traveled to France with the explorer the previous year. La Forest informed Tonti that the king had returned Fort Frontenac and Fort St. Louis to La Salle and that Tonti had been promoted "captain of foot, and governor" at Starved Rock. Tonti was invigorated—ready to take on the new challenges at Fort St. Louis, ready to remove Baugy from power and the fort, and eager to conduct business at the fort in keeping with La Salle's vision. Even more, Tonti learned that La Salle was traveling to the Gulf to build a post and establish a settlement near the mouth of the Mississippi.

Soon after Tonti and La Forest met, they formed a company "of 20,000 *livres* to maintain the fort."[16] Needing to get their own badly needed merchandise to the fort, they next contracted experienced voyageurs to escort several canoe loads of supplies to Fort St. Louis and to trade with the Indians. The first of these contracts was between Tonti and Jean Pacquereau who agreed to "go immediately to the said fort to trade with the Indians." For his part, Tonti would furnish Pacquereau the canoe, the provisions, munitions, and merchandise to trade. The profit was to be equally split between the two men. In addition, Tonti permitted Pacquereau to trade his gun, blanket, *capot* (hooded coat), and several shirts for profit, and promised him an *apichimo*, a gratuity, of ten beaver pelts.[17] The trader was required to remain at Starved Rock in Tonti's employ for as long as Tonti "shall direct." On October 14, Tonti and Jean-Baptiste Beauvais entered into an agreement whereby Beauvais would go among the local tribes and "trade well and faithfully the merchandises which will be furnished." A codicil advised Beauvais that he was responsible for any losses incurred by "misfortune or accident" caused by "dissipation and bad conduct by debauch, gambling, or in some similar way." Like the agreement between Pacquereau and Tonti, all profits were to be divided equally and Beauvais was allowed to trade some personal items for profit.[18] With affairs in order in Quebec, La Forest left for Fort Frontenac to assess the damage to La Salle's interests there.

Tonti and La Forest were finally reaping the benefits of their perseverance, patience, and diplomacy. Backed by the King of France, and having overcome seemingly insurmountable obstacles, the two men had been granted new authority to carry on La Salle's work. The next chapter of French and Indian history at Starved Rock was ready to unfold.

5

1685–1691:
TRADE AND THE BEAVER

(Ataweeyoni ci amehkwa)

Because it was late in the season, Tonti was forced to wait until the spring of 1685 to begin his return journey to Starved Rock. When Tonti arrived at Fort St. Louis, he had the pleasure of notifying Baugy that he, Baugy, was no longer in command. Tonti presented Baugy with orders to report to the governor at Quebec. In Tonti's view, justice had been served. Despite the best efforts of La Barre and others to use their political influence to commandeer La Salle's enterprise and benefit from the profits it generated, the interlopers had failed. Firmly in control, Tonti and La Forest immediately faced new problems.

During Tonti's absence and under Baugy's command, disputes that had arisen between the Miami and Illinois now threatened the stability of the Indian settlements. Baugy, who probably knew little about the long history of infighting between the two tribes, had done nothing to resolve the problem.[1] Because the situation was allowed to chafe without resolution, the disputes intensified and the tribes reached the point of combat. Tonti, acting to keep the peace between the tribes, attempted mediation.

Failing a truce, Tonti eventually agreed to pacify the two tribes by presenting them with merchandise valued at about one thousand dollars. With
this threatening and destructive situation effectively resolved, order was
restored. Tonti was free to work on sustaining and expanding the post's
trade operations, maintenance of the fort, and securing the cooperation of
his men with work and food.[2]

When not engaged in the day-to-day operations of the fort, Tonti's
thoughts were of La Salle. Two years had passed since La Salle had left
Starved Rock. Tonti, who was oblivious to La Salle's problems in Texas,
remained genuinely concerned for his well-being and that of the people
with him. Since the Illinois and Mississippi Rivers were direct routes to
the Gulf, Tonti was aware that he and the men at Fort St. Louis were the
only people who could assist La Salle should he need help. Having not
received any word from the explorer, Tonti was compelled to learn what
he could about La Salle's last voyage. Concluding that news might have
reached the French post at Michilimackinac, where information arrived
long before it did at Starved Rock, Tonti packed his gear and traveled
there with several men.

On his arrival at Michilimackinac, Tonti learned that there was no
news—neither fact nor rumor—about La Salle's expedition. It was at
this time that Tonti learned that La Barre had been summoned to France
and that he had been replaced as governor of Canada by the Marquis de
Denonville. Tonti was given a dispatch from the new governor, directing
him to go to Quebec to discuss plans to attack the problematic Iroquois,
who continued to attack French settlements.[3] Tonti was a good soldier,
but his first priority was not fighting another battle with the Iroquois but
seeing to the welfare of his chief, La Salle. In Tonti's judgment, if La Salle
were alive, he would certainly want to know that La Barre was gone. With
this rationale, Tonti made the decision to first search for La Salle and later
go to Quebec.

Tonti left Michilimackinac for Starved Rock with a group of woodsmen and a load of supplies, arriving in January 1686. About a month
later, he left for the Gulf with a crew of twenty-five or thirty Frenchmen
and several Shawnee Indians.[4] Reaching the mouth of the Mississippi,
they found no fort, no settlement, and no evidence that La Salle was in the
area. To expand his search, Tonti split his party into two groups—one to
search the coastline east of the Mississippi while the other was to search

west of it. Although each party explored the coast for about ninety miles, both failed to uncover any trace of La Salle or his missing expedition. Having done their best, they began their return to Starved Rock, hoping that some news of La Salle might have arrived while they had been away.

Working their way back up the Mississippi, the Frenchmen arrived at land that La Salle had given to Tonti in 1682, located at the mouth of Arkansas River. Being at the juncture of two major rivers and close to several others, it was apparent that this place was an ideal location for a settlement and a trading post. Ten men asked for permission to remain at the site. Because there was no place in the entire region where Indians could bring furs to trade, and because the site was directly north of where La Salle proposed to build a port on the Gulf, Tonti agreed to let "some" of his men stay, two of whom were Louis Delaunay and Jean Couture.[5] Leaving the Arkansas area, Tonti and the rest of his party continued to Starved Rock, arriving there in June.[6] It appears that while Tonti was away searching for La Salle, La Forest and a party of Frenchmen had arrived at Fort St. Louis, where La Forest assumed command until early 1687.

Soon after he arrived at Starved Rock, Tonti and two Illinois chiefs traveled to Montreal to meet with Governor Denonville. Once there, Tonti explained his delay in responding to the governor's summons for a meeting. Tonti recounted his fears for La Salle and the expedition as well as his own journey down the Mississippi in search of La Salle and his party. While it is likely that Tonti expected that the governor would have been angered by his tardiness, the opposite was true. Denonville wrote the French Minister of Marine, Marquis de Seignelay, "That officer [Tonti] has been as far as the mouth of the River Mississippi in search of Sieur De La Salle without having received any news of him." The Minister replied, "His Majesty is very impatient to receive news of Sieur de La Salle. Let him communicate every particular he will learn of that gentleman, and afford him every protection he will stand in need of, should he return."[7]

Tonti and the governor also discussed plans to strike the Iroquois by marching into Iroquois homelands. By December, Tonti had returned to Starved Rock. He dispatched agents to the Illinois, Miami, Shawnee, and other local allies telling them to "declare war against the Iroquois" and inviting them to "assemble in good season at the fort." The agents also conveyed the message that the French governor, a title known as Onontio to the Indians, was going to war against their Iroquois enemies and that he needed the help of the tribes. In April, warriors gathered for a council at Starved Rock where Tonti told them that it was "the will of the King and of the Governor of New France" to defeat the Iroquois. Tonti told them that he was leaving, going east to fight, and he implored the tribesmen to join him. Tonti then stood up and in the company of sixteen Frenchmen and a Miami guide, left the fort. He set up camp about a half league upstream where he would wait for his allies to join him.[8] That night fifty Shawnee, four Loups, and seven Miami Indians came to Tonti's camp. The next morning over three hundred Illinois warriors arrived. But even though the Illinois wanted the Iroquois subdued, only half of those who appeared joined the campaign. Tonti's contingent of sixteen French and 210 Indians—a number that represented only a small percentage of tribesmen as there were many more warriors living in northern Illinois at this time—left the valley and journeyed east to rendezvous with La Forest, who had left Fort St. Louis sometime earlier with thirty men. Du Lhut, La Durantaye, and an assemblage of French and Indian fighters from the West traveled to Detroit to meet La Forest and Tonti. Fort St. Louis was left in the capable hands of two of Tonti's close associates, François Boisrondel and the Sieur de Bellefontaine.

The French and Indian army led by the governor himself marched into Iroquois territory. This campaign, like the one led by Courcelles and Tracy over two decades earlier, was indecisive. The Iroquois, who were aware that the French and their allies were coming, scattered before their enemies arrived. However, Denonville did burn several Seneca villages and destroyed their crops, cutting the tribe's winter food supply. One notable French success during this campaign, one in which Tonti was a participant, was the capture on Lake Erie of two English flotillas led by several Canadian "renegades" who were en route to Michilimackinac to trade with the Indians in lands claimed by the French.[9]

The Texas Survivors

After La Salle was murdered, his killers took refuge with the Indians while the other members of the party struggled through the wilderness, eventually reaching Delaunay and Couture's post on the Arkansas River. There, they reported La Salle's death, news which they realized should not have been disclosed. La Salle's name had been their security; with it, members of La Salle's party could borrow canoes and provisions and return to France. Without the asset of La Salle's name, none of these things would be possible. Careful to protect their tenuous support system and their hope of returning to France, the men agreed to tell no one else of La Salle's murder, reckoning that they would make a public accounting of events once they arrived safely back in France. Anxious to continue their journey the survivors, Abbé Jean Cavalier (La Salle's brother), Father Anastase Douay, Henri Joutel, Colin Cavelier (La Salle's nephew) and a man named Tessier were escorted north in canoes by four Arkansas Indians. Several weeks later, on September 14, they arrived at Starved Rock.[10] It had taken them a little over nine months to chop, float, swim, walk, and paddle their way from Matagorda Bay, Texas, to Utica, Illinois, a journey of about thirteen hundred miles.[11]

When the party arrived at Starved Rock, Tonti was away fighting Iroquois in the east. In Tonti's absence, the survivors were greeted by "a few Frenchmen," a group that included Boisrondel, the fort's keeper of the "merchandise and furs," a blacksmith, and two others.[12] Believing that La Salle was with the survivors, Boisrondel and the others with him pressed the Texas group for information about La Salle and his colony. Henri Joutel, the chronicler of the expedition, simply told them "that said *sieur* [La Salle] had led us a certain distance and had left us at a certain place forty leagues away from the Cenis," an Indian village located near today's San Pedro Creek in northwestern Houston County, Texas, and "when he had left us, he was in good health."[13] Strictly speaking, Joutel was being truthful—he never saw La Salle's dead body. The last time Joutel had seen La Salle, he *had* been alive. The survivors also told Boisrondel that La Salle had ordered the Texas survivors to sail to France, to give an account of the expedition to the Court, and obtain "succor" for the colonists. They added that La Salle was planning to return to the fort, but that they did not know when he would arrive.

The survivors were escorted into the fort. As soon as the group entered, Abbé Cavalier reportedly "asked where the chapel was, so that he could give thanks to God for having so happily brought us" to the fort. The group met Bellefontaine, who commanded the fort during Tonti's absence. Soon afterward, a group of Indians came to the fort "to shoot off guns at the door [of the fort] to express the joy," thinking that La Salle had returned to Starved Rock. Living arrangements were organized: the two priests, Abbé Cavelier and Father Douay, were assigned a room to themselves while the others were assigned quarters in the fort's storehouse. In relative comfort, the Texans bore the weight of the knowledge that the colonists back on the Gulf desperately needed help. To secure assistance, the group needed to sail to France as soon as possible, but according to Joutel, "there was hardly anyone at said fort, each having gone to war against the Iroquois." This represented an important setback. Because the route to Quebec was extremely hazardous, travel and navigation of the rivers of the Upper Country required experienced canoe men. About this, Joutel wrote, "for that water route was quite different from what we had just seen, in that there are many waterfalls and rapids to get through, where, if one missed the taking-out points where it was necessary to get out of the water above said rapids, one would certainly perish."[14]

The next day, the survivors observed that not everyone in the fort was pleased to hear their news, albeit false, of La Salle's expected return, including ailing Father Allouez.[15] The two priests and Joutel paid a visit to the bedbound missionary, who reportedly aggressively questioned them about La Salle, his whereabouts, and his colony. Joutel wrote that Allouez "was very ill-at-ease, and it seemed that this news did not please him too much." He was very concerned that La Salle might return to Starved Rock.[16] As an enemy of the explorer, he was worried for good reason. Allouez wanted to avoid any and all contact with La Salle, but due to illness and the absence of canoe men, he was unable to leave the fort at this time and to take refuge among his Indian friends elsewhere.

In addition to visits from Allouez, the survivors also met several Indian chiefs including a Kaskaskia, a Peoria, and a Shawnee, all of whom lived near Fort St. Louis. Apparently missing from the local tribal emissaries were representatives of the Miami. Joutel reported that one group of Miami were located about two miles upstream of the fort where they were reportedly "in a strong place, advantageous for building a strong town, being on a hill that is craggy all around, and where the rivers laps and passes at the foot of the rock, as it does at Fort St. Louis of the Illinois." The description of the site of the village of this Miami group is, no doubt, today's Buffalo Rock.

Because it was mid-September, a sense of urgency prevailed on the survivors to reach Quebec and sail to France before winter closed the waterways, and before word of La Salle's death destroyed their collateral for travel. The journey would be dangerous and difficult, one that included battling the turbulent waters of the Great Lakes, paddling wild rivers, and braving the cold, rain, and snow. Hunger, exposure, and misery would also be the order of the day, and they would be passing through lands where being captured or killed by the Iroquois was a distinct possibility. Regardless of the peril, the survivors felt an overriding necessity to leave the fort. Perhaps as compelling, because of their duplicity regarding La Salle's death, was their wish to leave Starved Rock before Tonti's return.

Surprisingly, three Frenchmen at the fort, one of them the fort's blacksmith, volunteered to transport the survivors to Canada. The nameless French blacksmith, Joutel wrote, was an important member of the French group at the Rock. The smith was reportedly "quite necessary to the fort, and he is the one for whom the Indians have the greatest admiration since he repairs their guns and tomahawks." Although this man's skill and expertise might be missed by the men at the fort, another individual agreed to replace the tradesman during his absence away from the fort.[17] Joutel also learned that a local Shawnee chief had agreed to provide several of his people to guide Joutel and the others and carry some of their provisions to Lake Michigan. Before leaving for Canada, the survivors gave the Arkansas Indians who had escorted Joutel's group to the Rock recompense for their services that included giving a gun to each man, and "two hatchets, a few knives, some powder and balls and a few other trifles."[18] Even though one of the Arkansas guides died at the fort, Boisrondel gave the other Arkansas the dead man's share of the payment, tokens of French friendship that would eventually be delivered to the deceased family or to members of his village. After learning that the Arkansas men were en route to their canoes to return to their village, someone inside the fort "learned that some scoundrels of the Illinois were waiting for them [the Arkansas] at the bottom of the river to rob them."[19] Fortunately, however, the Illinois plot to rob the Arkansas Indians never materialized.

The anxious survivors then prepared their canoe for the voyage to Canada. Ready to leave in the company of three Frenchmen from the fort and about a dozen Shawnee Indians, they bid Boisrondel and the small garrison at the fort *adieu*. On September 18, 1687, their race against winter had begun.[20]

On September 25, Joutel's group reached "Chicagou," a place that he wrote "took its name from the amount of garlic which grows in that area, in the woods."[21] Not long after reaching Lake Michigan, "a few Frenchmen" from the fort and the Shawnee Indians returned to Starved Rock, apparently leaving the survivors with one French guide and few provisions. The lack of rainfall that had left little water in the streams of northeastern Illinois that summer was about to be balanced by a deluge that was soon to hit the Lake Michigan coast.[22] For eight days Joutel and his group camped on the shore of the lake waiting for the storm to abate. During this time, one member of the French group was left physically uninjured, but not psychologically, when his musket exploded while shooting at a turkey. Beyond the difficult weather and the unfortunate incident with the musket, Joutel's group had to deal with the reality of their inexperience in Great Lakes wilderness survival. Despite their successful travel from Matagorda Bay, Texas, to Starved Rock, the odds were heavily against their successful journey to Quebec, given the lack of experienced guides and the oncoming winter weather. Joutel wrote that "Everything seemed in this manner to be going against our trip, which gave us much grief, me in particular, because I still felt a lot in my heart about carrying the news of the country to France."[23] The weather and the group's lack of survival savvy, combined with the great distance they had yet to travel and the lateness of the season, were factors that compelled the French party to return to Starved Rock. They would winter at the fort and leave for Canada in the spring when conditions allowed.

Before returning to Fort St. Louis, the Texans buried their ball, powder, a few beaver robes, and between 100 and 120 otter pelts they had carried with them. Joutel described the cache where the goods were buried:

> We dug a hole in the ground, at a place that was slightly elevated, so that water would not get in it, and we lined the bottom with stones and dried grass, and the sides as well, after which we put in our supplies, our furs and other things, such as powder and balls. We then made a kind of floor with stakes and dried grass on top; we put back still some of the soil that we had trampled on, so that water would not get in, and as one cannot stir up said

ground without one's noticing it, we knocked down an oak that was nearby, we made it fall on the said cache, we dug in the heart of the oak a hole, as if for grinding corn, which is done sometimes, everything done to not lead the Indians who could come to that place to think that there was a cache there. What was useful still was that the leaves were falling, and that contributed enough to hiding the upturning of the earth.[24]

On October 7, the survivors were back at Starved Rock. Joutel wrote that Abbé Cavelier was housed in a "private apartment" while Father Anastase Douay and the rest of Joutel's group were assigned living quarters in the storehouse. Joutel wrote that two Indian hunters supplied his party with venison, which they "did not lack during the autumn and a good part of the winter, that is to say, during the season that these animals and the other kinds of game are fat and good, since they eat the acorns and the nuts, of which there is an abundance, as well as a many other fruits."[25] "The wives of the Indians," according to Joutel, "brought us something every day at the fort, sometimes watermelons, pumpkins; sometimes bread that they bake under the ashes, or still some nuts or other similar things, for which people gave them some little present in exchange, as likewise they brought us wood to keep warm." Besides the great quantity of venison and the flesh of other game animals, Joutel observed that the Illinois countryside beckoned with wild apples, vines, hops, hazelnuts, and other kinds of fruit. Hemp also grew along the banks of the Illinois River, a variety that Joutel reported "grows very tall and people say that it is better than that in France; at least it is more resistant to water, when people make nets from it."[26] In addition, "the land of the Illinois is full-fledged, and that people there could have every necessary thing there for life and for upkeep, for to the beauty of which it is adorned it joins fertility." Around Starved Rock the Frenchman saw:

A prairie about a half league wide, in which the river takes its course, and which ends in hills of medium height. Very tall and big grasses grow in said prairie in abundance. There is also in the river many islands of different sizes, containing trees of different kinds; the Indians cultivate some of these islands on which they sow corn and other vegetables, which grow very well and in abundance on them. On the hills, the grass is finer there; the stones and rocks are like a kind of sandstone or gypsum, or at least they are shiny. On top of those hills there is a good six feet of soil that is darker and which seem very good; the trees that are on top are oaks and nut trees for the most part; behind those woods are great plains and countryside as far as the eye see, full of fine, beautiful grasses. However, there are on certain hills some places where there are pines and other kinds of trees, but the ground does not seem so good there, not to mention the rocks and kinds of sandstone and gypsums, which would be very good for building.[27]

Good coal was reportedly abundant. Seventeenth-century Illinois and the Starved Rock area were rich in natural resources that afforded people easy opportunities to draw off the wealth of the land, as Joutel reported, and this with little expense. Today, corn, soybeans, wheat, and rye grow in those same grassy fields, and limestone is quarried near Starved Rock. A century ago coal was mined across the valley and Lowell Crockery was produced upstream on the Vermilion River. What Joutel observed three hundred years ago became farms, mines, and quarries today. Even though communities have, in those years, exploited those natural resources, the groves of oaks and walnut trees still stand tall and the beauty of that valley is still a lovely sight to behold.

Not only did the Indians living near Starved Rock plant maize, beans and squash, the French too grew maize and also introduced wheat to the Illinois Country. Boisrondel had imported a small quantity of wheat from Canada to Starved Rock where the Frenchman harvested, during one season, seven to eight *minots*, a quantity of six or seven bushels.[28] To grind the grain, the men at Starved Rock used a "little steel mill" rather than mill the wheat by hand.

The Texas survivors would spend a restless winter at Starved Rock, troubled both by their shared secret of La Salle's death and by the knowledge that the colonists remaining in Texas desperately needed help. However, revealing the urgent needs of the colonists could possibly lead to an admission of La Salle's death. Each survivor passed the time with these thoughts in his own way. Joutel, for example, kept a journal in which he wrote down what he saw. About the site of Fort St. Louis and the configuration of the structures inside, Joutel wrote:

Nature has strengthened it, being steep and craggy all around with the exception of one rather difficult side where people climb up. The river passes at the foot of it, and M. de Tonty had four big pieces of trees placed so that people could draw water from above, in case there came an attack. The fortifications consist only of some palisades and a few houses, which are around the edge and which enclose it; the place is not more than an *arpent* and a half all the way around. There are several houses built of pieces of trees and others which are lighter and made only of stakes. . . . The houses went out all the way to the edge of the rock, and in the places where there were no houses at all, there were palisades.[29]

In addition, there were Indian cabins in the fort, huts where according to Joutel, the twenty-two Indian defenders and their families that had fled to the fort just prior to the 1684 Iroquois siege at Starved Rock resided.

It is interesting to note the difference between La Salle's description of Fort St. Louis, a post that he had designed and built for defense, and Joutel's observations, which contradict the description of a heavily fortified bastion. Joutel wrote of the defenses that the Rock was the fort's strategic advantage, not the structure that sat on the summit. Joutel further confirms this opinion by writing, "And that is all the fortifications that there were."

The French in the fort attended mass daily. Father Allouez reportedly held services in the fort's chapel while the two priests in Joutel's party "alternated saying mass there on feast days, one after the other."

Tonti, who had left Fort St. Louis to fight in Governor Denonville's Iroquois campaign, arrived back at Starved Rock on October 27. With him was his cousin, likely Pierre-Charles Delliette and several other Frenchmen. Not long after he arrived, Tonti relayed stories of his adventures, exploits that included the capture of several canoes of Englishmen led by French defectors who were carrying trade goods and a lot of brandy to the western tribes, while Joutel and the others revealed nothing of La Salle's death or the condition of the Texas colony.

Not all of the French who left Starved Rock to fight the Iroquois returned to Fort St. Louis. Some traveled to Montreal where they obtained merchandise to be delivered back to the fort at Starved Rock. Although some of these men could have been redirected by Canadian authorities to perform other duties back east, some Frenchmen attempted to paddle back to Starved Rock with canoe loads of goods and supplies, a dangerous undertaking (according to Joutel) as the Iroquois often ambushed these French convoys. In 1688 one such convoy was redirected to deliver goods from Montreal to Fort Frontenac. In this French group was d'Autray, La Salle's trusted confidant. Apparently, after delivering the goods to Fort Frontenac, d'Autray's party left the fort to travel back to Montreal. During the journey the party was ambushed by Iroquois Indians on the Saint Lawrence River and d'Autray was killed.[30]

In December two voyageurs from Montreal arrived, one of them the Sieur Juchereau, commandant at Michilimackinac while La Durantaye was away fighting the Iroquois. They told Tonti that their canoe convoy was stranded at Chicagou where low water and ice prevented further passage. Knowing just how important the goods were to the economy and protection of the fort and to the Indians of the Starved Rock area, Tonti convinced a Shawnee chief to recruit a group of his people to help extricate the convoy. Thirty Shawnee men were sent to help free the trapped canoes. Several days later the rescue party returned, with singing voyageurs and canoes full of merchandise. According to Joutel, Tonti and the others at the fort preferred the assistance of the Shawnee over the Illinois as the Illinois were "natural thieves." Joutel also wrote that the Shawnee were so honest that they "even take the trouble to let us know when they see that the Illinois are stealing something, which has caused a kind of jealousy to spring up between them."[31]

In addition to having been hired by La Forest to carry goods to the fort, Juchereau had also been invited by Tonti to hunt near Fort St. Louis, as the hunting there was much better than in the Michilimackinac area. Hunting, however, was not on Juchereau's mind when he arrived at Starved Rock. Instead he brought grim news: the Iroquois problem in the east was far from resolved, so much so, that Tonti feared he might be obliged to recruit another group of Indians and Frenchmen to return east to fight the Iroquois again.

With much free time to consider their plight and that of their comrades in Texas, Joutel and the others resolved to leave Starved Rock "with the melting of ice and snow," hoping to "take advantage of the river." The melting snow and ice would raise the level of the Illinois and Des Plaines Rivers, hopefully allowing canoes to pass over the rapids and avoid several portages. Joutel noted that for traveling money, Abbé Cavelier "had a note from his late brother, who had made it for him at some time I do not know when, in order to take a sum of money in furs at said Fort of the Illinois to use to get things one needed."[32] Traveling on the currency of La Salle's name remained a singular imperative for maintaining secrecy about La Salle's death.

During the months that winter kept the Texas party at Starved Rock, Father Allouez related disturbing information to Joutel that confirmed Jesuit intrigue pertaining to the stormy relationship between the Miami and Illinois Indians. According to the information Joutel learned from Allouez, the Jesuits had indeed intended to destroy La Salle's enterprise in Illinois by alienating the tribes allied with the explorer from each other. Jesuit ire with secular intrusion into their perceived domain motivated the order to cause ruptures between friendly tribes, and to use that breakdown in relations to nurture Indian animosity toward traders and others who were operating in the Illinois Country. In La Salle's case, by creating a chasm between the Miami and the Illinois, the success of La Salle's enterprise in the Illinois Country was made much more difficult in that he could not rely on either the Illinois or the Miami as allies or hunters. Joutel wrote that the Jesuits, employing the Miami as their proxies, wanted to "destroy Fort St. Louis, having built one at Chicago, where they had attracted some of the Indians, not being able in any way to take possession of said fort."[33] Allouez's admission means that the Jesuits had indeed recruited Indians to both destroy La Salle's operations in Illinois and to eliminate La Salle's Starved Rock fort. These facts reveal both an unflattering view of Jesuits in the Illinois Country and a disclosure of their culpability in creating distrust between closely related tribes. These facts also provide insight into the anxiety that Allouez felt in learning of La Salle's expected arrival at Starved Rock.

Joutel mentions in his journal that the Miami lived as a separate group upstream from the fort in a defensive village on the summit of Buffalo Rock, which offered them a point from which to look down upon the Illinois at Kaskaskia. To Joutel, the Miami were not emissaries of good will between their people and the French at Starved Rock; they were instead, an isolated group of Indians who kept to themselves. Unlike the Miami, the Shawnee and the Illinois were often in and around the fort and were involved in ongoing dialogue with the French at the fort and with each other. Having several months to wait before he and his group could travel to Canada, and with the plight of the other French in Texas daily on his mind, Joutel occupied himself by writing down his observations and perceptions of the customs and religious practices of the Shawnee and Illinois tribes.

Joutel wrote that although most Indians believe in an afterlife, neither the Shawnee nor the Illinois practiced a formal religion. As a Roman Catholic, a member of a religion that had built huge cathedrals filled with great works of art and stained glass windows, and where colorfully clad priests performed rituals amid the smoke of incense, ringing bells, and heavenly music, Joutel and other theists would naturally view people who gave simple thanks to a creator and who lived in the supernatural world of spirits and visions as having no religion. Although the spirituality of the Shawnee seems to have escaped Joutel's notice, he did write that they were faithful, hardworking, and frugal, having acquired more goods than the Illinois.[34]

Joutel also noted Illinois and Shawnee burial customs. He wrote:

> There are those who put their dead, when it is a question of important people, into a kind of raised coffin on four pillars, and there were, in the corn loft of the fort, the bones of a chief of the Illinois, who was the one who had received M. de La Salle and had made a kind of donation of the entire country that they occupied, recognizing him as their father.[35]

Illinois mourners reportedly "cry for the dead," whereas the Shawnee rejoice when death takes a member of their group. Joutel wrote that Shawnee mourners:

> Sing for twenty-four hours and have banquets to which they invite all their friends to come sing with them, and where those of the said assembly give presents to excite the young people and the warriors to sing well. The dead one being as if present in the lodge, they sit down in a circle, having a fire in the middle of them for the convenience of the smokers.[36]

The Shawnee also commemorated the dead at the end of the year or when family members of the deceased dream of the departed.

Still maintaining secrecy regarding La Salle's death, Abbé Cavelier, La Salle's brother, observed during his stay at the Rock the deteriorating conduct of the Frenchmen there. Cavelier believed that this behavior was directly related to the belief that La Salle was either "dead or lost." With an intimate knowledge of this wilderness and the men who sought their

fortunes and futures in it, Abbé Cavelier recognized the temptations of
these men in the absence of authority. As an example of this behavior, the
Abbé wrote that "all those who had some of his [La Salle's] belongings
acted as if they were their own, and for this reason I was unable to obtain
any account from them."[37]

By late February 1688, the Texas survivors, upon learning that a canoe
convoy would be departing the fort and heading to Michilimackinac, convinced Tonti to let them accompany the French canoes. Needing items to
trade for food and provisions during their trip to Quebec, the survivors
demonstrated the strength of their duplicity by requesting provisions and
trade items. Tonti loaned Abbé Cavelier "four-thousand livres in furs, castor, and otter skins, a canoe, and other effects." Tonti believed that his
generosity would be repaid by La Salle when the explorer returned to
Starved Rock.

Winter was beginning to release its grip on the Illinois Valley when
preparations to leave Fort St. Louis had begun. Joutel and his group,
the Sieur Juchereau, and Boisrondel departed for Michilimackinac on
March 21. Accompanying the Texas group to Canada and eventually
to France were four local Indians, two Shawnee and two Illinois. The
tribesmen's decision to make the journey was truly remarkable because
the journey would take them across an ocean to a place completely
unknown to them, and because the last two Indians who had traveled to
France with La Salle had never returned to the Illinois Country, having
died while they were away. From Joutel's point of view, their decision to
accompany the group derived from their deepest respects for La Salle.[38]
Anticipating the needs of a rescue effort to save what remained of La
Salle's Texas Colony, the Abbé planned to utilize the skills of these Indians to hunt and supply meat for the rescue party when they returned to
the Gulf the following year. The Abbé also planned to send the Indians
to Starved Rock to report to Tonti and announce to him that they had
returned to the Gulf.

After the Texas group and their Indian companions had traveled about
twelve miles, they encountered the rapids at the present-day town of Marseilles. There, as La Salle had reported a little over seven years earlier,
the rapids impeded passage upstream, so much so that the group had
to disembark from their canoes and pull them up the shallow and rocky

stream.[39] Joutel reported, "I can say that I had more trouble and pain doing this than during the entire trip, for, to start with, at that place where the rapid was, the bottom of the river was full of rocks and stones which were very uncomfortable, and notably for me."[40]

Six months after the group left Starved Rock, Jean Couture, one of the Arkansas post traders who had helped the survivors get to Fort St. Louis, arrived at Starved Rock in the company of two Arkansas Indians. It was from them that Tonti learned of La Salle's death. Tonti's reaction of surprise probably struck Couture as odd, as Couture likely assumed that Tonti had already known that La Salle was dead, since many months had passed since the Texas survivors had left the Arkansas post for the Fort St. Louis. Couture told Tonti that everything he knew about the incident came "from the lips of M. Cavelier" himself and he also told Tonti that there was a "young man," a Texas survivor who could vouch for everything he said.[41]

The news probably both saddened and angered Tonti. He had traveled a great distance to the Gulf in his search of La Salle two years earlier, and he had done this while disobeying orders from the governor. Every decision he had made had had La Salle's best interests at heart. Tonti had borrowed money and had gone deeply into debt, believing that La Salle would eventually reimburse him. Those scoundrels, Joutel and the others, had cheated Tonti out of money and merchandise. And they had done these things while Tonti had provided for them for an entire winter, and at the peril of the colonists still in Texas. Recognizing the urgency of reaching the Texas settlers, Tonti sent Couture back down the Mississippi to "Nicondiché," a Cenis Indian village, to find out what he could about the colonists.[42] Couture left immediately but not long afterward, his canoe wrecked on the Illinois River and everything on board was lost. He was forced to return to Starved Rock.

On December 3, Tonti, four Frenchmen, one Shawnee, and two "slaves," embarked in canoes for the Gulf of Mexico. After a difficult and cold journey south, in May, they reached the confluence of the Red and Mississippi Rivers. Confronted with weeks of heavy rains that had flooded the rivers, creeks, and bayous of the Gulf region, Tonti knew that it was impossible to continue his search for La Salle's lost colony. Tonti had no choice but to return to Starved Rock, arriving there in September.[43]

Trade at the Starved Rock Fort

Trade and travel to and from Fort St. Louis were complex affairs as was the daily management of the fort. Among Tonti's responsibilities were monitoring trade with the Indians, mediating occasional intertribal disputes, assessing rumors, safeguarding the fort, travel, and keeping check on British intrusion into French trade territory. Additionally, Tonti was responsible for communication with La Forest, who in Montreal was outfitting canoes, hiring voyageurs, and writing contracts with the canoe men who transported goods and furs between Canada and Starved Rock. It is important to note that in all probability, the reason why Illinois trade contracts drawn between 1684 and 1691 exist today is because they were legal documents that were written under the authority of La Salle's concession, and later, with the authority of Tonti and La Forest. These documents provide a historical record of the legal trade of La Salle's enterprise. In the years of 1683 and 1684, during which time La Salle had been away from Fort St. Louis and Tonti had been reduced to a position of no consequence, it is likely that some illegal trade had been conducted in the West with the acquiescence if not the support of Governor La Barre and his personal appointees, Baugy, La Durantaye, and Du Lhut. However, the scope and extent of this trade is uncertain. It is possible that Tonti had observed a few French canoes bearing illegal trade items arrive at and depart from Starved Rock. If such trade had occurred, Tonti, without authority and during Baugy's tenure at Fort St. Louis, was helpless to prevent such corruption. In fact, it is likely that the pillaging of the seven canoes on the Kankakee River in March 1684 became an issue only because Frenchmen had been attacked by the Iroquois. Had the canoe convoy not been attacked, it is unlikely that any record would exist documenting the invisible trade that continued, uninterrupted, to Fort St. Louis during the La Barre years. The contracts written by Tonti, La Forest, and Boisrondel provide proof of the resumption of legal trade and commerce in the West.

These contracts are like windows into the work of voyageurs and the fur trade in the seventeenth century at Starved Rock. Tonti and La Forest were not traders; they were commandants and administrators who had to rely on men experienced in the Indian trade business. Traders who worked for Tonti and La Forest usually signed two-year contracts to work at Fort St. Louis. In 1687, Jean de Broyeux agreed to work at the fort where, as stated in his contract, he would "have his aforesaid store, shall trade with the Indians of the country and with the various tribes in the best and most advantageous way that shall be possible." As a paid employee, compensated at 1,000 *livres* per year, he was to protect Tonti's and La Forest's interests only and was forbidden to conduct trade for his own profit. De Broyeux appears to have been the primary trader at Fort St. Louis between 1687 and 1689.[44] In 1691, de Broyeux was contracted again as a trader at the fort.

In a contract between La Forest and the voyageurs François Dumay and Louis Pichart, the latter were required to use a canoe that "La Forest shall assign." The two were also guaranteed that if they encountered low water, they would be "aided in carrying or dragging the said merchandise as far as the said Fort St. Louis."[45] A contract signed between La Forest and Laurent Barette also guaranteed help in case the river level was low. Since this stipulation of assistance was written into many agreements, it is probable that not only were voyageurs well aware of the navigational challenges of the rapids on both the Des Plaines and the Illinois Rivers, the traders and voyageurs likely had discussed the matter among themselves.

Some contracts included a provision that in the case of a voyageur or other employee remaining in the Illinois Country for more than the time specified in the contract, the individual would be paid for the extra duty. This provision was presumably added to protect traders or employees financially in the event that Indian hostilities, weather conditions, river levels or a poor fur harvest in the Upper Country prevented a trader or employee from returning to Montreal as initially planned.

By midsummer of 1688, most of the contracts drawn by members of La Salle's company with voyageurs were for the transport of goods to the fort and for hides carried back to Montreal. Voyageurs were typically required to subsist on their own. To trade with the Indians along their route to the Illinois Country for food and other provisions, they were sometimes allowed to bring the equivalent of two packs of beaver pelts with them.[46] With little time for hunting or fishing, bartering with the Indians for the few things that they needed shortened the traders' time traveling to and from Starved Rock, which in turn reduced risk and increased profit. Records also indicate that voyageurs carried some food with them such as dried grains and dried meat, as well as personal items. One contract specifically mentioned that each canoe man could carry a gun, a blanket, six shirts, seven pounds of tobacco, three pounds of powder, and three pounds of lead or ball. To keep these items secure, they were also permitted to carry a strongbox.[47] This made good business sense both for the voyageurs and La Forest. To ensure that they didn't bring extra merchandise to trade, some voyageurs, such as a man named Morin from La Chine, were required to give La Forest a list of the personal items that he carried to Starved Rock.[48]

In addition to contracts for supplies and merchandise for Fort St. Louis, contracts were drawn for special services. In July 1688 one such individual, François Tardif, a Montreal surgeon, agreed to "work his art and profession" at the Illinois fort. He was asked to "seek solely the profit of the said Sieur de La Forest and shall warn him of his loss if it comes to his knowledge." In return for his services, for the two years stipulated in his contract, he was to be fed, treated kindly, and paid eight hundred *livres* in "good beaver" for his service.[49] In 1688 La Forest hired three laborers to provide general services as required at the fort. Their names were Mathieu Rouillard, Jean Froment, and Jean Heurtebise.[50] In 1691, Sieur Claude Pinard was hired as a surgeon at the fort and Pierre Hunault was hired as the fort's gunsmith.[51]

The nature and terms of these contracts between La Forest and the voyageurs help us understand the scope of all that was required for an enterprise and for a person's very survival in the Illinois Country. They reveal the juxtaposition of finely detailed documents, drawn to govern circumstances that were unpredictable. It is important to note that these contracts stipulated beaver pelts, not the buffalo hides that had been solely stipulated in La Salle's five-year patent. This restriction had evidently been lifted from La Salle's second royal commission, and Tonti and La Forest appear at this time to have taken advantage of this modification.

Among his many responsibilities, Tonti was required to settle intertribal disputes, travel, and organize military expeditions on multiple occasions—with his own funds. These financial responsibilities caused Tonti to uncompromisingly protect the resources of the Illinois Country from other traders, because his income and expenditures were directly tied to the number of furs he acquired. Only *his* traders were allowed to operate in the Illinois Country. These actions attracted the attention of Governor Denonville. About this matter, the governor wrote Minister Seignelay that the "Said Sieur de Tonty will not permit the French to trade in the direction of the Illinois." Seignelay replied, "It is a ridiculous pretence on the part of Tonty, and I shall write sharply to him on the subject, as it is his Majesty's intention to preserve to the French the liberty of going to the Illinois to trade."[52] Denonville's solution was to allow a buffer zone of five leagues, about thirteen miles, as a reserve for Tonti's trade range.[53]

It is interesting to note the variety of goods that were transported at that time to Starved Rock for trade. One contract from July 1689 contains a list of items including blankets, *capots*, dozens of butcher knives, clasp knives, hatchets, gunpowder, lead, bacon, brandy, glass beads, kettles, tobacco, mirrors, and cloth. Some of these items were used exclusively by the French at the fort, while other items, like glass beads, were traded to the Indians. Many items were used by both the French and the Indians. In a way the fort at Starved Rock wasn't just a military compound, it was also the only place in the West where customers could purchase or trade for needed goods.

French traders used a variety of watercraft—canoes and boats—to navigate the waterways of North America in the seventeenth- and eighteenth-centuries. Bark canoes, the type that were primarily utilized by the French and northern tribes who lived in regions where birch trees were common, came in different sizes, and each variety was often used for a specific purpose. Some canoes, such as the *canot de maître*, a vessel used in the Upper Lakes region, could carry as many as eighteen people, could transport considerable cargo, and was better suited for use on large bodies of water such as Lakes Superior, Michigan, Huron, and Nipigon. Other canoes were smaller shallow-draft vessels, the type of craft better suited for traversing shallow and rocky streams and rivers like those of northeast Illinois that during most of the year were only a few inches deep, and coursed at this depth sometimes for several miles. Available evidence from written accounts indicates that French traders and voyageurs most often used a variation on this smaller type to transport goods and peltry between Montreal and Starved Rock during the time of Fort St. Louis, 1683–1691. As mentioned earlier, in March of 1684 the Iroquois had pillaged seven canoes and captured fourteen Frenchmen on the Kankakee River while they were en route to Starved Rock. The assumption is that each canoe carried two men.[54] Trade contracts written at Montreal for voyageurs traveling between Starved Rock and Montreal indicate time and again that small, shallow-draft canoes manned by two voyageurs were the preferred watercraft for traversing the shallow streams of northeastern Illinois.[55] It is interesting to note that La Salle learned first-hand the importance of shallow-draft vessels. During his first expedition to Illinois, the record indicates that LaSalle had used larger canoes, having noted on November 30, 1679, that he was in the company of *thirty men in eight canoes.*[56] A year later, La Salle wrote that the "Divine River [present-day Des Plaines and Illinois Rivers] is unnavigable for forty leagues, the distance to the great village of the Illinois [Kaskaskia]. Canoes cannot traverse it during the summer, and even then there are long rapids this side of that village."[57] When he returned to the Illinois Country in December 1680, he paddled down the Illinois River, searching for the missing Tonti, while in the company of six Frenchmen and an Indian, in *three* canoes.[58] The assumption that French traders and canoe men during this time had utilized large ten- to eighteen-man canoes has led to unrealistic estimates of the number of

Figure 5.1 The Vermilion River. The rivers of northeastern Illinois were rocky and shallow. During the seventeenth century, French voyageurs in the Illinois Country used small canoes, usually two-man, in Illinois waters. Photo: Mark Walczynski.

Frenchmen, as many as two hundred, who supposedly traded or lived at Starved Rock during Baugy's tenure at the post.[59]

Although there are no documents that describe trade transactions at Fort St. Louis, the best evidence indicates that trade was conducted in the spring, as soon as the Illinois and other tribes living around Starved Rock returned from their winter hunt, when they needed supplies. Their newly taken furs were the currency required to obtain what they sought. Contracts signed between La Forest, Tonti, and Boisrondel with the many voyageurs who brought goods to Starved Rock and pelts back to Montreal reflect this time-table. Contracts written during late summer and early fall months indicate that the voyageurs would soon leave for the Illinois Country before winter had set in and weather conditions made travel to Starved Rock difficult.[60] Other contracts, those that were signed during the spring, indicate that the voyageur would leave for Starved Rock when notified by La Forest or his agent to do so, and that said voyageur would return to Montreal during the following "spring" with a load of pelts from Fort St. Louis.[61] Like trade and currency today, supply and demand dictated the value of currency. Currency such as furs, exchanged for European trade goods—for example, steel knives—fluctuated in value. In years of poor hunts, the value of the yields increased. Conversely, an abundance of beaver pelts often made their value drop considerably. While the value of the currency fluctuated, so did the cost of European goods. When war between European powers erupted, naval blockades made trade items from Europe more expensive. Traversing enemy Indian territories and the associated increased risk of capture or death also caused the price of European manufactured goods to skyrocket. The Illinois tribesmen may have been disillusioned at times because of the fluctuating price of trade goods and the changing value of the hides and pelts that they traded to French traders. While the Indians might have felt that they were being exploited by French traders, the reality was that European knives and hatchets and other implements improved the lives of the tribesmen by making tasks and chores such as processing fish and game, felling trees, and building huts and cabins easier to do. Having been introduced to metal tools and weapons, it would have been difficult for the Indians to return completely to their pre-contact technology.[62]

With La Salle's powerful influence gone and the guiding hand of Tonti away on business, searching for La Salle, or fighting Iroquois, the restraint among the Frenchmen at the fort began to break down, especially among those unknown woodsmen to whom La Salle had awarded land grants. Governor Denonville wrote to Seignelay:

> M. de la Salle has made grants at Fort St Louis to several Frenchmen who reside there since many years without desiring to return. This has given rise to infinite disorders and abominations. Those to whom M. de la Salle has given grants are all young men without any means of cultivating the soil; every 8 days they marry Squaws after the Indian fashion of that country, whom they purchase from the parents at the expense of the merchants. Those fellows pretending to be independent and masters on their distant lands, every thing is in disorder.[63]

Concerned that the lapse in communication might be construed by some of the French woodsmen in the West as a sign that La Salle had established his own empire on the Gulf, the governor further apprised Minister Seignelay, writing, "They have not been able to learn any news of Sieur de la Salle's expedition, but it is greatly feared that the lawless Coureurs de bois among the Outawacs and Illinois will adopt the resolution to go and join him."[64] Just as with the Iroquois and the English, the *coureurs de bois* presented yet one more problem for French authorities. Their lawlessness among both the Indians and French threatened the tenuous hold French authorities had on their own people in the region.

While trade flourished in the Illinois Country, intertribal bickering and squabbles tore at the fabric and cohesion of the Indian settlements. Old enmities between the Illinois and the Miami were renewed. Moreover, competition grew more intense for the region's dwindling supply of natural resources. As a result, by 1689 nearly all of the non-Illinois tribes had left the Starved Rock area for their old villages. With the departure of the Miami subtribes, the Shawnee and the Otoe, only the Illinois who lived at Kaskaskia remained.

It was during this time of discord and emigration that Jesuit missionary Jacques Gravier arrived at Kaskaskia. Gravier came to Canada in 1685. A few years later he was appointed to replace an aging Allouez in Illinois. Gravier began his work at Kaskaskia in 1688, and in time, despite the intrigues of the village medicine-men, he had reportedly "molded his flock into a model Christian Church."[65] Historians have mistakenly claimed that Gravier was the author of the massive Illinois-French dictionary, but it was actually composed the Jesuit yeoman and brother Jacques Largillier.[66] While Gravier would certainly have contributed to this dictionary, he did not write it. Indeed, it is unknown and probably unknowable how much he did contribute to its creation.

Largillier arrived in the Illinois Country in 1688 as an assistant to Gravier at Kaskaskia. Like Gravier, Largillier was an adept of linguistics who provided newly arrived Jesuits with an understanding of the Miami-Illinois language. In his capacity as a Jesuit scribe, he likely assisted the missionaries in collecting, analyzing, and interpreting much of the "raw data on the language."[67] Previously, Largillier was with Allouez at the Jesuit mission at Sault St. Marie in 1671. He was a member of Jolliet's and Marquette's famous voyage and as a member of that team of discovery was one of the first Europeans to have seen Starved Rock. He was at Kaskaskia with Marquette again two years later, and was with the missionary when he died. It was Largillier who provided information about Marquette's final journey that was included in the missionary's unfinished journal. In 1677, Largillier returned to Kaskaskia as a Jesuit brother with Allouez. He was again at Starved Rock in 1684, arriving as a member of La Durantaye's relief party, leaving with Allouez in 1688. Largillier was a familiar face in the Starved Rock area, and was privy to the relationships and business of the area's missionaries, Indians, and traders. He was well-positioned to assist the second wave of Jesuits that came to the Illinois Country, beginning in the waning years of the seventeenth century, including Fathers Pinet, Mermet, Marest, and Gravier.

In the spring of 1690, La Forest left Canada and sailed for France to petition the Court for La Salle's Illinois trade concession, in which both he and Tonti were heavily invested. While La Forest was away, Boisrondel, Tonti's clerk at Starved Rock, hired voyageurs to haul goods and furs to and from there, and administered contracts.[68] At times, he was also responsible for borrowing money to pay business expenses.[69]

La Forest's mission to France was a success. He and Tonti were granted La Salle's Illinois concession, which included the fort on Starved Rock and all surrounding lands. They were now in control of the Illinois trade—with one stipulation in the grant: they were required to "send the Illinois and other nations against the Iroquois."[70] The stipulation was a tangible expression of the frustration experienced by the French government in their failure to halt the continuing attacks by the Iroquois. Even though Denonville had attempted to resolve the Iroquois problem, the Iroquois were still, in the eyes of French authorities, as arrogant as ever. The Iroquois viewed Denonville's failure to engage and defeat the tribe as a sign of French weakness. In fact, it even emboldened them to attack a French settlement at La Chine near Montreal, where 1,500 Iroquois burned a French village of 375 people. During the raid, twenty-four colonists were killed and more than seventy were taken prisoner, most of whom were later tortured to death. The Saint Lawrence Valley and the Montreal area in particular became dangerous places for French settlers, missionaries, and canoe men.

By early 1689, Denonville was weary and exhausted. He was reportedly "worn out by his exertions," so much so that he asked to be replaced as governor. Returning to Canada to take the reins of government from the weary Denonville was Louis de Baude, Comte de Frontenac, the man who had governed Canada from 1672 to 1682. In 1689, Frontenac faced a host of problems that threatened French Canada's very security. Enemies were both Indian and European. Apart from the devastating and reoccurring Iroquois assaults on French settlements, the growing threat of attacks by the English added to his concerns. Indian allies also required attention. Frontenac was required to provide arms, supplies, and military aid to French-allied western tribes. The challenge of protecting a vast region with few men, far from the power and resources of France, was immediate and immense. Acting on these problems, Frontenac first ordered attacks on English settlements. Although these attacks helped to raise French morale in Canada, the victories also served to unite the English, who in retaliation mounted an unsuccessful naval assault to capture Quebec in 1690.[71] To strengthen the Illinois alliance that French authorities valued, and understanding the significance of Fort St. Louis in the Illinois Country in maintaining that alliance, Frontenac ordered Tonti and La Forest to give the Indians ammunition and "small presents" in order to ensure "their natural hatred against the Iroquois." The gifts were also intended to motivate the Illinois and the Miami to attack the Iroquois. Tonti and La Forest were ordered to personally fund the request of gifts and ammunition to the Indians, all at no cost to the crown.[72]

To protect the citizens of Canada, and to provide the military bases from which to operate, the colonial administration launched a plan to pay for construction of new forts and fortifications. Although Canada's Intendant, Jean Bochart de Champigny de Noroy de Verneuil, agreed with Frontenac's plans to secure the citizenry of Canada, defeat the Iroquois, and keep the alliance of the western tribes, he had to determine how to fund the construction of the new forts and fortifications. He suggested to the new Minister of Marine, Louis Phélypeaux de Ponchartrain, that the Crown issue more permits to trade in the West. De Champigny wrote:

> Nothing more is necessary than to appropriate to that purpose [the construction of forts] the twenty-five licenses usually issued every year for trading in the Outawas Country, each of which produces a thousand livres; they are bestowed gratuitously to settlers and are of no benefit to his Majesty. The public interest cannot be better advanced than by applying them to that use. Fifteen more can be issued for the Illinois trade, each of which will also produce a thousand livres, and thus an annual fund of forty thousand livres would be obtained, provided peace existed and we could send to those Tribes.[73]

By 1691, recognizing the significance of Fort St. Louis at Starved Rock to Franco/Indian relations in the West, the king ordered an accounting of the situation from both Governor Frontenac and Intendant de Champigny. He was most interested in the extent of success achieved by Tonti and La Forest in persuading western tribes to attack the Iroquois. Writing to Frontenac and de Champigny, the king requested that they provide a report "of the state of Fort St Louis of the Illinois; of the conduct of Sieur de la Forest who obtained the grant of it for himself and Sieur de Tonti; and of the movements in which said Sieur de la Forest will have engaged the said Illinois against the common enemy."[74] Ultimately, the king's planned contingent of western tribes, inspired by La Forest and Tonti, never materialized because the two Frenchmen could not rally the Illinois and Miami.

In the spring of 1691, Tonti traveled to Michilimackinac for business. Before leaving, he placed his young but very capable cousin, Pierre-Charles Delliette, in command at Starved Rock. He also informed the principal Illinois chiefs at Kaskaskia that Delliette would assume command in his absence. Tonti's endorsement had no small influence on the chiefs. Delliette later wrote, speaking from the perspective of a seventeenth-century

French commandant, "never had Indians been so submissive as they were during this time."[75]

While Tonti was away, the Illinois Indians living near Starved Rock were considering their future. What they saw around Kaskaskia was over-exploitation of the natural resources—the scattered Indian settlements had taken their toll on the environment. Disappearing were the groves of trees that had been used as fuel for fires that burned twenty-four hours a day, six to eight months of the year, inside and outside Indian lodges for light, heat, cooking, and to repel swarms of mosquitoes during summer months. Deforestation caused wildlife such as elk and deer, two of the three most important large game mammals utilized by the Illinois, to move elsewhere.[76] Removal of the canopy provided by trees altered the ecosystem as some plants need more-or-less sunlight than others, which in turn impacted the fauna that fed on the plants and lived in these ecozones. Delliette himself wrote that one of the two primary reasons for the French and Indian exodus from the Starved Rock area was the scarcity of firewood.[77] The paleo-channels and adjacent marshes had been hunted, trapped, and fished out. Nutrients in the soil where the Indians had planted their crops were depleted from continuous farming. Illinois women now had to venture farther and farther away from camp to find places to plant their crops which, in turn, subjected them to enemy ambush.

According to Delliette, "several [Illinois] women complained that their maize had been cut, and others, that they had found Iroquois moccasins in their fields."[78] A find such as this was cause for serious concern. Delliette suggested to the principal village chiefs that they send out scouts to verify the reports of the women. The chiefs readily agreed. Eighty Illinois warriors left Kaskaskia to find the intruders, searching the rivers and trails that led to the village. Returning to the village four days later with two Iroquois prisoners, the scouts reported that they had found the enemy, three hundred of them, and had engaged them in a brief yet intense skirmish. Even though they had lost four of their own comrades, the ferocity of the Illinois attack had forced the Iroquois to withdraw. Delliette reported that these prisoners "had cut corn for the last time" as they were tied to a post and were unmercifully tortured to death by the Illinois. By complete happenstance, a group of French woodsmen who had been sent out by Tonti earlier that year returned to the fort with four more Iroquois prisoners.

The Illinois at Kaskaskia recognized that their lands were no longer tenable and that Iroquois harassment threatened the peace. As a result, many clans and family groups began leaving Kaskaskia for new camps at Lake Peoria. By 1691, only about a thousand people remained in the village.

The French command at the Rock was also concerned about an Iroquois attack and siege on the fort and the problem of obtaining water during a siege, a realistic concern given the Iroquois siege of the fort in 1684. With a shared understanding of the concerns, Delliette was not surprised when the Illinois chiefs made their decision to relocate to "the end of Lake Pimitoui," Lake Peoria, where the other Illinois groups were living.

After the village maize had been harvested, the remaining Illinois at Kaskaskia moved to their new homes downstream. With the Illinois gone, Fort St. Louis on Starved Rock became a costly and superfluous outpost that served no purpose. The French recognized that their role in the Illinois Country was to trade with the Indians and to help defend the village should the Illinois be attacked. With the Indians of Kaskaskia gone, manning the fort made little sense. As a result, Delliette and his Frenchmen followed the Illinois to Lake Peoria, abandoning the fort.

Exactly when Tonti left Michilimackinac and returned to the Illinois Country is unknown. What is known is that when he arrived at Starved Rock, the fort's garrison was gone and everything of value had been carried away. At Lake Peoria, a new fort had been built, and by 1699 chapels had been erected at each end of the village.[79] For the decade following the French withdrawal from Starved Rock, Lake Peoria would become the primary focus for French traders and missionaries. Although a few Indians and some traveling Frenchmen would stop at the Rock, it would be the activities around Lake Peoria at this time that would take precedence in the unfolding story of Illinois history.

Part 2

STARVED ROCK INTO THE EIGHTEENTH CENTURY

1692–1712:
The Rock Is Abandoned

(Neekarenta aašipehkwa)

Most of the Illinois subtribes, including the Kaskaskia and Peoria, were now well established at Lake Peoria. The Tamaroa and Cahokia were living in villages on the Mississippi River in 1698. In 1700, the Kaskaskia and their Jesuit associates left Lake Peoria, relocating along the Mississippi River, first at Des Pères Creek in today's St. Louis, Missouri, and then a few years later a short distance from the confluence of the Kaskaskia and Mississippi Rivers near a place that would eventually be called Kaskaskia, the site of Illinois' first state capital.

For the next two decades, the Peoria would remain separate from the other Illinois groups. It was this segregation that in fact engendered their ultimate survival. Unlike the Kaskaskia, for example, who allied themselves closely with the French, especially the Jesuits, the Peoria were indifferent, even at times hostile toward Christianity, sometimes responding violently to the missionaries' attempts to convert them. Missionaries who served at Lake Peoria—such as Fathers Gravier, Marest, and Mermet—described the challenges and difficulties they confronted when dealing with Peoria shamans. Two such incidents involved Father Gravier, and the second in 1705 eventually led to his death. Shot in the arm with an arrow released by a Peoria Indian, Gravier suffered a serious wound that was made worse by the stone arrowhead that remained lodged in his arm.[1] Reportedly nothing could be done in Louisiana to help Gravier so he sailed to France in hopes of having the projectile removed. With Gravier's departure from Lake Peoria, the Peoria mission was closed. On his arrival in France, Gravier learned that even the best surgeons could not remove the arrowhead. Returning to North America, the unfortunate missionary died of the wound three years later at Mobile Bay, Alabama, in 1708.

According to a linguistic study of the meaning of the name Peoria by Michael McCafferty of Indiana University, "PE8ARE8A," as the name was transcribed by the earliest French Jesuits signifies "someone who dreams in relation to, with the help of, entities in the spirit world."[2] This translation provides a justification of the sometimes inexplicable actions of this subtribe, who held their traditional spiritualism and the role of the shaman in very high regard. Like other native tribes the Peoria, before the coming of the Jesuits, already had strong, long-held, spiritual beliefs, ones that they were not anxious to abandon. The interpretation of dreams, the role of good and bad spirits, and the Peoria's understanding of their place in the universe were beliefs that were held as tenaciously by the Peoria people as the Catholic faith was by the missionaries.

With the Indians and the French gone, the land in the Starved Rock area began to heal. In the barren prairie border lands, new life sprouted from the earth. Pockets of flora that had survived the human tenure of the site and had adapted to these changing conditions became habitat for deer and other animals. In the abandoned and unproductive fields along the river, seeds hidden deep in the soil burst open with new life and vitality. In the autumn, these unharvested grains and browned foliage became compost, laying down a new layer of nutrient-rich soil. In the paleo-channels, the wildlife and marine life that had survived the hunter and the fisherman were now reproducing and thriving. Redhorse, catfish, snapping turtles, beaver, mink, and raccoon became plentiful again. Flocks of migrating birds such as ducks and geese were now safe in these shallow waters and like the other creatures, lived unmolested by man. During this time, nature did what nature does best—reclaim what had been taken from it.

Figure 6.1 One of the many paleochannels of the Kaskaskia—Starved Rock area. Paleochannels are the remnants of ancient conduits of the Illinois River that provide habitat for the area's fauna and flora. Photo: Mark Walczynski.

Human activity at Starved Rock between 1691 and 1712 appears to have been very limited, as are any surviving records that could provide knowledge of the site's occupation. Exactly what happened to the fort remains a mystery. From reports, it appears that a few remnants of it were still visible as late as 1721. Richard Hagen, an archaeologist who excavated the summit of Starved Rock in 1949 and 1950, speculated that Indians may have removed the fort's palisades to use them for firewood.[3] He reported that he had uncovered "tradebeads, brass kettle parts, iron gun parts, hawk's bells, etc." in post-holes that were once part of the fort, indicating that there had been human activity at the site not long after the palisades had been removed.[4] Regardless of the fort's fate, new life— grass, bushes, and trees—eventually sprang from the nooks and crannies on Starved Rock's summit as the last vestiges of human activity, like the surrounding countryside, were reclaimed by nature. The site that had once been the center for French and Indian activity in the West had become nothing more than a geographical landmark.

Occasionally a party of canoe men or Indians passed the once-famous Rock, and some of them surely told of what they had once observed there. One of the more interesting accounts occurred in November 1698, when four canoes en route to the Mississippi from Michilimackinac passed Starved Rock. At that time, three missionaries of the *Société des Missions Étrangères* (Society of the Foreign Missions)—Fathers Jean-François Buisson de St. Cosme, Antoine Davion, and François Jolliet de Montigny—made their way down the Illinois River, guided by none other than Tonti.

Of Tonti's leadership, St. Cosme wrote, "he greatly secured our passage through many nations, securing us the friendship of some and intimidating others—I mean the nations who through jealousy or the desire to pillage us sought to oppose our passage."[5] He also wrote that Tonti "performed those [duties] of a zealous missionary, entering into all our views, exhorting the savages everywhere to pray and to listen to the missionaries." As a role model for the tribes, Tonti went to mass and performed "devotional exercises" to encourage the Indians to do the same. St. Cosme's journal records that Tonti had a great rapport with the *Société des Missions Étrangères* and was eager to help whenever he could. This was apparently not the case with other Catholic orders like the Jesuits, with whom Tonti, admittedly, had quarrels and whom he had accused of rendering "bad services."[6]

Dragging, carrying, and pushing their canoes down the shallow and rocky Illinois River, the party camped at the old Kaskaskia site where they were surprised to find two cabins of Indians wintering. Among these tribesmen lived a woman who was reported by St. Cosme to have been a "thoroughly good Christian," an observation that the missionary was eager to point out. This reference demonstrates that the village site had still been used from time to time, by small groups of wintering Indians.

The following day, the flotilla continued its slow trek down the river where it passed, according to St. Cosme, "a place called the Old Fort. This is a rock on the bank of the river, about a hundred feet high, whereon Monsieur de la Salle had caused a fort to be built."[7] Although part of the fort was still visible at this time, St. Cosme's observation refers to Starved Rock, not the old fort.

St. Cosme's perceptions recorded in his journal are interesting as they provide insight into his concerns regarding the deteriorating relations between the French and the Mesquakie. These observations also describe how that relationship changed the group's route from Lake Michigan to the Mississippi. The last thirty years of the seventeenth century would be a transformative period for the Mesquakie Indians. The arrival of the French in the Upper Country would forever change the dynamics of Mesquakie culture, economy, and polity.

The Mesquakie, also known as the "Red Earth People," divide their history into two categories: the legendary and the historic. The legendary history began in Canada's province of Quebec, where Mesquakie oral tradition places the tribe at Lac St. Jean, located about 130 miles north of Quebec City. Sometime later, the tribe moved south and established a village along what appears to be the Blackstone River, near the state line that separates Rhode Island and Massachusetts. Next the tribe moved west, first to the Niagara Falls area and then south along the Allegheny River to the Ohio River. The Mesquakie followed that stream until they struck north, up the Scioto River in today's Ohio. After reaching the Scioto headwaters, it appears that the Mesquakie continued their northward trek overland until they reached today's Michigan where they settled in the area of Detroit.[8] It is at Detroit, according to Mesquakie tradition, that the tribe's legendary history ends and the historical one begins.

How long the Mesquakie occupied the Detroit area is unknown, perhaps long enough to have developed a fond affection for the region. Having been forced to flee Michigan because of repeated attacks by Ojibwe, Iroquois, and other enemies, the Mesquakie traveled north, crossed the Straits of Mackinac, and headed down into Wisconsin. By the 1650s the tribe had established a village along the Wolf River and by the 1680s they were living along the Fox River.[9]

The first *known* Mesquakie contact with French missionaries occurred at La Pointe in 1666. It was there that Father Allouez ministered to a collection of tribes that included Illinois, Mesquakie, and about ten other tribes who wintered near the south shore of Lake Superior. In 1670, Allouez encountered a village of Mesquakie located on the Wolf River in Wisconsin, where the priest established the Mission of St. Marc. While the missionary found initial success in converting the Mesquakie to Catholicism, the tribe, likely due to the missionary's failure to adequately establish a firm foundation of Catholic instruction in the tribe, came to reject Allouez and his faith.[10] During this same period, the Mesquakie experienced ebbs and flows in relationships with their neighbors, at times peaceful while at other times embroiled in wars with the Sioux, Ojibwe, Miami, and Mascouten. Natural disasters such as early spring frosts killed Mesquakie crops, and European-borne disease ravaged Mesquakie villages. Exacerbating matters were French canoe men and traders who paddled waterways that traversed Mesquakie territory to trade with the large Sioux tribe, effectively cutting off the Mesquakie from trade items that, by this period in their history, the tribe had come to depend upon. The Mesquakie attacked the convoys, which created friction between the French and the tribes who remained on good terms with the French.[11] Fighting intermittent warfare on several fronts and seeing their waterways commandeered by French traders who traded with and armed the Sioux, the Mesquakie tribe grew increasingly protective of its territory. This state of affairs eventually precipitated a change in tribal dynamics that, in one way, manifested itself in the diminished role of civil chiefs and elders and the increased rise of power and prestige of the war chief.[12] This would prove to be disastrous for the Mesquakie, because tribal elders represented the wisdom acquired through the years, through times that were lean, prosperous, and/or sometimes bloody; it whittled away at the Mesquakie sense of tribal stability that came from the knowledge and understanding gleaned from tribal chiefs and elders; and it fostered actions based on emotion, rather than practicality. Since aggressive young warriors were now making military decisions for the tribe, the Fox and Wisconsin Rivers became dangerous for French traders and tribes allied with the French. In his journal, St. Cosme wrote that the Mesquakie who live on the Wisconsin River "will not allow any persons to pass lest they might go to the Sioux, with whom they are at war, and consequently have already pillaged several Frenchmen who tried to go that way."[13] The Wisconsin River was an important thoroughfare, a stream that, in conjunction with the Fox River, connected the Great Lakes to the Mississippi. Restricted from safe access to the Wisconsin River by the Mesquakie warriors, St. Cosme and Tonti were forced to travel hundreds of miles south, down the shallow and at places rocky Des Plaines and Illinois Rivers. Even though these skirmishes in Wisconsin had no direct bearing on the activities at Starved Rock at this time, they would eventually evolve into a series of battles that lasted nearly twenty-five years, making the Illinois River and the Starved Rock area dangerous places to be for French traders, travelers, and missionaries, and their Illinois allies.

Tonti guided St. Cosme and the others safely down the Illinois and Mississippi Rivers until they reached their destination, the Indian village on the Arkansas River. After visiting his nearby trading post, Tonti traveled back north to Lake Peoria. The party's three missionaries also set off to different destinations. Montigny went to the Taensa and the Natchez Indians but found the tribes too indifferent to conversion. He left Louisiana and eventually served in different capacities in France, China, and Rome. Davion went to the Tunica Indians where he was initially greeted with scorn and contempt. However, his second attempt at converting them was more successful. He reportedly labored among the tribe for eighteen years. In 1707, St. Cosme became the first Canadian-born missionary to be martyred when he and several companions were murdered while they slept along the Mississippi by a party of Chitimacha Indians.

Other convoys made the long and arduous journey from Montreal to the fort at Lake Peoria and then back again, passing Starved Rock on every tour. A few of the hardy men who led them were J. B. Depeyras, François Picard, Le Pailleur Laferté, Bertrand Viau *dit* L'Esperance, Jacques Simon *dit* Lapointe, Nicolas le Tellier, Paul-Charles Dazé, and Gabriel Benoist. The Jesuit missionaries Sébastien Râle, Julien Binneteau, and Pierre-François Pinet each passed the Rock on their way to Lake Peoria and later, to the Mississippi. Like Marquette, these missionaries did not mention Starved Rock in their reports, primarily because no one lived at or near the site at the time that they passed by. To these men, the bluff was only a part of the natural landscape.

With many of the same goals as those of the French administrators in the Illinois Country, Antoine de la Mothe Cadillac founded a French post at Detroit in 1701. This new post resulted in the closure of the fort at Michilimackinac and the relocation of the Jesuit mission to Detroit. At Cadillac's invitation, many tribes including the Sauk, Miami, Wendat, Potawatomi, and several northern tribes, resettled in Lower Michigan to be closer to the new French post. For the next decade, trade in the Upper Lakes would center on Detroit, a sparsely manned outpost that stood amid large villages of Indians. The new post would one day become the epicenter of a raging American Indian conflict, some of it involving Peoria Indians from Starved Rock.

The European access to Starved Rock, previously exclusively French, was altered in 1710 by the arrival of a nineteen-year-old named Joseph Kellogg, the first known Englishman to see Starved Rock. Kellogg worked for the French as an interpreter, having learned an Iroquoian tongue during his six-year captivity among the Mohawk Indians. Not long after his release, he was a passenger in one of two French canoes that traveled the southern trade route to deliver trade goods and supplies from Montreal to the French post on the Arkansas River. At the head of the Illinois River, the chronicler of the expedition noted that Kellogg saw "fine large Savannahs or Meadows of forty Miles in length, Some of the Richest Land the World affords" and in these "Thousands of Buffalo" and "wild cattle" lived in large herds. Waterfowl was everywhere as he saw an "Infinite number" of "Cranes, Geese, Ducks, and Swans" that "feed upon wild oats [which] are called by the Indians Mauahomine, by the French Falavoine." And along the river's course they viewed "wild apple trees and plumb-trees, the apples bitter and Sower, but the plumbs good; & a fruit much like Cucumber that grow upon Small trees or Shrubbs. They call "em Raisimins."[14] While Kellogg aptly described the area of the Illinois Country, Starved Rock itself was not mentioned in his account.

Another visitor to the area, Jesuit missionary Father Pierre-Gabriel Marest, did mention Starved Rock in his report. Marest first passed the place in 1698 while on his way to the Lake Peoria mission, where he and Father Binneteau gave the St. Cosme party "the best possible reception" when they arrived.[15] Marest had a great aptitude for learning and understanding Indian languages. According to Binneteau, "Father Gabriel Marest is doing wonders; he has the finest talent in the world for these missions; he has learned the language in four or five months, so that he can now give lessons to those who have been here a long time."[16] Marest left Lake Peoria in 1700 with the Kaskaskia Indians, landing at the new Kaskaskia in 1703 where he served until 1711. After learning that the Peoria sincerely regretted their part in the death of Gravier, and recognizing that the Indians were in need of trade goods and a market for the furs that they could offer in trade, Marest traveled to Michilimackinac, which had been reopened in 1712 to meet with his superior and brother,

Joseph Marest, to make an argument for reopening the Peoria mission.[17] Although what transpired at their meeting is not recorded, what is known is that the following year, Marest returned to the Illinois Country and to the Peoria Indians.

After stopping at Father Chardon's mission on the Saint Joseph River, Marest's party portaged to the Kankakee and paddled that stream to the Illinois. Arriving in the Illinois Valley, the missionary wrote, "At last we perceived our own welcome country; the wild oxen and the herds of deer were roving along the bank of the river, and from the canoe we shot some, now and then, which served for our repast."[18] His party was several leagues east of Starved Rock when it encountered a large group of Peoria Indians who greeted them and escorted them to their village—offering protection to Marest's party from enemies that were reportedly in the area. Drawing closer to the village, one of the canoe escorts went ahead of the flotilla to announce the missionary's arrival. The year was 1712; the Peoria Indians had returned and were once again, living at Starved Rock.

The exact location of the Peoria village in 1712 is not known. It is doubtful that it was at old Kaskaskia since there is no clear archaeological evidence of Peoria occupation of the site from this period. It is possible that the 1712 Peoria village was located along the south shore of the river, near today's Starved Rock seawall.

When Marest arrived at the village, the Peoria and the few Frenchmen living with them greeted him and his party with a volley of musketry. He later wrote that "joy was actually painted on their faces, and they vied in displaying it in my presence." The visitors were invited to a feast given in their honor provided by the French and the "most distinguished men" of the village, including Chachagouache, the "grand chief of the Illinois Rock village."

Chachagouache, was a civil chief and influential leader who was reported by French authorities to have been "a good man" who had "much authority" with his people.[19] Village chiefs sought the good will of their people, and they led by way of consensus. They met in council with the village elders, the oldest and wisest men in the camp, to ensure that all important matters were discussed openly and honestly. Chachagouache's authority would have also extended to that of his organization. During summer buffalo hunts, his experienced leadership was valued both for the success of the hunt and for the safety of his people.[20] Chachagouache's position was hereditary; he was the latest in a long line of respected village leaders.

In this position of leadership and respect, it was imperative that Chachagouache be the individual to convey to Marest the regret felt by the Peoria regarding Gravier's death. Of the incident, Marest wrote, "the keen grief that they felt for the unworthy manner in which they had treated Father Gravier; and he besought me to forget it, to have pity upon them and their children, and to open for them the door of Heaven, which they had shut against themselves."[21] The missionary was deeply touched by Chachagouache's genuine plea for forgiveness. In Marest's judgment, the matter was settled—the Peoria had asked for forgiveness and the priest had granted it. With the Peoria matter resolved, Marest left two days later for his Kaskaskia mission with a joyful heart. There he would continue his work.

What Marest witnessed during his visit to Starved Rock and later recorded in his report documents that the Peoria had returned to Starved Rock. What remains unclear is whether or not they or any part of their subtribe were concurrently living at Lake Peoria at this time. According to Joseph Zitomersky's population study of the Illinois Indians, "we can only speculate as to whether Pimitouy [Lake Peoria village] continued to exist after 1712 and before 1718, when we have evidence again of an Illinois settlement there."[22] In either case, we do know that after a twenty-one-year hiatus, the Starved Rock area would again host at least one band of Illinois Indians.

Father Marest's post at Starved Rock was filled by Father de Ville, a fellow Jesuit. The Peoria Indians and their French associates, however, rejected the new missionary. They wanted Marest, a priest whom they knew well, one who had served them at Lake Peoria for two years and a man who had won their hearts and minds. They were reportedly "accustomed" to Marest. Eventually, despite their opposition, de Ville ably won over the reluctant Peoria tribesmen with his zeal, spirit, and commitment.[23]

It is likely that beyond de Ville's sincere and effective efforts, his acceptance by the Indians was due in part to his acceptance by French traders who were living among the Indians at Starved Rock. These Frenchmen were often held in high esteem by the Indians because they represented access to trade goods that the Indians both desired and needed. This access often elevated these Frenchmen to positions of influence with the Indians, so much so that sometimes they married Indian women and became kin, establishing not just friendly relations with the Indians but blood kinship bonds. The traders sometimes served as intermediaries between the tribes and French authorities. Although illegal traders were known to have disrupted life among the tribes and were perfidious among their own countrymen, other traders, like those at the Rock in 1712, were likely influential in counseling, advising, and at times leading the Indian community.[24]

Marest, in recounting his journey to the new Kaskaskia, mentioned enemy tribes in the Illinois Valley. He wrote that the day after his party had left Starved Rock, heading downstream and toward the Mississippi, they encountered a large Sioux war party that had been camped along the riverbank. Marest surmised that the Sioux warriors had ignored his party because they had likely already struck their intended target and were returning home. Whether or not the Sioux had attacked the Peoria at this time is unknown, though it is possible that they could have used the Illinois River as a route to strike another regional tribe. What is known is that 1712 was a pivotal year for the Starved Rock Peoria as a new series of skirmishes, ambushes, and clashes was begun that turned the Illinois Country, at times, into a battleground. For the next two decades, the Peoria would be embroiled in a bloody conflict with the Mesquakie Indians, hostilities that historians today call the Fox Wars.

1712–1730:
STARVED ROCK AND THE FOX WARS

(Mihšikatwi Aašipehkonki—Mahkwaskimina)

In Wisconsin, the ongoing conflict between the Mesquakie and the Sioux continued, as did the Mesquakie raids on French *coureurs des bois*, illegal traders who carried goods to markets in Sioux country. The few items that the Mesquakie were able to purchase from French traders sold for exorbitant prices. Feeling themselves slighted, the Mesquakie, at the instigation of friendly Iroquois, considered trading with the British. To counter potential British inroads into French trade turf, and to nullify the effects of illegal traders in Wisconsin, Cadillac invited the Mesquakie to settle near his new post at Detroit, in the Lower Peninsula, where other regional tribes had previously settled. It is also possible that the Mesquakie considered returning to Detroit because, other than being offered better trade opportunities at the French fort, the tribe had formerly lived there. The memory of life at Detroit was not far removed from the present. This had been *their* territory. Having been forced to flee the Detroit area in order to protect their villages from attack and their noncombatants from capture, the Mesquakie may have been nostalgic recalling good times under better circumstances in the past, and this may have influenced their decision to return.

Unfortunately for the tribe, by the time the first Mesquakie group—led by a chief named Pemoussa—arrived at Detroit in 1712, Cadillac was no longer commandant of the post. He had been sent to a new assignment in Louisiana and had been replaced by Charles Regnault Sieur du Buisson, a French officer who had little use for the Mesquakie and who considered the tribe a nuisance.[1] Pemoussa's band arrived at Detroit, apparently sporting a bit of bluster and audacity. Upon arrival they established camp approximately fifty yards from the fort. Soon after the Mesquakie had settled near the fort, they created unrest by stealing livestock and taunting other tribes. The situation worsened when Mascouten survivors of an Odawa (Ottawa) and Potawatomi attack on their St. Joseph River village arrived at the Mesquakie fort, an incident that enraged the Mesquakie because the Mascouten were not only heir linguistic cousins, they were also allies. The French at the fort, who only numbered about thirty men, eventually received reinforcements from Missouri, Osage, Potawatomi, Odawa, and Illinois warriors, likely Peoria from the Starved Rock village.[2] Together they surrounded the Mesquakie fort, cutting off Mesquakie access to food and water. Pemoussa and two others went to the French fort under a flag of truce to meet with the post's commandant, du Buisson. Once inside the fort, du Buisson escorted the Mesquakie representatives to the parade grounds where he then assembled the chiefs of his Indian allies. Pemoussa opened the council by presenting du Buisson a wampum belt and two slaves. He first asked the French commander to "have pity" on his children, Pemoussa's people, and then asked for a two-day truce to permit his elders to find a way to turn away the commandant's wrath. Du Buisson told Pemoussa that he believed the hearts of his people were "yet bad," and that before he would even listen to the chief, the Mesquakie must first release their women hostages—a demand du Buisson's Indian allies supported. Several Frenchmen then escorted the chief safely back to the Mesquakie encampment.[3]

Two hours later, two Mascouten and one Mesquakie delivered the hostages to du Buisson. The Mascouten and Mesquakie Indians also told the commandant that they "would not eat them [the hostages], thinking you would call us to an account for it." They next asked that du Buisson tell his Indian allies, who were still assembled in the parade grounds, to allow the Mesquakie to obtain provisions for their women and children as "many" of them "die every day." With the women hostages now safely released, a cocky du Buisson told the Mesquakie that had they eaten them, "you would not have been living at this moment." He also told them that as far as their situation was concerned, du Buisson's Indian allies would determine the Mesquakie fate.[4]

It was at this time that an Illinois chief named Makouandeby, probably from the Starved Rock village who was "appointed by the chiefs of the other nations," stood to deliver a message to the Mesquakie delegates. In a commanding voice he told the Mesquakie chiefs, "Now listen to me ye nations who have troubled the earth. We perceived clearly by your words, that you seek only to surprise our father du Buisson, and to deceive him again, in demanding that we retire. We should no sooner do so, but you would again torment our father, and you would infallibly shed his blood." Makouandeby continued, "You are dogs who have always bit him . . . You have thought, wretches that you are, that we did not know all the speeches you have received from the English, telling you to cut the throats of our father, and of his children."[5] He also told them that "as soon as you shall re-enter your fort, we shall fire upon you." This threat, coupled with du Buisson's chide, would inspire the Mesquakie to attack the Illinois for years to come.

As promised, the Peoria and their allies renewed their fire on the Mesquakie camp. The Mesquakie fought back with arrows, some of them flame-tipped, igniting the straw roofs that threatened to burn down the entire French settlement. The siege wore on until a violent late-night thunderstorm drove the besieging Indians to cover, allowing the Mesquakie to escape. Once free, they headed to the shore of Lake Saint Clair where they set up an ambush for the French and Indian allies who they knew would soon take up the chase. The initial Mesquakie assault struck down a score of pursuing Indians. However, the Indian allies recovered and eventually surrounded the Mesquakie. The besieged Mesquakie again found themselves outmanned, outgunned, and without hope of reinforcements, so—they surrendered—a decision they would soon regret. The Indian allies gave the Mesquakie no quarter, killing the Mesquakie men and taking prisoner the women and children. About one hundred Mesquakie men managed to escape.[6]

The Mesquakie who had survived the massacre returned to Wisconsin, carrying news to the other bands about the treachery of the French command at Detroit. Soon afterward, the Wisconsin Mesquakie sent war parties back to Michigan where they ambushed and killed unsuspecting Frenchmen and Indians in the Lower Peninsula. Hunters were afraid to leave the safety of their villages to hunt and trap. Even more threatening, the Mesquakie problem had multiplied when the Kickapoo and Mascouten tribes who were allied with the Mesquakie, joined the Mesquakie in war against the French and their Indian allies. The addition of the Kickapoo and Mascouten tribes nearly tripled the strength of the Mesquakie.

Mortal enmity was now sealed between the Mesquakie and their allies and the French and their Indian allies. Makouandeby's insults were added to a long list of grievances that the tribe held against the French and now, against the Illinois. This affront to Mesquakie honor was yet another reason why the Fox Wars grew to become so violent. It ensured that the Starved Rock Peoria would become targets of Mesquakie wrath and reprisals.

The Peoria had yet another enemy—the Miami. The old feud between the two tribes had never really ended. In Detroit, the French command had recognized that if they could broker a peace between the Peoria and the Miami, the combination of about fifteen hundred warriors would present a substantial force, one that could strike a decisive blow against the Mesquakie. If successful, this alliance could reopen both the French fur trade and navigation on the Wisconsin and Illinois Rivers. An international motivation lay behind uniting the Miami and the Peoria—the Miami had threatened to move to the Ohio River, "precisely where the English are about to erect a fort."[7] The French could not afford to lose the Miami and their furs to the British. It required three difficult years, but in 1715, peace between the two tribes was finally achieved.

By the time Marest stopped at the Peoria village at Starved Rock, attacks by the Mesquakie and others may have occurred on an intermittent basis. In Indian society, every member of the group had a job, a role to perform. If a member of the group was killed, lost, or incapacitated, the other members of the group had to work harder to compensate for the loss. Protection of the group was paramount. This culture, coupled with the climate of uncertainty brought about by attacks from warring tribes, prompted the Illinois to make changes to secure the safety of the group.

For example, sometimes the Peoria moved to an island such as Plum or Leopold Island in front of Starved Rock. An island location forced enemies to cross a shallow and wide open river channel without cover or concealment to reach their intended victims. The Indians on the islands benefitted by having scouts and lookouts and by the warnings of barking dogs should intruders openly approach on the water, allowing ample time to prepare for an attack. Just as those who sought protection made changes in the face of wartime uncertainty, so too did warriors. Rarely would a warrior take the unnecessary risk of approaching an enemy on an island without cover or concealment, especially when he could capture or kill an enemy on the mainland at some future time. This understanding was one more reason that Indians like the Peoria often chose islands for village sites during times of war.

In 1713 the Mesquakie attacked and destroyed "several cabins at the Illinois." During this same time they killed several Wendat Indians and three Frenchmen at Detroit. They also killed a French trader named L'Épine at Green Bay. As a result of the Mesquakie attacks, the Western tribes were supplying fewer furs to French traders. Additionally, French officials worried that the English, who remained on good terms with the Mesquakie, might make inroads into the Upper Country fur trade. The consequence of these two trade considerations was the planned destruction of the Mesquakie. In the words of Canada Governor Vaudreuil and Intendant Bégon, "it is absolutely necessary to take all possible measures for destroying them."[8]

Assembling the scattered Indian bands and sending them against a consolidated, fortified, and determined Mesquakie in Wisconsin would be a daunting challenge. Claude de Ramezay, acting governor of Canada during Vaudreuil's absence between 1714 and 1716, knew that the tribes had to be "sustained" and "animated" by French authorities to ensure their cooperation. One way to do this was to give illegal traders in the West amnesty so that they could convince their Indian brothers and kin to join a French-led alliance. Louis de la Porte de Louvigny was chosen to lead a French and Indian force into the Mesquakie homelands. His goal was to convince the troublesome Mesquakie to ally with the French. If the Mesquakie refused, de Louvigny would attack them and destroy their villages.[9]

French envoys had convinced the Illinois and Miami to dispense with their quarrels and, as in 1683, unite against a common enemy. With the two long-time archrivals united, the French command hoped to assemble the tribes at what is now Chicago and then lead them, if necessary, to battle at the Mesquakie capital located near Wisconsin's Big Lake Butte des Morts. Concurrently, canoe men, voyageurs, and militiamen would bring maize, canoes, and other goods to the rendezvous site.

But the plan immediately unraveled. De Louvigny fell ill and could not command.[10] A measles epidemic struck the Miami at Detroit killing several warriors including a principal chief. Measles also battered a French contingent led by Ramezay's son Maunoir and by Dudoncour de Longeuil that was en route to a Miami village on the Wabash. The disease spread throughout the village, killing between fifteen and twenty Indians every day. Maunoir, doing his best to keep the expedition viable, left for Starved Rock to recruit a company of Peoria warriors. Before leaving, Maunoir ordered Longeuil to lead his (Longeuil's) Miami to Chicago and to wait for him there. Unfortunately for the French, Longeuil was delayed when he fell ill with the disease. Several more days passed, and of the anticipated two hundred warriors promised by tribal leaders, only twenty or thirty remaining Indians led by Longeuil were able to begin the trek to Chicago. Along the way, Longeuil's men stumbled across a Mesquakie trail, a dangerous omen as they were forced to proceed more slowly and cautiously to avoid an ambush. When the group finally arrived in Chicago, Maunoir and the Peoria were not there and neither were the canoes or further orders. In Chicago, with the forces and command in such disarray, the Miami abandoned Longeuil and returned to the Wabash.[11]

As these events were unfolding, Maunoir was traveling as fast as possible to Starved Rock. When he was about six miles from the village, he sent ahead his aide, a voyageur named Bisaillon, to tell the Peoria that Maunoir was coming to their village and would soon be there (a common practice used by the French to avoid startling the Indians). Rather than wait for Maunoir's arrival, two hundred Peoria boarded dugouts and headed upstream to greet him. After the two groups met and exchanged greetings, the tribesmen reportedly "carried him [Maunoir] to their village," an act of reverence that was the Peoria's "greatest mark of honor." At Starved Rock village, Maunoir spoke to the crowd of Indians, exhorting the young men to join him against their Mesquakie enemies. After listening to Maunoir's speech, about 450 Peoria accepted his appeal and left to rendezvous with Longeuil and his Miami at Chicago.[12] When Maunoir and the Peoria arrived in Chicago, they found no other Indians or French. There were no supplies, food, or canoes. These Peoria warriors had left home to risk their lives, to attack their well-fortified enemies, with a Frenchman who had promised everything but delivered nothing. Unable to find an explanation, Maunoir returned to Starved Rock with the Peoria to ascertain what could be done.

Several other Frenchmen leading three groups of Wendat and Potawatomi Indians from the Great Lakes also found Longeuil absent at Chicago. Unsure about what to do next, they headed to the closest village of allies in the region, the Peoria encampment at Starved Rock, hoping to find Maunoir and Longeuil there. When these parties arrived at the Rock, they learned that Maunoir and Longeuil were not there. Recognizing that the disheartened and embittered Peoria wanted no part of another uncoordinated foray against the Mesquakie, the two men had paddled to the Kaskaskia, in southern Illinois, to recruit more warriors there. Once at Kaskaskia, Maunoir became very ill with a debilitating sickness that rendered him "unable to march or write."

When he regained his health, Maunoir received news from Illinois scouts that Kickapoo and Mascouten were "hunting along a certain river."[13] Unable to attack the primary Mesquakie force in Wisconsin, Maunoir may have thought that a successful attack on Mesquakie allies would be a significant contribution to the French strategy of eradicating the Mesquakie threat to trade. He sent Bisaillon and other Frenchmen back to Starved Rock to convince the Peoria, Wendat, and Potawatomi to strike the enemy tribes at the river. Bisaillon convinced the Indians to attack and the assault was successful, as they reportedly chased the Mesquakie allies to a "steep rock where they were entrenched," a location likely located in southern Wisconsin. There the Illinois reportedly "killed more than 100 of them, and carried away 47 prisoners, without counting the women and children."[14] In spite of the success of the French and their Indian allies, the Mesquakie sent four hundred of their warriors to reinforce the Kickapoo and Mascouten. The reinforced Mesquakie allies skirmished with the Peoria and the other Illinois and in the melee, both sides suffered casualties. The attempt to chastise the Mesquakie and their allies could be considered a success, but overall, the 1715 campaign was a dismal failure in that the Mesquakie threat remained unchanged.[15]

While French officials tried to organize a more effective campaign against the Mesquakie, the tribe readied to defend itself against the formidable army that would be coming. In anticipation of the inevitable attack, the Mesquakie dug a moat and erected a palisade of "triple stakes" around their Big Lake Butte des Morts village.[16] They also secured a cache of food, gunpowder, ammunition, and other supplies as preparation against a siege. Their choice for the site of their fort complimented their defense strategy because it encompassed a flowing spring that provided the Mesquakie people with a reliable, safe water supply—an obvious lesson learned from their defeat four years earlier at Detroit. They also sent messengers to their allies requesting aid or reinforcements.[17]

The preparations were both timely and relevant. In 1716, a better prepared and better organized French and Indian force led by de Louvigny marched on the fortified Mesquakie village and set up siege operations. The French command was determined to capture and destroy the Mesquakie fort and to kill all of the fort's inhabitants. According to reports, French sappers dug trenches to undermine the palisades and bombarded the palisades with small cannon fire.[18] Despite their preparations, the Mesquakie recognized that ultimately, their fortifications would fail. Besieged by their enemies again for the third time in four years, and knowing the bloodshed and anguish they would soon suffer, the Mesquakie agreed to terms with de Louvigny.

Whether or not any Peoria from Starved Rock were in de Louvigny's force is unknown. What is known is that one of the conditions of surrender required the Mesquakie to return all prisoners, including Illinois prisoners. They complied with this demand, likely with the assumption that the Illinois would reciprocate and release Mesquakie prisoners that they held. The Illinois, however, claimed that they held no Mesquakie captives. The Mesquakie accused the Illinois of lying and keeping the Mesquakie people prisoners against their will. In the future, the subject of prisoners would remain contentious between the two tribes.

Prisoners were people who were captured in war or who were traded between tribes; they were essentially slaves who lived at the mercy of their captors. They were also important components in the Illinois Indian trade, culture, and in the fostering and maintenance of good relations with French officials and with other tribes. To the Illinois, prisoners were more than just captives who were held against their will. Prisoners were sometimes used as hostages to ensure good behavior as they were when the Iroquois arrived at Kaskaskia in 1680. Sometimes they were adopted by the tribes to replace lost members of the group. Chiefs sometimes gave honored guests in their company such as Marquette and La Salle slaves as tokens of friendship. However, the Illinois in particular were known for trading slaves to northern Great Lakes tribes, including the Odawa, in exchange for European trade goods.[19] About the Illinois Indians, historian Carl Ekberg wrote that the tribe captured slaves such as the Pawnee west of the Mississippi and traded them to the Odawa for guns and other trade items. According to available data, "sixty-eight percent of Indian slaves in Canada for whom tribal designations are available were identified as 'Panis [Pawnees]' which is an astonishingly high number even when taking into account that 'Panis' was often employed generically to mean 'Indian slave.' "[20] It also appears that women and children were more likely to be captured and held as slaves than men. Furthermore, historian Brett Rushforth maintains that "Fox [Mesquakie] men, women, and children captured in. . . . raids continued to stream into Montreal even after the French-brokered peace [of 1716]."[21] Considering that the Illinois were fully immersed in the Indian slave trade, it appears that the Mesquakie had good reason to suspect that the Illinois did indeed hold Mesquakie prisoners.

The agreement also required the Mesquakie to "make peace with all the nations dependent on the king with whom the French trade" such as the Peoria at Starved Rock and the other Illinois subtribes.[22] From the evidence, it appears that the Mesquakie had stopped their attacks on the Illinois but the Mesquakie allies, the Kickapoo and Mascouten, had not, a reality that eroded the truce.[23] The fragile peace was further damaged when the Illinois took inappropriate and unfair advantage of a treaty oversight. It was the Mesquakie, not their allies or the Illinois, who were required to obey the dictates of the accord. During 1718 and 1719, Illinois warriors killed over twenty Mesquakie, Mascouten, and Kickapoo tribesmen in ambushes and attacks.[24]

Intertribal discord was further complicated by the Illinois Country's jurisdictional transfer in 1717 from Canada to the new colony of Louisiana. Starved Rock was situated along the boundary of the two French colonies. Being at the distant northern end of Louisiana and the extreme southwestern edge of Canada, the Illinois Country represented the farthest reaches of French territory—a huge holding that lacked any authoritative or sizeable French presence.[25] It appears at this time that the Peoria at Starved Rock and the Peoria band living at Lake Peoria were the only people, save for a few Frenchmen, who were living in semi-permanent summer villages along nearly two hundred miles of the Illinois River.

Life in the Illinois Country at Starved Rock, while isolated, had structure and social order. An anonymous memoir written in 1718 provides insight as to what a traveler might have seen at the village there: "Le Roché [Starved Rock]. The jlinois live here on the bank of the River, and the French live on the Rock, which is very High and impregnable. . . . The jlinois nation of le Roché number 400 men, and are eighty Leagues from the ouyatanons [Wea, a Miami subtribe], and more than one hundred and fifty Leagues from the Renards [Mesquakie]."[26] They use bow and arrows a "great deal," dress in deer skins or buffalo robes, and wear furs of the "wild-cat, wolf, pole-cat, beaver, or otter skins." And they were heavily tattooed. As they had been doing for millennia, they made everyday items from whatever nature provided.

This passage is revealing about the Peoria Indians who lived in the Illinois Country during this time. First, the Illinois (the Peoria) are directly associated with Starved Rock itself. Starved Rock is not just a tall landform along the Illinois River; it is the home of an Indian tribe. The reference to "the Rock," means the people who live there, as well as the place. In the passage it is seen that these Peoria live on the bank of the river, while the Frenchmen who also lived at Starved Rock lived separately from the Peoria on the summit of the bluff, probably as a means of safeguarding their goods and valuables from thievery. The passage reports that there were about four hundred Peoria men living in the village in 1718, which means that the village had a total population of about two thousand people, a figure demonstrating that the Starved Rock Peoria village was larger than the Peoria Village at Lake Peoria.[27] It also reveals that the Peoria lived about 175 miles from their Ouiatanon cousins, a Miami subtribe whose village was located about five miles southwest of today's Lafayette, Indiana, and that the Peoria, "the Dreamers," still kept some of their ancient ways such as the use of the bow and arrow and their animal skin clothing, even though other options could be provided by French traders. Even more culturally insightful, the writer notes that the Peoria at Starved Rock were "very clever," a reference to their wit and humor.

In fact, when Jolliet and Marquette visited a Peoria village on the Des Moines River in the summer of 1673, the two explorers asked the tribesmen the name of the group of Indians who were living at a village some distance away. Their Peoria hosts replied that they were the *mooyiinkweena* (history's Moingwena). What Jolliet and Marquette didn't know was that *mooyiinkweena*, a word that they took for the name of an Illinois Indian subtribe, literally meant "shit-face." The name endured. Today, nearly all books, articles, and other publications written about the Illinois Indians include the "Moingwena" as an Illinois subtribe.[28]

The Peoria took full advantage of the Illinois Country's isolation and of the remote authority governing the region by continuing their unwarranted attacks on the Mesquakie. By 1719, however, the tipping point was reached and the Mesquakie finally began exacting revenge against the Illinois, primarily the Peoria. In separate ambushes east of Starved Rock, the Mesquakie killed a Peoria named Joucherinenga and three women, and later killed two Illinois men and one woman, taking three children prisoners. According to an Illinois chief, a group of Mesquakie invited a delegation of Peoria from Starved Rock to enter their camp under a flag of truce. Once inside, the Mesquakie reportedly turned on their guests, burning eleven of them to death and smashing the skulls of four others. Two other Peoria prisoners observed the slaughter and, assuming that they would soon be next, stabbed themselves to death. The rest fled for their lives, thirty of whom were captured and killed by the Mesquakie.[29] Intertribal warfare had returned to the Illinois Valley.

The Mesquakie attacks continued. In 1721, they struck Kaskaskia in southern Illinois.[30] However, the Illinois and French regrouped, rallied, and drove away the attackers. Taking up the chase, the Illinois and French eventually overtook the Mesquakie war party. After a brisk but intense fight, over thirty Mesquakie were taken prisoner. It appears that these warriors were eventually handed over to the Starved Rock Peoria, the people who had suffered the most from Mesquakie attacks.[31] The Peoria burned to death their prisoners including Minchilay, the nephew of a principal Mesquakie chief named Ouashala.

While this turmoil occurred in the Illinois Valley, a group of French canoe men paddled through the Great Lakes, ascended the St. Joseph River, portaged to the Kankakee, and eventually entered the Illinois Country. In the escort was the Jesuit teacher and historian Pierre-François

Xavier de Charlevoix, acting under the guise of a traveling missionary but really reconnoitering the West as an informant for the King of France. The journal that Charlevoix kept during this voyage is an important source of information about the manners, customs, and religions of the Indians of the period.

Charlevoix's journey through Illinois began with his observations on the *Theakiki*, the Kankakee River, where hostile tribes like the Mesquakie and the Sioux ambushed unsuspecting victims. His party, he observed, passed the *River of the Iroquois*, a reference that documents that the river was well-known by that name in 1721.[32] Another significant site Charlevoix passed was the fork of the Kankakee and Des Plaines Rivers, where his party entered the Illinois River, about which Charlevoix wrote, "it is not possible to behold a finer and better country than this which [with] its waters, at least as far as the place whence I write."[33]

About thirty-five miles west of the Forks, the party passed the mouth of the *Pisticoui*, the Fox River, where Charlevoix noted a "fall, or a rapid stream, which is called *la Charbonière*, or the *Coal-pit*, from the great quantity of sea coal found in the places adjacent." Incidentally, the first name of the city of Ottawa, where Charlevoix noted the coal pit, was Carbonia.[34] Three miles below the *Pisticoui*, on the north side of the river, the party gazed at a high bluff that the Jesuit called the *Fort of the Miamis*, today's Buffalo Rock, where some Miami Indians lived between 1683 and 1689. Two miles downstream, Charlevoix noted "another rock, quite similar to the former, and which has got the simple appellation of the Rock" (*Le Rocher*), Starved Rock.[35] Viewing *Le Rocher* in late afternoon, he described it as "steep on all sides" and that at a distance "one would take it for a fortress." He saw that some of the old palisades were visible on its summit and that the Indians had "cast up an entrenchment" there that could be easily repaired to in case of attack.

According to Charlevoix, the Peoria Indians were no longer living along the southern shore of the Illinois River as indicated in the anonymous 1718 memoir, but instead were living on an island at the foot of Starved Rock, what is now Plum Island. This relocation of the Peoria village could have been the result of the 1719 Mesquakie attacks. At the village, Charlevoix met the village chief, whom he described as "a man of about forty years of age, well-made, of a mild temper, a good countenance, and very well spoken of by the French."[36] He also encountered some of his

Figure 7.1 Jesuit Pierre-François Xavier de Charlevoix described the Starved Rock site as "steep on all sides" and noted that at a distance "one would take it for a fortress." Photo: Mark Walczynski.

"countrymen, who were trading with the Indians." After greetings were exchanged, the Jesuit next climbed to the top of Starved Rock "by a pretty easy but narrow ascent."

Once on the summit, Charlevoix recognized that the site could be easily defended—it was level, it was steep on all sides, and it was large enough for a fort "Twenty men," he wrote could "defend themselves against all the Indians of Canada, provided they had fire-arms." Since it is unlikely that a fort on the summit of the Rock could be taken by direct enemy assault, Charlevoix understood that the site's natural defenses would work to the advantage of the defenders. He wrote that although an individual warrior will wait "with pleasure for eight or ten days behind a bush in the hope that someone may pass," a group of them are less inclined to remain idle for long periods of time.[37]

Looking around, the priest eyed a ghastly spectacle which reportedly struck him with horror. Below him he saw the remains of two Mesquakie prisoners who had been burned to death by the Peoria and whose bodies had been left to be devoured by the birds. These victims may have been the remains of two of the thirty Mesquakie captured by the French and Indian party after they attacked Kaskaskia. While the repugnant sight was disturbing to Charlevoix, it was one that typified the fate of enemy warriors who were captured alive.

Charlevoix wrote that when a Peoria war party returned to their village with prisoners, a council was held to determine the fate of the captives. Sometimes prisoners were spared while at other times they were killed. When they were spared, their hands were untied, they were rushed to the river where they were thoroughly washed and then taken to the people for whom they would serve as slaves. When a prisoner was condemned to die, a loud cry informed the village that an execution would happen soon. The Indians then gathered to watch the exhibition or they helped torture the victim to death. When this happened, the captive was stripped naked and tied to a "square," two vertical wooden posts in the earth with a cross beam about two feet above the ground, and another cross beam about six feet above the first. The condemned was then fastened spread-eagle fashion on the square where he was burned on all parts of his body by the men, women, and children. When the tormenters were bored with the prisoner, they either dispatched him with an arrow or covered him in tree bark and set it on fire. The Peoria then returned to their cabins where they beat the inside walls and furniture with rods to prevent the prisoner's soul from taking up residence. After their cabin had been exorcized, they passed the remainder of the night rejoicing.[38]

Charlevoix's observations concerning the torture of prisoners seem brutal and unnecessary to the Western mind. But like any endeavor, be it a game, a process, or a method, unless the rules are understood by the observer, the actions of the participants in the game, process, or method make no sense. It is the same with torture perpetrated by Indians, typically torture by fire, on other Native Americans. It is unfortunate that nearly all written accounts of Native American torture in the Upper Country are from the European perspective, many of these written by Jesuit missionaries who viewed these practices as not only evil, but evil in regard to spiritual sensibilities. What is ironic is that it is in this spiritual dimension that Native Americans conducted ritual torture.

Unlike torture by fire that used to punish criminality, heresy, treason, or to extract confessions from suspects who had been accused of offenses against the church or state, torture by fire in Native American tradition, in the words of researcher Adam Stueck, "dealt with a complex sequence of Amerindian mourning customs, religious ideas, and a community expression of aggression, as well as a means of revenge. The event of torture allowed the entire community, men and women, young and old, to engage in a relationship with an adversary that, in the Amerindian cultural context, temporarily resided between the worlds of the living and the dead."[39] In other words, the victim and the captor who administered torture understood that the act of torture by fire pushed the boundaries of the world of the living closer and closer to that of the world of the dead.

The time of day and the method of torture used by the captor were important factors in the torture ritual. According to Stueck, "all evidence indicates that the opportunity to torture a captive by slow fire had a great deal to do with Amerindians' religious beliefs regarding the relationship between day and night."[40] When the captive was tortured at night, the captor would continue the process until dawn. If the captive showed fear or screamed during torture, they were usually killed by his or her captors while it was still dark. It appears that an important incentive for the captive to withstand torture stoically and maintain the "dualistic balance" between life and death was the belief that if they did, their *sken*, as it is called in the Wendat language, would "torment" their captor's community after their death, something akin to an "angry ghost" that caused chaos in the village. This explains why the Peoria, as Charlevoix had written, beat the inside walls of their cabins with rods after a captive died from his or her torture.[41] Torture therefore had to be administered in such a way as to produce the most pain in order to reach the cusps between life and death, yet slow enough to keep the victim alive until dawn, the symbolic boundary between life and death seen in the physical world, in order to prevent the deceased *sken* from terrorizing the village.

Charlevoix spent a relatively uneventful night at the Peoria village, although he was awakened in the middle of the night by the cries, wails, and shouts of a mourning Peoria woman who was grieving for a son who had been lost some years earlier. In the meantime, the rest of his party camped outside of the village to keep a watchful eye on their possessions. Even though the supplies were guarded, some enterprising Peoria managed to steal a musket and a few other items that were never recovered. At about 4:00 p.m. the next afternoon, Charlevoix's party left Starved Rock and traveled down the Illinois to Lake Peoria. Arriving there, Frenchmen informed the Jesuit that his party could go no farther downstream, nor could they go back upstream as several roving Mesquakie bands were reportedly in the area. Incredibly, Charlevoix's group had safely passed between the war parties. With this first-hand experience, the priest could accurately report to the king that the Illinois River—like the Fox, Wisconsin, and Mississippi Rivers—was indeed a perilous place.

While the reason that the Peoria had been living at two locations, Lake Peoria and Starved Rock, is not known, it is understandable that the two groups merged for their own protection following the presence of the Mesquakie war parties in the Illinois Valley. United they lived at Starved Rock. Documents indicate that Peoria groups often lived in separate villages. In 1666–1667, one band of Peoria lived at La Pointe, in northern Wisconsin while the others lived presumably near the confluence of the Des Moines and Mississippi Rivers.[42] In 1673, two Peoria bands lived in separate villages near the Des Moines River, where Marquette and Jolliet encountered them during their voyage down the Mississippi. In 1712 one Peoria group returned to Starved Rock, while the other group stayed either at Lake Peoria (where there was no French contact with them to verify their existence there) or had moved to Starved Rock and then moved back to Lake Peoria in 1718. In 1722, the Lake Peoria group merged with the group at Starved Rock, where they lived together.

On May 23, 1722, a French expedition in search of copper mines in the Illinois Valley left Fort de Chartres in southern Illinois and journeyed up the Mississippi then continued up the Illinois. François Philippe Renault, French superintendent of mines, led a small contingent of French soldiers and an army officer named Legardeur Delisle, who kept a journal of their voyage.

Taking the same route traversed by Jolliet and Marquette forty-nine years earlier, the French *bateaux* entered a very quiet, serene, and uninhabited Lake Peoria. Having learned at Cahokia that the Lake Peoria band had joined the others at Starved Rock, Renault dispatched an Indian and ten Frenchmen to go to the village at Starved Rock to find anyone who knew the location of a coal mine near Lake Peoria, where copper had also reportedly been found. For some unknown reason, the remaining group did not wait for the Frenchmen and their Indian guide to return but instead continued up the Illinois. Three days later, they reached the mouth of the Vermilion River. Seeing that the Starved Rock rapids prevented their boats from any further passage, the Frenchmen left the bateaux

Figure 7.2 A photograph of today's Starved Rock and Plum and Leopold Islands. In 1721 the Peoria Indians lived in a village located on an island "at the foot of Starved Rock," likely today's Plum Island. Photo: Mark Walczynski.

under guard and set off on foot along the south shore of the river, toward the Peoria village three miles upstream. Delisle reported that the Peoria village was no longer located on Plum Island, as noted by Charlevoix the year before, but had been relocated to the south shore of the Illinois River next to Starved Rock.[43] When the French group arrived at Starved Rock, most of the Peoria men were away hunting. When the hunters returned the next day Delisle, through an interpreter named Bourdon, presented them with a gift on behalf of Louisiana's governor. It was during these interactions that Delisle noted the tension between the two Peoria bands. Delisle wrote in his journal that although the two groups had been living together, they were "not agreeing well together."[44] Later that day, an Indian brought Renault two copper nuggets, one that allegedly had been found about three miles from the village. The news animated the crew. The next day they began excavating the site but after two days of fruitless digging, they reportedly had found nothing but a coal mine.

After returning to the Rock, Renault walked the bluffs behind the Peoria Indian village in search of copper. Likely treading several miles through forests and swamps and climbing the hills and bluffs of present-day Starved Rock State Park, Renault's exploration was unsuccessful. Finding nothing and without an Indian guide to help locate the coal mines at Lake Peoria, the frustrated miner left for the French fort on the Mississippi.

Even though the Renault expedition was a failure in that no copper had been found, Delisle's journal of the mission contains important demographic, historical, and geographical information that scholars use today.

While French officials traveled, searched for ore, traded, and observed, and while intra-tribal issues continued to affect the interrelation between the two Peoria bands at Starved Rock, the hatred between the Mesquakie and the Peoria and other Illinois subtribes continued to fester. The 1721 burning of Minchilay, nephew of Mesquakie chief Ouashala, by the Peoria was about to escalate intertribal war to a broader and more brutal level. In Wisconsin, the Mesquakie were planning to avenge the horrific death of Minchilay.

The ongoing warfare between the Mesquakie and the Illinois had to some extent weakened Ouashala's influence, especially among his young men. The chief had maintained an arm's-length relationship with the French—one that tolerated them, but his stance changed markedly when he learned about the capture and burning of Minchilay and the Mesquakie prisoners. Set on revenge, Ouashala assembled a large war party and set out for Starved Rock, hoping to destroy their village completely [the Starved Rock Peoria village] and to spare no lives whatever.[45]

Much of the information pertaining to the Mesquakie raid at Starved Rock is vague, confusing and sometimes contradictory. Drawing from multiple sources, it appears that Ouashala's war party was very large and may have included warriors from other tribes including the Sioux, Winnebago, and Sauk Indians, and may have also included women and children who prepared food, carried supplies, and performed tasks to help the warriors.[46]

No known account describes the initial Mesquakie assault on the village. Since the shallow, rocky river protected the front of the village while the steep bluffs behind secured the site's rear, the attackers may have waded across the river and attacked the Peoria village before or at sunrise to escape detection. Trapped between the river and the cliffs and awakened by gunshots, cries, and war whoops, the Peoria men would have likely scrambled to organize a defense, providing time for the non-combatants to flee to the apparent safety of the summit of Starved Rock. Following behind the women, children, and elderly were the men who eventually joined the others on the Rock. In the melee, the Mesquakie captured several Peoria prisoners, including some children.[47]

The Peoria who had survived the attack were now on Starved Rock and surrounded by enemies. Having had no advance warning of the Mesquakie raid, they had brought no provisions with them. They were fortunate to have reached the summit of the Rock with their lives. A waiting game had begun.

According to Ouashala's account, the Peoria recognized that they were trapped without food or water and were without the resources to obtain them. The Peoria also realized that they had no choice other than to appeal to the Mesquakie and convince them to let them live as they were, according to one source, reduced "to such extremities that they were Obliged to Sue for their lives."[48] Before Ouashala could negotiate with the Peoria, he had to convince his young warriors to allow him to do so. Given the complete helplessness of the Peoria on the Rock's summit, the young Mesquakie warriors were initially opposed to any negotiation. Eventually, Ouashala was able to convince his men to hear what the Peoria had to offer. Shortly thereafter several Illinois chiefs in the company of three interpreters, asked the Mesquakie war party to "withdraw, as they were reduced to the last extremity."[49] Ouashala's warriors heard the pleas of the Illinois ambassadors but remained unmoved in their resolve to finish off the Peoria. Ouashala, however, tried to convince his people to spare the Peoria their lives. He reminded his warriors of the mercy de Louvigny had shown the Mesquakie people when they had been besieged in similar fashion at Butte des Morts in 1716.[50] Navangounik, Ouashala's brother, came forward to support the chief. Eventually, these two Mesquakie elders persuaded their warriors to grant the Peoria their lives and to withdraw from Starved Rock. The siege was ended and Ouashala and his war party returned to Wisconsin. After the Mesquakie had gone, the Peoria descended Starved Rock and fled to the Mississippi River, in southern Illinois, where they lived for the next several years among the other Illinois subtribes.

Period documents substantiate the belief that the Peoria had been besieged on Starved Rock at this time. Vaudreuil later wrote to the French

Minister that "The Renards [Mesquakie] last year [1722] besieged The Ilinois of Le Rocher," Starved Rock.[51] When Ouashala and his war party returned to Wisconsin, he told Montigny, French commandant at the Green Bay post, "I pressed them [the Peoria] very hard, and it depended only upon myself to carry out my project fully; for, finding themselves on the verge of destruction, reduced by hunger, and deprived of all means of getting water, so that they were beginning to die of thirst."[52] Other period French sources, including the journal entry of Inspector General of Louisiana Diron d'Artaguette, corroborate these reports. In fact, d'Artaguette even dispatched two rescue parties to liberate the trapped Illinois.[53]

Ouashala also told Montigny that he could have destroyed the Peoria, that although he and his men could have counterattacked the French force and escaped their predicament at the Butte des Morts siege in 1716, the Starved Rock Peoria did not have that option. They had been trapped, without hope of escape.

Attempting to persuade Montigny that the Mesquakie were not French enemies, the chief told the French commandant that he made sure that no harm would befall any French they encountered during their march to Starved Rock. Ouashala pleaded with Montigny to relay these things to "Onontio," Governor Vaudreuil. He ended his speech by promising that "the wars are all ended today," that is "unless we are first attacked."[54]

While there is no record of Ouashala's thoughts, the chief, motivated by the tortured death of his nephew wanted to kill many Starved Rock Peoria. By launching a surprise attack on the Peoria village, he had assumed that he and his warriors would kill many Peoria Indians and return victorious to Wisconsin. He had not expected that the Peoria, rather than stand their ground and fight, would instead flee to the Starved Rock summit. He certainly did not anticipate that he would have the entire village at his mercy, trapped without provisions. Even though his warriors could not scale Starved Rock to attack on the summit, there had been no need to attack—without provisions, time and siege would have effectively killed his adversaries. Ouashala could boast complete victory with few if any casualties. In fact, Ouashala could boast the greatest military victory in all Native American history, one that could more than double the losses inflicted by Indians on Arthur St. Clair's troops in 1791.[55] Had Ouashala continued the siege, more than two thousand people would have perished, and an entire subtribe of Indians would have ceased to exist. The lure of these possibilities must have been great.

Nonetheless, Ouashala recognized that the Illinois were allies of the French and that the French could unite the many Indian tribes in the Upper Lakes region to make war against the Mesquakie. Beyond the defense of their Indian allies, the French had a vested interest in maintaining their already-established trade opportunities with the Illinois. Ouashala was understandably concerned that French and Indian forces would retaliate and possibly fight a war of extermination against the Mesquakie. With the facts and risks considered, Ouashala chose to show mercy to the Starved Rock Peoria and to leverage that mercy to convince the French governor of Ouashala's compassion. One day, French assistance might be required.

Montigny then spoke to the chief and the Mesquakie chiefs seated with him. He first told them that "the war which you, with all those who have accompanied you, have just waged against the Ilinois is very unjust, having no other pretext than to avenge the death of Minchilay—who brought about his own death very foolishly, having attacked people with whom he was not at war." He also said that those Mesquakie who "engaged him in this war were more to blame than the Ilinois." But in burning Minchilay "as cruelly as they did [the Peoria] they were wrong, because they showed by this unworthy action that they wished for no reconciliation with this nation."[56] He also promised to relay the chief's message to the governor, that Ouashala had shown his enemies mercy. He finished by telling Ouashala, "I will say to you that it is to be desired for your nation that you be faithful in all your promises, since you will by this means obtain from us in the future the pity that you desire."[57]

At the conclusion of the meeting between Ouashala and Montigny, the men parted. Following this outcome, Ouashala surely wanted to live out the rest of his days quietly, but ultimately he would not. Sometime afterward, his unruly warriors attacked some Ojibwe on the Saint Joseph River, creating even more intertribal enmity. Ouashala was present but only to ensure that the warriors did not harm any Frenchmen that they encountered.[58] The French would remain allies and trade partners with the Illinois even though Governor Vaudreuil believed that they, not the Mesquakie, had been responsible for much of the chaos in the West. The Peoria would make southern Illinois their home but would return to Starved Rock again.

By late 1722 the Peoria Indians were living on the Mississippi, several hundred miles from Starved Rock. Distance, they assumed, provided relative safety from Mesquakie attacks as did their numbers. At this time about seven hundred Illinois warriors lived in the area among three villages.[59] Early in 1723 an Illinois Indian reported to French Inspector General d'Artaguette that Mesquakie were heading to Starved Rock to establish a village there.[60] The Illinois, who considered Starved Rock to be within their territory, were outraged. In hopes of stopping the Mesquakie before the main body of the tribe arrived, the Illinois dispatched thirty warriors to strike the Mesquakie vanguard. The Mesquakie, aware that their occupation of Starved Rock might be fiercely opposed by the Illinois, were ready for the skirmish and reportedly drove off the Illinois war party. On June 1 d'Artaguette, learning of a report that six hundred Mesquakie were en route to attack the Illinois at Cahokia, sent reinforcements from Fort de Chartres to the small French post at Cahokia. The preparations though were for naught because the Mesquakie army never appeared; throughout that summer, however, there were scattered ambushes and killings along the Mississippi.

Throughout this period, a continuing obstacle to peace was the Mesquakie belief that the Illinois continued to hold Mesquakie prisoners and that the Illinois refused to release them. In 1724 this belief fueled raids by the Kickapoo, Mascouten, and Sauk Indians, all Mesquakie allies.[61] What further heightened Mesquakie outrage was the knowledge that Ouashala could have taken hundreds of Illinois prisoners at the Rock, but had chosen not to do so, and that in 1716 the Mesquakie had returned all of the Illinois prisoners that they had held. The Mesquakie continued their raids, forcing French officials to act.

The following year Claude Charles du Tisné, French officer and one time commandant of Fort de Chartres, wrote Governor Vaudreuil that "Our Illinois have no Slaves belonging to the Renards [Mesquakie] and have Never acted Treacherously toward them."[62] The Jesuits also spoke on behalf of the Illinois in a letter written to du Tisné, as Fathers Boullenger and Kereben wrote, "We Certify that in our Illinois villages there are no renard [Mesquakie] slaves, except one girl who is with the Chief of the metchicamias [Michigamea, an Illinois subtribe]; and the latter has promised to surrender her as soon as they give up to him His son Vensa."[63] The Illinois also restated their claim that they held no Mesquakie prisoners.

The verbal standoff in the West was about to erupt into war. Emotion, not reason, was causing young Mesquakie men to discard the advice of their elders and lash out at the French and the Illinois. Rather than follow the traditional method of council, discussion, and analysis to find a solution, the incensed Mesquakie warriors prepared for battle, alienating themselves from the more conservative chiefs who recognized that they were losing control of a significant portion of their tribe. This fracture led to an avoidable and even more costly conflict.

Through alternating years of peace and war, accusations and apologies, treaties and violations of treaties, it seemed that there was little that French officials could do to stop the intertribal conflicts in the West. Given the strained and potentially explosive relations between the Mesquakie and the Illinois, and the resulting impact on trade, French authorities were compelled to act. Charles le Moyne de Longueuil, acting Governor of Canada, sent Captain de Lignery to Green Bay with orders to meet the Mesquakie, Sauk, and Winnebago chiefs in an effort to stop the attacks on the Illinois. At the conclusion of the meeting, the tribal leaders told de Lignery that they "have given their promise to maintain peace." In a letter to Charles-Henri-Joseph Tonti, Sieur Desliettes—cousin of the Delliette (the last names of the Delliette cousins are spelled differently) of Starved Rock fame—de Lignery briefed Desliettes about the meeting's outcome. De Lignery directed Desliettes to return any Illinois-held Mesquakie prisoners to the Mesquakie people. De Lignery planned, if the peace lasted through the year, to host a general conference with all Western tribes at Chicago, Starved Rock, or Green Bay.[64]

Charles de la Boische, Marquis de Beauharnois, arrived in Canada in 1726 as the colony's new governor. Immediately apprising himself of the Indian issues, he developed his own strategy to control the potentially destructive situation. While he appreciated the peace that de Lignery had achieved, he further understood that maintaining that peace would be expensive. French traders would need to provide the tribes with goods and services, essentially bribery, in exchange for preserving the peace, and would also be required to intervene in tribal affairs by helping chiefs like Ouashala control their young men. In fact, this intervention was already urgent. Ouashala's warriors had reportedly formed a war party and were preparing to strike the Illinois again.

In the meantime, Desliettes had replied to de Lignery, writing that the "surest method" of dealing with the Mesquakie was not to bribe them to be civil, but to "destroy them." Disagreeing with Beauharnois, Des-liettes' position was that French forces should pursue the Mesquakie, destroy their villages and their crops, and ultimately destroy the tribe. Beauharnois recognized the logic of Desliettes' position but he also was very aware that if the Mesquakie knew that the French military planned to attack them, the Mesquakie would flee to the protection of their friends, the Sioux or Iowa, who would in turn harass Frenchmen in the Upper Country, making the situation even more difficult.[65] As the friction and animosity between the Mesquakie and the Illinois increased with every Mesquakie skirmish and harassment, the French under Beau-harnois were pushed to action.

While French officials were developing a plan for dealing with the Mes-quakie, the Mascouten and Kickapoo severed ties with their long-time Mesquakie allies over the fate of some French prisoners. The departure of the Mascouten and Kickapoo from the Mesquakie alliance reduced the number of warriors the Mesquakie could muster against the Illinois, limiting the tribe's ability to wage war on multiple fronts. Making matters worse for the Mesquakie, the Mascouten and Kickapoo joined the Illinois against their former allies.

In August 1728, acting on their plan to destroy the Mesquakie, about 1,450 French and Indians marched through Mesquakie lands in Wis-consin, but the Mesquakie were gone, having fled before the French and Indian contingent arrived. However, the Franco-Indian force destroyed Mesquakie villages and burned unharvested the maize, and that of the nearby Winnebago as well. For the first time in over a decade, French offi-cials were in a powerful position to negotiate peace with the Mesquakie.

While the French position was strengthened against the Mesquakie, so was that of the Illinois, whose numbers had grown by the same number as those of the Mesquakie had diminished, with the defection of the Mas-couten and Kickapoo to the Illinois. In addition, the Ojibwe and Odawa from the Upper Lakes along with the Winnebago and some Menominee joined the ever growing anti-Mesquakie cause. Together, these tribes attacked a Mesquakie village, killing over one hundred people. Early the next year, the same allied group attacked a second village, killing more than three hundred Mesquakie men, women, and children.[66] They also attacked a large party of Mesquakie who were returning from a buffalo hunt in Iowa.[67] Abandoned by their allies, surrounded by enemies, and pursued by their French adversaries, Mesquakie diplomats convinced the Seneca Iroquois who lived in present-day western New York State to grant them asylum. Having done this, the Mesquakie next had to traverse allied-controlled country to secure safety.

The Mesquakie chose to get to Seneca country by traveling south into Illinois and then heading east through Indiana, Ohio, and Pennsylvania.[68] Although this route was longer and required permission of the Miami to allow them to pass through their lands unmolested, it seemed safer than the Great Lakes route because the wilds of the Great Kankakee Swamp, once the second largest wetland in the United States, would mask their retreat. It was important that a safe route be chosen because the Mesquakie group, in addition to warriors, also included women, children, the elderly, and people who had a variety of different ailments and disabilities. Their group moved slowly, only as fast as the slowest person could travel.

The Mesquakie were not the only Indians on the move. It had been eight years since the Peoria had been besieged and during this time the Mesquakie had been abandoned by their allies. Further, French authorities were planning the Mesquakie destruction. This news may have given the Peoria a sense of security. The Peoria and a group of Cahokia Indians, another Illinois subtribe, slowly made their way up the Illinois Valley and eventually arrived back at Starved Rock.

In 1730 the Mesquakie made their way from Wisconsin to their Seneca asylum by following the Fox River of Illinois, a route that took them to Ottawa, nine miles east of Starved Rock. Reaching this milestone, it is probable that they hunted to replenish their food supply, repaired their clothes and footwear, and rested to refresh the struggling members of the group.[69] In the upland prairies near Starved Rock, Mesquakie hunters, probably believing the Starved Rock area to have been abandoned by the Peoria since their siege, were surprised when they encountered some Illinois hunters. A short skirmish ensued that resulted in the Mesquakie capturing seventeen Illinois who were brought to the Mesquakie camp. This victorious skirmish was a miscalculation on the part of the Mesquakie. Several other Illinois had escaped through the tall grass and had raced to the Starved Rock village to spread the alarm and plan an attack. To make matters worse, the Illinois reported that one of the captives taken by the Mesquakie was a son of a Cahokia chief.

The Mesquakie recognized how perilous a situation they were now in. They had hoped to skirt around the bottom of Lake Michigan by using the interconnected waterways and the Kankakee Marsh to conceal their passage to reach the Seneca lands undetected, or at least to remain undetected until they had entered Miami territory. Now, because of the unexpected encounter with the Illinois hunters, the Mesquakie had been discovered by the Illinois. It was imperative that they allay the fears of the Peoria and Cahokia of Starved Rock by convincing them that the Mesquakie meant them no harm. The Mesquakie likely hoped to persuade the Illinois to let them pass peacefully through the eastern extent of Illinois land, unannounced to other tribes and the French, until the Mesquakie had traveled at least some distance from the Starved Rock area. To this end, a small Mesquakie delegation went to the Starved Rock village to plead their case to Illinois leaders, presumably planning to bargain with their seventeen Illinois prisoners. It is also possible that the Mesquakie representatives unveiled their plan to reach the Seneca by way of Miami territory in order to demonstrate to the Illinois that the Mesquakie had no intention to remain in the Starved Rock area for long. But this would not be the case. Such enmity existed between the two tribes that in the council chambers an unruly Illinois attacked a Mesquakie delegate with a tomahawk and hunting knife, superficially wounding him. The attacker was quickly subdued and escorted from the lodge, but no agreement was struck. The Mesquakie delegation returned to their camp where a few days later they burned their Illinois captives to death. Illinois runners were dispatched to Fort de Chartres to notify the French command that the Mesquakie had assembled *en masse* and were vulnerable and isolated on the Illinois prairies.[70] It also appears that during this time the Peoria sent messengers to the Potawatomi, Kickapoo, and Mascouten Indians, advising them the location of their Mesquakie enemies.[71]

The Mesquakie had few options. They could not continue east as planned as their route would take them perilously close to the French fort on the Saint Joseph where the French contingent would undoubtedly recruit the Miami to fight against the Mesquakie. They found themselves in a distant and hostile land, far from their homelands in Wisconsin. They were without allies and knowing that if they remained where they were or if they attempted to leave the Starved Rock area, the French and their Indian allies would pursue them. Confronted with the reality that their options were extremely limited, the Mesquakie headed south, traveling blindly through the Illinois prairie. As they chopped their way through the tall grass made worse by the scorching summer sun and swarms of flies and mosquitoes, Cahokia and Peoria snipers, time and time again, shot into the Mesquakie group. For days the Mesquakie endured these hardships until they saw that their passage was blocked and that they were surrounded by their enemies.[72] Besieged again, this time at a site believed by researchers to be near Arrowsmith, Illinois, surrounded by St. Ange's Frenchmen, Potawatomi, Sauk, Illinois, Wea, and Piankashaw warriors, the Mesquakie reportedly "begged for their lives" but to no avail.

Eventually the Mesquakie, having exhausted their food and water supply, were forced to eat "dressed hides." Though they knew that death was inevitable, they hoped that their enemies would have mercy on their young. With this expectation, they threw about three hundred of their children over the walls of the Mesquakie earthworks. It is believed that their besiegers adopted the Mesquakie children into their tribes.[73] As the siege wore on, about two hundred Illinois, impatient with the standoff left for home. The French command, however, was determined to defeat the Mesquakie. It appeared that all hope for the besieged Mesquakie was lost when an unexpected event provided for their escape.

The assistance came in the form of a tremendous evening storm that struck the Illinois prairies, like the tempest that had belted Detroit in 1712. When the besieging allies ran for cover, the Mesquakie made their escape. Into the fury of darkness, wind, and rain they ran without a plan. In the turmoil, they lost all sense of direction. Gathering in groups for safety, they negotiated the unfamiliar terrain, wandering aimlessly in the vast ocean of alien prairie, trying to avoid those who would kill them if they were discovered.[74] Rather than chance running into a Mesquakie ambush, the allies waited until daybreak to take up their trail. When the allies finally did catch up with their "prey," they showed them no mercy. Most of the Mesquakie who had fled their fort were captured and gunned down where they stood or were tortured to death. About fifty to sixty warriors who escaped the ordeal returned to Wisconsin where a few of their kin who had not left to join the Seneca were still living. The actual number of Mesquakie who had been killed at the Illinois "Fox Fort Siege" is unknown as the reported number of casualties varies between four hundred and twelve hundred people.[75]

The Mesquakie threat to Starved Rock and the Illinois Valley was finally over. The irony in all of this is that the tribe that had besieged and could have exterminated the Peoria at Starved Rock in 1722 had been besieged themselves in 1730 and had been nearly exterminated.

8

1730–1776:
We Leave, Never to Return

(Nimecimehkaamina)

By 1730 Starved Rock was a well-known landmark, and as such was a familiar reference point in the vast wilderness of the West. The site gave travelers, traders, missionaries, and French officials a sense of geographical perspective. For example, in a document written by the commandant at Detroit, the Mesquakie were reported "fighting with the illinois," between *Le Rocher* (Starved Rock) and Ouiatanon, a designated place between two *known* points amid a great expanse of wilderness.[1] Governor Beauharnois and Intendant Hocquart used Starved Rock as a reference in writing to the French minister about the death of a great Cahokia chief's son, "some of their people" had been burned near *Le Rocher*, on the Illinois River. In 1731 the Intendant wrote to the French Minister that the Mesquakie had been defeated in a plain located between the Wabash and Illinois Rivers, about sixty leagues south of the southern shore of Lake Michigan, "to The East South East of *le rocher* in the Illinois Country."[2] Further, as a noteworthy and recognized place, Starved Rock had been chosen as one of three possible sites where the French administration in Canada had considered hosting a grand council of the tribes from Louisiana and Canada.[3] *Le Rocher* was an important geographical marker, a notable and unmistakable landmark, and a point on the globe that was familiar to Frenchmen and Indians alike.

By 1732 nearly all Peoria Indians were living at villages in the Illinois Valley, at either Starved Rock or at Lake Peoria.[4] That year, according to one account, there were sixty cabins of Peoria, or about 1,200 people, resettled at Starved Rock.[5] It is unlikely that 1,200 people were living at Starved Rock at this time as there were only approximately 1,700 Peoria Indians alive a decade earlier, a point in time that marked a decade of dramatic decline in population of all Illinois subtribes.[6] This does demonstrate, however, that some Peoria Indians had returned to Starved Rock to establish a semi-permanent summer village.[7]

For the Illinois, especially the Peoria and possibly some Cahokia living at Starved Rock, it appeared that the Mesquakie threat had been extinguished. Realistically, the upper Illinois Valley should have been a safer place to live. French and allied engagements against the Mesquakie now would be offensive, to utterly destroy the tribe if necessary. To this, Canada governor Beauharnois wrote, "Although I have granted [the remnant of the Foxes] their lives on the condition that I have the honor of mentioning to you [French Minister of Marine], The savages [the French allies] appear to me to be inclined to wipe out that race, and I shall Maintain them in that disposition if the Renards [the Mesquakie] fail to do what they promised me."[8] The village at Starved Rock would be a base of operations for these actions.

During the winter of 1731–1732 a war party of Christian Iroquois and Wendat, with logistical support provided by Henri-Louis Deschamps de Boishébert, commandant at Detroit, attacked a Mesquakie village located in southwest Wisconsin, killing approximately seventy men and eighty women and children. They also captured approximately one hundred-forty women, children, and elderly.[9] Fifty-six of these prisoners, mainly children and the elderly who could not keep pace with the rest of group, were killed by their captors while they were being escorted east by the Iroquois and Wendat. When the Wendat and their prisoners arrived at Detroit, the French second-in-command at the post, Jean-Charles d' Arnaud, met with the Wendat headmen and ably convinced them that the captured Mesquakie were "snakes in their bosom, particularly certain individuals." The Wendat considered the words of Arnaud and shortly thereafter killed the remaining Mesquakie prisoners.[10]

In 1732 the Starved Rock Peoria joined Potawatomi, Mascouten, and Wendat warriors in attacking a fortified Mesquakie village at Lake "Marameg," possibly today's Pistakee Lake in Lake County, Illinois.[11] In a brisk action there the Mesquakie bravely defended themselves and their village, repulsing the attackers and counterattacking when their enemies fled the field. The confrontation ended in an agreement between the tribes in which the Mesquakie agreed to meet with French officials at either Detroit or on the St. Joseph in the following year.[12]

Having no one to help defend his people from the incessant onslaughts of the French and their Indian allies, Mesquakie chief Kiala and the few elders who remained decided to leave their village and move to Green Bay where they would seek protection among ancient friends of the Mesquakie, the Sauk Indians. Like the Mesquakie, the Sauk, according to legend, left their camps in Quebec and relocated to Massachusetts. Together the two tribes took the same route west and eventually settled in Michigan, the Mesquakie at Detroit and the Sauk in the Saginaw Bay area. Crossing the Straits of Mackinac, the Mesquakie and Sauk moved south, both tribes settling in eastern Wisconsin, the Mesquakie along the Fox River and the Sauk in the vicinity of Green Bay. The two tribes shared a legendary and historic past, sometimes as partners while at other times rivals. Not long after the Mesquakie reached the Sauk village, French officer Nicolas-Antoine Coulon de Villiers, acting on the instructions of governor Beauharnois arrived with Indian allies to "gather all the Mesquakie and escort them to Montreal to be scattered among tribes loyal to the French." If the Mesquakie did not comply, de Villiers was instructed to "destroy them" to "kill Them without thinking of making a single Prisoner, so as not to leave one of the race alive in the upper Country If possible."[13]

De Villiers appeared at the Sauk fort and demanded that the Sauk relinquish the Mesquakie hiding inside. The Sauk refused. De Villiers and the Frenchmen who were with him attempted to force their way into the Sauk compound. Angered by the intimidating strong-arm tactics of de Villiers and his unjustified attempt to force his way into their village, the Sauk opened fired on the officer and his men. Shots were exchanged between the two sides. When it was over, de Villiers, a son, and a son-in-law had been killed, as were several other French. French native allies, who had been stationed around the Sauk fort to prevent the Sauk and Mesquakie from escaping, left their posts and joined their French comrades. They too were unable to enter the Sauk fort. A stalemate ensued.

Three days later the Sauk and Mesquakie fled their Green Bay village and headed west to avoid French retaliation. A combined force of French soldiers and allied warriors took up pursuit. Catching up to the Sauk and Mesquakie along the Fox River at Little Butte des Morts, the two groups exchanged gunfire. When the smoke cleared, twenty-seven French and allies lay dead or wounded. The Sauk and Mesquakie suffered thirty-five casualties.[14] The French command called off the chase and returned to Green Bay.

During the summer of 1734, Beauharnois directed Captain Nicolas-Joseph des Noyelles to lead a Franco-Indian expedition to locate the Sauk and Mesquakie to "separate" the two tribes and, if possible, seize the Mesquakie.[15] Leaving Montreal Noyelles arrived at Detroit, where he learned that some of his more reliable allies—including the Odawa and Ojibwe—refused to join his expedition, while other warriors who had accompanied him to Detroit decided to abandon the group. After leaving Detroit, intertribal disputes broke out among some of the allies. Making matters worse for the French-Indian group was the dearth of provisions that were needed to feed and support the expedition. Finally, in April 1735, Noyelles and his "dispirited" men located the Sauk and Mesquakie in east-central Iowa, where several skirmishes were fought between the two sides.[16] Finding themselves outnumbered by a better supplied and more motivated group who had no intention of surrendering, Noyelles asked the Sauk to meet with an envoy to discuss relinquishing the Mesquakie to him.[17] After two days of talks, the Sauk proposed to Noyelles that they would surrender the Mesquakie if the French and their allies would withdraw. Safe from French retaliation, the Sauk said they would then return to their Green Bay village and deliver the Mesquakie to them.[18] Knowing full well that the Sauk had no intention of returning to Wisconsin, Noyelles considered his situation: his men were hungry, cold, and dispirited; they were without adequate provisions or means to obtain them; and he realized that some of his allies including the Kickapoo might switch sides and join the Sauk and Mesquakie. Noyelles decided to quit the siege; he and his men then withdrew to the Illinois Country.[19]

Rather than continue their campaign of genocide against the Mesquakie, the French administration decided to utilize its resources where
they were needed most—in the lower Mississippi Valley against the fierce
Chickasaw tribe, who were allies and trade partners of the British. The
Chickasaw would deliver several major defeats to French forces and their
Illinois allies, but in a little more than twenty years the Illinois would
again meet the Mesquakie, who in the company of other tribes would
emerge victorious against them.

With Mesquakie attacks on the Peoria in the Illinois Valley abated
and their own existence more secure, the Illinois, Miami, and other tribes
renewed old rivalries that had gone dormant during the wars with the
Mesquakie. No longer fearful of Mesquakie attacks, thirty warriors from
the Starved Rock village who were en route to attack their ancient enemy,
the Sioux, stumbled upon a mixed group of Ojibwe, Menominee, Sauk,
and Nipissing Indians in Wisconsin. For reasons unknown, the Illinois
attacked the group and killed three men, three women, and a child "in a
cradle." They also captured two young girls. The older and wiser Peoria
chiefs realized that this unwarranted and senseless assault on Indians with
whom they were not at war put the entire Peoria village in danger of a
retributive attack.[20] Consequently, four chiefs from the Starved Rock village traveled to Michilimackinac where they relinquished the two children
to Montigny, the fort's commander, hoping both to seek French assistance
in mediating the crisis and to demonstrate remorse and good faith in order
to mitigate enemy retaliation. The chiefs also gave Montigny a "collar"
and begged him to have "pity on Them and to speak to the nations to
induce them to forget the evil Deed that their young Men have Done."
Montigny reported that he sent orders to the commandants of the French
outposts to "Prevent the nations from Attacking Them [the Peoria] until
this matter can be settled."[21]

It was important for the French colonial government to have as accurate
an estimate as possible of the number of Indians living near French settlements. With this information, the French administration could determine the number of Indian allies who could be relied upon in times of
war as well as the volume and extent of trade from and trade goods required for the tribes. From a defensive standpoint, the census provided
relevant information should tribal allegiances change. With knowledge

of Indian population numbers, French forces were able to better respond tactically to military threats. The missionaries also wanted to know population counts. These numbers translated into converts or potential converts in each village, and allowed the missionaries to efficiently distribute their limited manpower.

When French officials wanted to know how many Indians there were in any given village, it was not necessary to count every individual. Instead, they applied general information to a given village to extrapolate population. As we have explained in chapter 3, French officials and Catholic missionaries calculated that the Illinois, for example, had a four-to-one ratio: every warrior represented a group of five people, or a family. Extrapolating further, the French had observed that there were approximately two families of five persons to one fire; there were two fires per cabin, thereby concluding that each Illinois cabin housed about twenty people. Using this methodology, missionaries like Marquette, Allouez, Membré, and others, counted cabins when they arrived at Indian villages. This same method was later employed by the British and the Americans.

By 1736, there were only about fifty Peoria warriors, or about two hundred fifty people, reportedly living at the Starved Rock village.[22] The census that enumerated the numbers of Illinois Indians at this time failed to take into account the Peoria tribesmen who lived at Lake Peoria, a group that was probably larger than the band of Peoria who were living at Starved Rock. By way of comparison, it was reported that there were at this time, about one hundred Kaskaskia warriors, or about five hundred people, and about two hundred combined Cahokia and Tamaroa warriors, or about one thousand people, living along the Mississippi River.[23]

Even though the Sauk had been a menace to French interests because they had protected the Mesquakie from extermination and had killed several French soldiers, some Sauk had fallen on hard times. According to Paul Louis Dazemard Sieur de Lusignan the commandant at the Saint Joseph River fort, a delegation of Sauk Indians arrived at his post, reportedly "quite naked and in tears," and "to offer him [de Lusignan] a Calumet and to beg for their Lives." Arriving to aid the downtrodden Sauk were the Potawatomi, Miami, Illinois from Starved Rock, and Odawa who had seen their plight and tried to help them by giving them food.[24]

The tolerance and peaceful coexistence demonstrated by this event was short-lived. Similar to the pointless 1732 attack by the hot-headed young warriors on the already-vanquished Mesquakie, which had resulted in Peoria elders seeking pardon and intervention by French officials to keep the peace, so too was the indiscriminate killing of a Frenchman "in the Ilinois," an incident that occurred in 1738. According to one account, a group of Winnebago Indians arrived at the Sioux Company post on the Rock River where French officer Paul Marin de La Malgue was told by the tribesmen that a war party of Sauk and Mesquakie Indians led by a Mesquakie chief had killed a Frenchman. The murder had occurred inexplicably while the perpetrator's village chief, a man named Mekaga, was at Montreal pleading his people's case before French authorities, attempting to reconcile past Mesquakie misdeeds. When the chief learned that some of his people had senselessly killed a Frenchman, he became so enraged that he reportedly had to be "restrained." Calling to his people, intent on sending a message to the murderers, the chief yelled, "You Are Dogs; while I go to beg for your lives, you kill a Frenchman." The killers claimed, however, that they did not know that their victim was a Frenchman as they had shot at him "from a great distance."[25] The uncalled for and unapologetic murder of the Frenchman in the Illinois Country plainly demonstrated the dysfunctional societal splintering of the Mesquakie people as the young men sought only self-gratification without considering potential consequences to their own people for killing without motive or forethought and for shunning the wisdom and advice of those who knew very well how this episode could bring down the wrath of the French and their allies upon the Mesquakie people again.

In 1741, in an apparent case of mistaken identity, believing that they had encountered Missouri Indians, the Sauk killed nine Peoria and captured five others. When the Sauk learned that their captives were Illinois and not Missouri, the Sauk stated, "My brothers, we Are sorry for what has happened. If you Had named yourselves, we would not have attacked you."[26] Immediately the Sauk sent messengers to the Peoria at Starved Rock and Lake Peoria to tell the tribesmen that they had "no share in the affair which Had occurred, and that they wished to live in peace with them." It appears that war was averted even though the French administration in Illinois and the West feared that the incident might lead "to open War between the two nations."

The above reference to the Peoria Indians living at Starved Rock in 1741 is the last known period source that identifies a semi-permanent summer village of Peoria at Starved Rock. Whether it was because the Indians at Starved Rock had again exhausted the area's resources, because they enjoyed improved relations with their kin, or possibly because their dwindling numbers left them vulnerable to attack by other tribes, nearly all of the Starved Rock Peoria had migrated and settled again at Lake Peoria.

In spring 1751 a Potawatomi and Ojibwe war party that included a few Mascouten and Menominee descended the Illinois River, intent on striking the Lake Peoria village. According to one account, the group first landed at Starved Rock at daybreak where they found four Peoria cabins, likely the remains of a winter hunting camp, but found no Peoria people. The only soul around was a French trader named Jean Brossac. Seeing that his comrades intended to kill the Frenchman, one Ojibwe grabbed Brossac by the arm to protect him from the others. Just when he did, a shot rang out. The ball hit the trader and killed him. In their zeal to attack the Peoria, this misjudgment of murdering Brossac was one that the war party immediately recognized. The Ojibwe sought the forgiveness of M. Duplessis, French commandant at Michilimackinac. Duplessis concluded that the event was not a mistake, calling it "a piece of rank treachery." When news of the murder reached Canada, Governor Jacques-Pierre de Marquis de la Jonquière, ordered Duplessis to tell the Ojibwe that "I will not leave the death of this Frenchman unpunished, that it is absolutely necessary that they come to Montreal themselves next year to deliver up the murderer to me at discretion, and that if they fail in it I shall revenge the death and shall give them no quarter."[27] He also told him that "Next year I shall examine into this matter quite closely, and if this Indian has really done this deed by treachery, I shall have him tomahawked as this disposition of the affair is indispensable." After leaving Starved Rock, the war party continued to Lake Peoria where they were ambushed and driven away. During the incident, three Potawatomi Indians and a Mascouten were captured by the Peoria but were later released.[28]

During the early 1750s the Lake Peoria Indians seemed to draw attacks from Ojibwe and Potawatomi war parties. As a result, the Peoria became hesitant to leave the village to hunt, limiting the tribe's food supply, which was further compromised by a severe drought in 1752 that destroyed much of their harvest.[29] Although these Peoria were the most numerous Illinois subtribe at the time, their numbers were declining.[30] They had few allies to help them fight the powerful "Three Fires" alliance (Ojibwe, Odawa, and Potawatomi), which was now moving into northern Illinois. With little chance of victory against the Three Fires, the Peoria instead chose to attack the Sauk of the Rock River, a reprisal "justified" because the Sauk had recently participated in a deadly attack on a Michigamea village south of today's Cahokia. The fact that there were far fewer Sauk warriors than warriors in the Three Fires created favorable odds of a victory. The Sauk of the Rock River were also much closer, making war not only more convenient but within relative reach of the safety of the Peoria village should circumstances require. The plans, however, were cancelled as the newly arriving French commandant at the recently re-established French post at Lake Peoria convinced the Peoria not to attack the Sauk. Nonetheless, the Sauk learned of the Peoria war plans and traveled to Lake Peoria, where they delivered several Illinois prisoners to the Peoria including a man, three women, and a child. The Peoria returned the gesture by giving the Sauk several horses. The two tribes agreed to peace and formed an alliance. Pleased by the alliance, the Sauk promised to send messengers to the other Sauk villages to seek the return of thirteen more Illinois prisoners held at those camps. If successful, the Sauk were to bring the newly released prisoners and join the Peoria in their summer buffalo hunt "toward" Starved Rock.[31] It appears, though, that although both tribes had the best intentions, the Sauk did not secure the release of any more Illinois prisoners and there was no hunt near the Rock.

By about 1755 the Peoria Indians had left their semi-permanent agricultural villages at Lake Peoria and had settled in the lower Illinois Valley near what is now Naples, Illinois, while others continued south and built camps alongside the other Illinois on the Mississippi. For the next fourteen years, the Peoria would continue to sojourn in the Starved Rock area, living out of temporary winter hunting camps, but with the exception of an occasional war party or canoe convoy of French traders, Starved Rock was deserted.

The Illinois Indians' long journey into semi-obscurity was paralleled by an astonishing population decline. Only a hundred years earlier there had been about fourteen subtribes. By 1758 there were only four, the Cahokia, Michigamea, Kaskaskia, and Peoria—the others were either lost to history or had been absorbed into the four remaining subtribes. Around the time of first contact with the Europeans, there were an estimated 9,600 Illinois Indians, not counting the Michigamea who later joined the Illinois alliance as a subtribe. Less than a century later, there were only about 2,300 Illinois, including the Michigamea. Of the 2,300, the 1,250 Peoria were by far the largest Illinois group.[32] The longevity of the Peoria way-of-life was likely the result of their isolation from the other subtribes. Living separately on the Illinois River for much of the eighteenth century, the "Dreamers" kept much of their traditional culture and sometimes limited their reliance on Europeans. While some French traders and a few missionaries lived among the Peoria, their numbers, when contrasted with the number of traders and missionaries in Illinois camps and French settlements on the Mississippi, were very small. At Fort de Chartres, Prairie du Rocher, Saint Anne, Kaskaskia, and Cahokia, French, Catholic, and commercial presence and influence dominated. The Illinois who lived at or near these places were losing their own culture and were being assimilated into something new. As with the Illinois people as a whole, the Peoria subtribe too, experienced a shrinking population. This population loss, coupled with fighting enemies without the assistance of other Illinois subtribes, convinced the Peoria to migrate to the apparent security of the southern Illinois camps.

In Europe, the French became embroiled in a conflict with the British known as the Seven Years' War (1756–1763), a conflict that spilled over to North America, where it is commonly and incorrectly called the French and Indian War. This was the last of a series of skirmishes, battles, and sieges between French forces and their Indian allies, fighting against the British and their Indian allies. During the struggle, it appears that the Illinois Indians participated in raids against the British in Pennsylvania, Virginia, Georgia, and the Carolinas.[33]

While the Seven Years' War raged in the East, French traders in the Mississippi Valley had a difficult time providing the Indians with trade goods and gifts as nearly all resources went, instead, to the war effort. This came to the attention of Canadian officials like Governor Vaudreuil, who wrote "The English being vigilant, profit by our scarcity of goods. They have invited the Illinois Nations to go to trade at The Rock."[34] The British already understood the value of the Illinois trade and Starved Rock.

In 1760 Captain Sieur Passerat de la Chapelle and his command of over two hundred French militia and Indians at Detroit had been dispatched to reinforce the French military at Montreal. Approaching the settlement, they were told by fleeing "fugitives" and several Jesuits that "Montreal had capitulated" to the British. Rather than continuing on to surrender his men, La Chapelle chose instead to retreat to New Orleans and ultimately to France. His route to the Gulf took him down the Illinois River and to Starved Rock.

When La Chapelle arrived at Starved Rock, the season was late. He planned to winter at Fort St. Louis (La Salle's fort 1682–1691) but when he arrived he saw "There was no fort; it had been burned a long time ago."[35] La Chapelle wrote that Starved Rock "did not offer any natural means of defense against a possible attack of the English coming from the east." This was a remarkable statement as nearly every other person before La Chapelle who visited the site and recorded their observation mentioned Starved Rock's suitability for defense. In any case, the French officer moved his people to nearby Buffalo Rock where they built Fort Ottawa, a name given in honor of the mixed-blood Odawa militia company of his command.[36]

While the fort was under construction, La Chapelle met a group of Peoria Indians who were wintering in the area and who, after he had given them a few gifts, helped his men build the fort and provided them with badly needed food. As a gesture of understanding between the two parties, La Chapelle soon set to work trying to learn the Illinois Indian language. He wrote that he "conciliated the good will" of one of their chiefs. Apparently the chief was so impressed that he presented the French commander with a "roll of skin" enclosed "in a sheath of wood." Unrolling the scroll, La Chapelle saw words written in French that read, "We Cavellier de la Salle, representing his Majesty, the king of France declare in his name a fair and perpetual alliance with the Nation of the Illinois. Cavellier de la Salle."[37] The scroll was authenticated, still bearing the badly worn imprint of La Salle's wax seal. Seizing the opportunity to flatter the chief, La Chapelle told the chief that like La Salle, he, too, represented the king of France and that he and his men "would always be faithful allies of his people." The chief, according to the officer, "declared that his ancestors had always respected this alliance and that his nation would continue it." La Chapelle then set his signature beneath that of La Salle. On February 11,

1761, La Chapelle and a detachment of soldiers left Buffalo Rock for New Orleans, arriving there on April 20. La Chapelle's reference to the Illinois Indians at Buffalo Rock is the last credible account of the presence of any Illinois Indians in the Starved Rock area.

The Seven Years' War ended with Britain victorious. As a result, nearly all lands claimed by the French east of the Mississippi became British possessions. French officials would soon be replaced with British agents, military men, and traders. The Illinois Indians would come to rely on them for supplies, support, and ultimately, protection. Although the Illinois had claimed large swaths of this territory for centuries, the British would be making the important administrative decisions there including that of trade and security.[38] Starved Rock was now part of the British Empire.

Even though French soldiers, missionaries, and explorers were gone from Starved Rock, there were still a few French traders living in the Starved Rock region. Many of these *coureurs des bois* plied the waters of the Illinois River to get to the trading post at St. Louis, an interesting account of which appears in an unpublished French trader's itinerary of a journey from the Saint Joseph River through the Illinois Country to Cahokia. The document, likely from the early 1760s like the journals of St. Cosme and Delisle, details the place-names traders passed while journeying down the Illinois, such as Massane ou L'endroit aux orties (Mazon River), La Charbonniere (the coal pit noted by earlier Frenchmen), La Riv: des Renards ou le tchestigon (the Fox River), Le Rocher fin des rapides (Starved Rock and the end of the rapids), and Le Vermillion (the Vermilion River).[39] It is interesting that this journal presents the name of the Fox (Renards) River, making it among the earliest references to the name of that waterway.

Another interesting document entitled the "Minutes from the Journal of Mr. Hamburgh's Travels in the Michigan and Illinois Country 1763," describes a journey from Detroit to Kaskaskia. Taking up the trek from the Saint Joseph-Kankakee portage, the journal describes the Kykaggy (Kankakee) River as "Running Exceeding Crooked for a Bout 30 Miles When it inlarges and Deepens" until it reaches the "Chycacoo River" (the Des Plaines River at the Forks) where it becomes the Illinois. "The Chief Hunting ground of the Battowaymes" (Potawatomi), according to the journal "is along this River for about 200 Miles Down to a Place Called Le Rocher [Starved Rock]." It is interesting that the Potawatomi are now said to have claimed land along the Illinois River as their hunting grounds, having begun around this time to infiltrate the Illinois Country, filling the void left by the Illinois Indians. Hamburgh's journal states what generations of French and Illinois had known: that the Starved Rock area has "the greatest Plenty they have here is Racoons, Otters, Some Bever, Elks and Dear, and Buffilows in Abundance."[40]

In 1773 Patrick Kennedy, an Englishman, led an expedition up the Illinois River in search of copper mines. They left Kaskaskia on July 23, arriving at "the little rocks," or Starved Rock, on August 9. Because low water at the Starved Rock rapids prevented further passage upstream by boat, Kennedy continued east on foot, still searching the Illinois and Fox Rivers for copper. Walking to within fifteen miles of the Forks, his group encountered several French traders camped on an island. Kennedy asked them what they knew about the alleged mines, but the traders were silent, either knowing nothing or telling nothing about the ore. A long way from their boat and unsuccessful in their quest, Kennedy hired one of the French traders to take his party back to Starved Rock.[41] From there Kennedy and his party headed back to Kaskaskia, arriving in late August.

Kennedy's journal contains important information, such as his report of French traders in the King's territory. It reveals that there must have been persistent rumors of copper mines in the region (as Delisle had earlier sought them), and it provides us with the place name "Little Rocks," as Starved Rock and the local bluffs were collectively known. Kennedy's journal is insightful also in what is not mentioned. He neither provides information about any people—Indians or French—living at Starved Rock nor makes any mention of Indians living anywhere else in the upper Illinois Valley, something he would have surely learned from the French traders and recorded.

By 1777 the Potawatomi were firmly ensconced in the Illinois Country.[42] Within a few years they had established villages on the Kankakee, Des Plaines, and Fox Rivers, and on smaller streams such as Indian Creek and Big Bureau Creek. Unlike the Illinois who lived in large agricultural villages for most of the year and who supplemented their agrarian diet with meat, fish, and what they could gather, the Potawatomi of the eighteenth century were hunters and fishermen first. In comparison to the Illinois, the Potawatomi lived in smaller groups and in smaller villages. As hunters and fishermen they required a lot of territory, abundant with natural resources in order to feed and clothe themselves. When a group grew too large to be adequately accommodated by the local resources, a number of Potawatomi would leave the village and establish another village elsewhere, not too distant from the original location. They did grow crops but not to the extent grown by the Illinois. While the Potawatomi practiced agriculture, it appears that they may not have necessarily depended on it to survive.[43]

Like the Potawatomi, the Mascouten and Kickapoo Indians also moved into Illinois. None of these groups, however, established themselves at Starved Rock. Yet another group of people would soon come to the Starved Rock area, one very different from those who had lived there in the past. These would be the Americans. They would change the entire dynamic of the history, culture, and occupation of the Starved Rock region.

Part 3

Starved Rock into the Nineteenth and Twentieth Centuries

1777–1840:
THE BIG KNIVES WILL BE IN CONTROL

(Tipeerinkiiwaki kata mihšimaarhsaki)

While the Potawatomi, Odawa, and Ojibwe were migrating into Illinois, the American colonists in the eastern reaches of North America were fighting for their national independence from the British. The war ended in 1783 with the victorious Americans founding a new nation. Four years later, the US government organized a swath of land that included parts of Illinois, Indiana, Ohio, Wisconsin, Minnesota, and Michigan into what is known as the Northwest Territory. Located within the boundary of this new jurisdiction was Starved Rock, which officially became part of the Northwest Territory in 1787.

For millennia, Native Americans had traveled the continent's waterways, understood the interconnectedness of the rivers and streams, and had been intimately acquainted with trails and portages. In time, the French had gained this knowledge, as had the British. Now it was incumbent on the Americans that they too, learn about this new land. It was imperative that the Americans explore, record, and understand the region's geography. To do this, the new US government dispatched soldiers and cartographers, charging them with that responsibility. One of these expeditions, including one by Lieutenant John Armstrong, passed through Illinois in 1790 from "the carrying place of Chicagou" to the Mississippi. During this mission, members of the Armstrong expedition, a constituent of the US Army, mapped the course of the Illinois River and included a three-page description of what the expedition had observed. Although the official report did not mention Starved Rock, their map did include what its anonymous author called "Small Rocks": Starved Rock and adjacent bluffs.[1]

The Armstrong expedition was not the only group to chronicle its journey down the Illinois at that time. In 1790 a pair of canoes carrying French-Canadians and a British trader named Hugh Heward left Detroit bound for the Mississippi. Rather than take the familiar Great Lakes route to the Chicago River, the group traveled south on Lake Erie, then traversed Michigan's Lower Peninsula through a series of rivers and portages, eventually arriving on Lake Michigan at today's Grand Haven. From there, the party headed south and entered the Chicago River. They portaged to the Des Plaines and paddled that stream to the forks of the Des Plaines and the Kankakee where they met the local Potawatomi and a French trader named Belhumour, who was living with the Indians. To help ensure the party's safety and to secure the chief's help if it were needed in the future, a man in Heward's party named Goodhumour presented the chief with tobacco and gunpowder. The party purchased four sacks of maize from Belhumour and loaned him shirts on credit. Belhumour, Heward noted, was so pleased to receive the shirts that he gave Heward his dog, a tea kettle, nine eggs, and a leg of venison. Leaving the village, Heward's party entered the Illinois River, where they passed what he called "Demi Charge" and "Rapid of Mamor," at the LaSalle County town of Marseilles, then the mouth of the Fox River, and later, the mouth of the Vermilion.[2]

Despite directly passing Starved Rock, Heward never mentioned the place in his journal, nor did he comment on people living near it. His written observations, though, provided other interesting information. In mentioning Belhumour, he verified that at least one French trader was operating in American territory in the Illinois Country. Further, he recorded "Demi Charge" and "Rapid of Mamor," two seldom-expressed place-names identifying the Marseilles rapids. Heward also recorded information about salt ponds across the river from the mouth of the Vermilion, something that, heretofore, had not appeared in a written record.

At this time in America in the late eighteenth century, with the Industrial Revolution still decades in the future, the vast majority of men were farmers, and farmers desired land—land that had to first be purchased from the Indians. The political significance of this majority was the Treaty of Greenville in 1795. The Treaty set aside a large tract of land in Ohio and Indiana for the exclusive use of the Indians.[3] Although the treaty included the Shawnee, Kickapoo, Kaskaskia, several Ojibwe bands, Odawa, Potawatomi, and Miami bands, and what remained of the Wendat, it did not include the Sauk or the Mesquakie, a matter that led to major land losses for these tribes nine years later. While on the surface the treaty seemed to protect the land for the Indians, it only provided these protections as long as the federal government owned the land. Once the land was sold to American settlers, the treaty for that land and the protections it included for the Indians would be rendered invalid. It would be just a few years before the Americans moved into these territories, purchasing Indian land for themselves.

In 1803 the US government bought over 800,000 square miles of land from France in a transaction since referred to as the Louisiana Purchase. Overnight, American territory nearly doubled in size. While most of the new nation's population was concentrated within the boundaries of the original thirteen colonies, the people of many sovereign Indian nations lived between these communities and the Mississippi. Dating as far back as the Jefferson administration, the US government consciously and consistently schemed to "legally" move Indians from land by using unscrupulous means. One effective method was to trade with the tribes on credit, offering guns, ammunition, knives and other necessities, all the while knowing that the Indians could never repay the debt. The government officials were well aware that in time the Indians would agree to resolve the matter by ceding their lands to the United States, thereby extinguishing tribal title to the land.[4] Another method was to simply deceive the tribes. US government officials would offer the Indians explanations of what was included in land sale documents, advising the Indians that it was in the Indians' best financial interests to agree to the sales when in reality, none of the promised benefits were established in the agreement.[5]

Still another method of deception employed by the US government was to formalize a land sale agreement between and itself and an Indian tribe. In these agreements, the US government, well aware that the land to be sold to the United States did not belong to the tribe with whom the government was dealing, easily struck these agreements. The lands, now legally owned by the United States, had never been the lands of the Indian tribe that entered into the agreement. At other times, when the government was dealing with a less powerful tribe, they simply told the tribe what the agreement would include. Officials such as future president William Henry Harrison were shrewd and at times openly confrontational with tribal negotiators, who were acting in good faith on behalf of their people. As the Indians became more disaffected with the Americans, the British—from whom the Americans had just wrested a nation—allied themselves with the Indians.

The British enjoyed a semi-amicable relationship with the Sauk and Mesquakie, since both tribes had been allied with the British during the American Revolution. To keep their friendship bonds intact, the British gave gifts to the Indians, a lesson in diplomacy that they had learned from their French predecessors. To the chagrin of the Americans, British agents, having fostered good relations with these tribes of the Upper Lakes, were permitted by the Indians to travel freely in this Indian territory. By the early nineteenth century, the Sauk and Mesquakie journeyed annually from their Saukenuk village, located near the mouth of the Rock River, to the British fort at Malden, Ontario, across the river from Detroit, to receive gifts from their British friends and renew their friendships. This well-established route of travel through northern Illinois to Malden is known even today as the "Sauk Trail."

Then in 1804, at a settlement near the Cuivre River, not far from St. Louis, a war party of Sauk Indians killed three American settlers. Soon after, a council was held between William Henry Harrison and a party of Sauk civil chiefs who had come to secure the release of one of the Sauk raiders. The Sauk also hoped to make restitution to the victim's families in some way. Harrison, exploiting the death of the Americans and taking advantage of the Sauk's sincere interest in restitution to the victims' families, further victimized the families of the dead Americans to advance the interests of the US government. Harrison did not want to squander this position of power over the Sauk on mere reparations for the victims' families. Recognizing that the Sauk and Mesquakie had never signed the Treaty of Greenville and that the Sauk and Mesquakie still held claim to land east of the Mississippi, Harrison instead forced the tribes to cede claims to these lands with one stroke of the pen. While history did not record the Sauk's interpretation of the Treaty of 1804, the Sauk chiefs unknowingly—as later accounts indicate, and without authority to do so—signed away an enormous expanse of property to the US government.[6] According to the Treaty of 1804, the Sauk and Mesquakie relinquished their rights to land that lay north from the mouth of the Illinois River and past Starved Rock to the mouth of the Fox River; then up the Fox to a location near the Wisconsin state line that angled to the Wisconsin River; then down the Wisconsin to the Mississippi to the mouth of the Illinois. In addition the Sauk ceded a large tract of land in northwest Missouri. For this the two tribes were to receive $1,000.00 in goods annually, were to have access to a government trader, and were under the protection of the United States. They were also to be allowed to live and hunt on the ceded land while it remained the property of the US government.

The chiefs had been duped. When they learned what had transpired they, like all of the tribal members, were outraged. Years later, at a council with General Edmund P. Gaines, Quashquame (Jumping Fish), one of the Sauk signers of the 1804 treaty, told the commander:

> I do not know what was put upon paper at the talk. . . . Some time ago I sold a part of the land of the Sauks to release one of our Braves who was in jail; but neither I nor any of my braves know of any sale of *all* our lands East of the Mississippi river. I am a red skin & do not use paper at a talk, but my words are in my heart, & I do not forget what has been said.[7]

This faithless and duplicitous treaty ultimately contributed, nearly thirty years later, to the 1832 Black Hawk War.

While the Sauk and the Mesquakie remained outraged by the treachery and deception of American government officials, a question remained and remains today: whether the lands that were ceded in the Treaty of 1804 were really Sauk and Mesquakie lands at all. It appears that by the mid—eighteenth century, the Sauk were firmly ensconced in northwest Illinois, southwest Wisconsin, and eastern Iowa. The lands described in the 1804 treaty were lands where they had lived seventy to eighty years earlier.

By 1804 in the ceded lands, the Sauk and Mesquakie lived only in small groups in a few scattered villages. Their primary town was Saukenuk, and their winter hunting grounds were located in Iowa. Potawatomi Chief Black Partridge charged in 1815 that the lands ceded by the Sauk and Mesquakie were not theirs to cede but were lands of the Potawatomi. He reportedly "sent a message to the President" stating that "no Part of this River does or ever did belong to the Sacks that whatever sale they have made was wholly unauthorized." Those lands, according to the chief, belonged to the Potawatomi and were "the Principal Hunting ground of our Nation."[8] These claims were not the ranting of an angry chief who, like most other Indians, cared little for Harrison or most other government officials. In fact, the claims of Chief Black Partridge were supported by Illinois Territorial Governor Ninian Edwards as well as by businessman and Indian treaty negotiator himself, Auguste Chouteau, and by Missouri Territorial Governor William Clark of Lewis and Clark fame. The next year representatives of the Three Fires, including Black Partridge, ceded those same lands to the United States along with land in northeast Illinois, which effectively ended the matter.[9]

The federal government was acquiring land and subdividing it as fast as circumstances would allow. In 1800, the Indiana Territory was carved out of the Northwest Territory and became a separate entity. Following suit, the Illinois Territory was established in 1809. The territorial governor was empowered to "act as commander-in-chief of the militia and was authorized to appoint militia officers below the rank of general and civil officers for counties and townships." He was also authorized to appoint an Adjutant General to oversee military enlistment, records, and attend military reviews. In addition, the Adjutant General was required to report to the governor regarding the condition of military equipment. This was an important position because the United States at this time did not have a large standing army. States typically had to supply their own protection under the direction of the Adjutant General. When trouble erupted, one's livelihood was temporarily abandoned—be it farm or shop—as citizens volunteered in the local militia company, usually for thirty to ninety days. These volunteers often brought their own horses and muskets to the battle. When the threat, uprising, or conflict ended, the militia disbanded and soldiers went home to continue where they had left off in private life.

Into this newly defined and defended Illinois territory came Americans, newcomers who enthusiastically headed west for cheap land. The Indians had many reasons to be agitated, and the tribes of the Illinois Country, with a bit of impetus from the British, decided to act. By 1811 William Clark feared that the Indians might start an uprising against the United States. In particular, he was very concerned with the "Bands on the Illinois River." Territorial Governor Ninian Edwards and "those under him" also believed that an Indian war was indeed possible.[10] Problem villages, as indicated by Illinois authorities, included Gomo's village (Potawatomi), located approximately twenty miles north of Lake Peoria and the large Kickapoo village near the head of that lake. In 1812 war erupted. At Chicago, Potawatomi Indians ambushed about ninety-six Americans who were evacuating Fort Dearborn, killing fifty-three and wounding many others.[11] In retaliation Governor Edwards led strikes on the Potawatomi and Kickapoo villages in the Illinois Valley. In 1814 Sauk, Mesquakie, and Kickapoo warriors attacked a three-boat US Army flotilla at Campbell's Island on the Mississippi, near today's East Moline, killing sixteen men, one woman, and one child while wounding fifteen others.[12] About a month later, a war party of Sauk, Mesquakie, Winnebago, and Sioux, reinforced by British soldiers, attacked a flotilla led by Zachary Taylor at Credit Island, near present-day Davenport, Iowa, mortally wounding three soldiers and wounding eleven others. The Sauk/British alliance effectively framed the Sauk as the enemy in the American perspective as, conversely, the American chicanery involved in the Treaty of 1804 established the Americans as Sauk enemies in the Sauk view. By the end of the War of 1812, most citizens of Illinois wanted these Indians and the problems that accompanied coexistence with them removed, as did the War Department of the federal government. In 1817, Illinois Territorial Governor Edwards was ordered to begin proceedings to extinguish the title of Indian lands "east of the Illinois River" (land south of Starved Rock).[13] Yet, when Illinois was admitted to the Union in 1818, sporadic raids and ambushes still occurred. These were no longer tolerated by state and local governments. Unoccupied and uncontested, Starved Rock existed quietly alone amid beautiful pines, soaring eagles, and tumbling waters.

Farther east, in 1818, Gurdon Hubbard, an influential city father of the future metropolis of Chicago, was hired by the American Fur

Company. Not long after he joined the company, Hubbard and a group of traders boarded keel boats and began their voyage down the Des Plaines and Illinois Rivers. That year, the water was so low that the Marseilles and Starved Rock rapids were impassable. To proceed downstream, the group had to unload their boats and carry supplies and gear on their backs while pushing, prying, and pulling their vessels over the rocks. Eventually they arrived at Starved Rock, a site Hubbard called a "romantic and picturesque spot." Hubbard and his party didn't stay long at Starved Rock. After they had rested from the rigors of the portage, they continued their journey, stopping at trading posts and Indian villages along their route.

The US government negotiated for more Potawatomi land in 1821 at a council held near Fort Dearborn in Chicago. This negotiation included territory in southern Michigan and northern Indiana. Representing the United States was Michigan Territorial Governor and Superintendent of Indian Affairs Lewis Cass. Also negotiating for the United States was the geologist, Indian agent, and a man considered by many to have been America's first ethnographer, Henry Schoolcraft.

To get to the council, Cass's and Schoolcraft's party traveled up the Mississippi from St. Louis, and then ascended the Illinois. When the group reached the Vermilion River, low water compelled them to continue their upstream trek on foot, pulling their vessels behind. They eventually reached Starved Rock, where they set up camp. Several men in the party were sent out to locate and borrow horses so that Cass's and Schoolcraft's group could continue their journey to Chicago.[14]

Schoolcraft later wrote that the French called Starved Rock "Le Rocher and Rock Fort." He described it as "an elevated cliff on the left bank of the Illinois [south bank of the river], consisting of parallel layers of white sandstone. It is not less than two hundred and fifty feet high, perpendicular on three sides, and washed at its base by the river," and "the effect upon the observer is striking and imposing."[15] The fourth side, he wrote, "is connected with the adjacent range of hills by a narrow peninsular ledge, which can only be ascended by a precipitous winding path." The summit is "level and contains about three quarters of an acre." It was also covered by "a growth of young trees." Probing the surface of the Rock, Schoolcraft reported that he found "broken mussel shells, fragments of antique pottery, and stones which have been subjected to the action of heat resembling certain lavas."[16] He also recorded that he saw an entrenchment, a linear mound of earth that corresponded to the edge of the bluff; a feature that he believed had been built by the Indians.

Schoolcraft's journal includes a tale of a band of Indians who, tradition says, had been chased to the top of the Rock by their enemies. After their enemies had cut all means to obtain water, the besieged tribe surrendered, a fateful decision as they were reportedly all killed by their foe. Although his description of this incident was without gruesome and sensational details, he did write that the surrender precluded the "total extirpation of the band," meaning that these Indians had died while others of the same tribe lived elsewhere.[17] Schoolcraft's reference to this incident is one of the very first versions of the famous legend of Starved Rock, one that has taken many different forms over the years as it has passed from storyteller to storyteller.

After the men returned with horses, Schoolcraft's group left Starved Rock and continued to Chicago, guided by a Potawatomi chief named Peerish. Their route took them along the northern side of the Illinois where Peerish pointed out what Schoolcraft described as "ancient sites of several Indian villages." These were old Kaskaskia and "a romantic tabular elevation called the Buffalo Rock." About these sites Schoolcraft wrote:

> These curious landmarks are calculated to recall an epoch in the history of the Indian tribes, when they were powerful in point of numbers,—when the bow and arrow were adequate to their subsistence, and when they cherished with pride the rude arts, the customs, and the simple manners of their fore-fathers, undismayed by the superior attainments of Europeans, and uncon-taminated by the evils resulting from the introduction of ardent spirits and other civilized vices; an epoch which affords a very melancholy contrast with their present enfeebled and depopulated condition.[18]

Schoolcraft's journal entries pertaining to his brief time at Starved Rock are important. In addition to giving us one of the very first refer-ences to the legend of Starved Rock, they detail significant anthropo-logical information about the human occupation at and near the site. Schoolcraft's description of Starved Rock becomes the template that later writers use for books and articles that will be read across America for the next twenty years.

In 1823 the first Americans settled in the Starved Rock area. That year, a man known only as "Dr. Davidson" became the Starved Rock area's earliest permanent American resident, building a log cabin on the south shore of the Illinois River approximately five miles upstream from Starved Rock.[19] More Americans arrived in the area, many whose names are synonymous with the area's geographical landscape today. New arrivals included Thomas Covell (Covell Creek), Lewis Bailey (Bailey Falls), and Simon Crosiar (Crosiar's Landing). Several of these new arrivals built cabins and established their businesses near the south shore of the river at Ottawa. It was there in 1827 that the settlers built a temporary fort to protect themselves from marauding bands of Indians during a disturbance known as the "Winnebago War," a brief and insignificant scuffle between Indians and settlers that occurred on the Mississippi River. Since news traveled slowly and was oftentimes mingled with fanciful fiction and rumor, the residents of the Starved Rock area thought it prudent to build a fort should the war move eastward. The post sat "back from the bluff in South Ottawa, far enough from the timber to prevent the enemy from attacking under its cover, and commanding a supply of water."[20]

From this odd mix of cultures that lived in the frontier villages and the Indian camps that dotted the tall grass prairie wilderness of northern Illinois emerged LaSalle County, a unit of government that was officially organized on January 15, 1831. The new jurisdiction, which at the time included parts of Livingston, Marshall, and Kendall Counties, and all of Grundy County, was carved out of Putnam County.[21] In March the first county elections for sheriff, county clerk, and a board of three county commissioners were held. That summer the county's first grand jury met in the shade of a tree along the south shore of the Illinois River and, happily, no indictments were returned. So pleased was presiding judge Richard M. Young that he reportedly complimented the jurors for their "high moral character" and then sent them on their way.

Also, in 1831, Schoolcraft's observations about his 1821 visit to Starved Rock received national attention when a portion of it was published in the *Monthly Repository and Library of Entertaining Knowledge*. The *Repository* also included one of the earliest images of Starved Rock, a likeness made from a woodcut.[22] Even though the illustration's excessively square dimensions and idealistic setting are more abstract than real, the unknown artist effectively expressed the Rock's strength, formidability, and stature.

In 1832 Timothy Flint's *History and Geography of the Mississippi Valley* made its debut in the literary and reference world. The book provided a state-by-state review of the nation's lands and waterways. Flint had a keen interest in the natural sciences, geography, and geology, and worked as the editor of the *Monthly Western Review*. He also wrote assorted "lectures on natural history, geology, chemistry, and the arts," and authored books including *Ten Years in the Valley of the Mississippi, Indian Wars in the West,* and *Memoir of Daniel Boone.*

In his *History and Geography of the Mississippi Valley*, Flint described the climate, marine life, and rivers of the United States and its territories. In the "Illinois" section, Flint's description of Starved Rock mirrors that of Schoolcraft. Flint, however, added an uplifting and poetic twist to Schoolcraft's simple and unadorned description of the site. He wrote:

> At the foot of Rock Fort, on the land side, the eye reposes on a verdant carpet, enamelled [sic] with flowers of surpassing beauty. To relieve the uniformity, from which even this beautiful view would suffer, the forest boundary of the opposite side of the prairie, presents its gracefully curved line, and offers, from the noble size of the trees, and the thickness and depth of verdure of their foliage, that boundless contiguity of shade, sought after by the poet.[23]

As a reference book, Flint's *History and Geography* provided an inspiring account of Starved Rock and its environs, one that piqued the curiosity of travelers, writers, and romantics.

While Flint's book was being published in the relative safety of Cincinnati, Ohio, the Starved Rock region in 1832 erupted in the violence known as the Black Hawk War. The conflict began as a Sauk Indian response to American settlers moving onto lands ceded in 1804. By 1830, the US government had sold lands ceded in the treaty to private individuals. This meant that the Sauk and Mesquakie were obliged to move west of the Mississippi. Most complied, with the exception of one band that had crossed back into Illinois led by the war chief Black Hawk. His unwelcome return riled the settlers around Saukenuk, near today's Rock Island,

Illinois, who petitioned Governor Reynolds to call up the Illinois militia. Within a few days, the militia was organized and it, as well as federal troops who had been stationed at Fort Armstrong in Rock Island, took up the pursuit of Black Hawk and his band.

In the meantime, Black Hawk's band slowly moved up the Rock River until they had reached a site near what is now Stillman Valley, located about thirty miles from Dixon's Ferry, or Dixon, Illinois. There the undisciplined and overzealous militiamen attacked an unarmed Sauk delegation which had likely come to conduct the militia to Black Hawk's camp so that both sides could discuss Black Hawk's return to Iowa. With the militia in pursuit, the surviving Sauk delegates raced back to their camp where Black Hawk and his men not only defended themselves gallantly, but also successfully counterattacked, chasing the militia, who sped away on horseback. Even though only about eleven militiamen were killed during the skirmish, the incident so completely demoralized the volunteers that most, upon reaching the safety of Dixon's Ferry, did not stop but instead continued south and fled for the safety of their homes and farms.

One week later a group of Potawatomi attacked the Davis settlement on Indian Creek, located about twelve miles north of Ottawa. Angry that the settlers had constructed a dam that prevented the redhorse carp migration, a major food source for the tribe, the Potawatomi killed fifteen men, women, and children. Although this incident had nothing to do with Black Hawk's return to Illinois or the fight at Stillman Valley, the settlers in the Starved Rock area and on the Illinois frontier were in a state of panic. Settlers built small stockades at present-day Plainfield, Naperville, and Hennepin in Illinois and in Wisconsin at Blue Mounds, near Mineral Point, and at Wiota. Two of the largest Black Hawk War forts were near Starved Rock: Fort Wilbourn (built by the US Army) near today's Oglesby and Fort Johnson (built by the local militia) on Ottawa's south bluff.[24] These two forts served as US Army command headquarters, protected local settlers from Indian attack, and were depositories for food, supplies, and troops.

It is interesting that Starved Rock, located between Forts Wilbourn and Johnson, was completely ignored by the US Army as a military site. Unlike Fort Johnson which was located near a prairie population center, and Fort Wilbourn, which was easily accessible by steamboat, Starved

Rock in 1832 rose above the sparsely populated lands, with river access limited by shallow water and unnavigable rapids. During the previous century, when bark canoes and wooden dugouts were the primary means of transportation, French voyageurs could usually paddle right to Starved Rock, making it an important outpost where goods and supplies could be delivered and stored. By 1832, the shift in population centers and modern transportation methods had rendered the formidable Starved Rock of only a century earlier useless as a military post.

When the Black Hawk War ended in August, nearly all the Indian tribes of Illinois, Indiana, and Michigan were forced to move west of the Mississippi. Realizing that the US Army was an imposing force, one with the ability to muster larger numbers of soldiers than tribes could gather warriors, the tribes preferred to negotiate with the government rather than beg for concessions later. US Army officials such as General Winfield Scott met with tribal leaders. Eventually the officials negotiated treaties with the Winnebago (September 15, 1832), the Sauk and Mesquakie (September 21, 1832), and the Potawatomi (October 27, 1832). The following year at Chicago, the Potawatomi agreed to resettle west of the Mississippi, in what would become Kansas. With the ratification of the 1833 Treaty of Chicago, Starved Rock would never again be home to the Indians.

The departure of the Indians was captured in colorful accounts of discovery, drama, and bloodshed—sagas that often presented fiction as exciting and enthralling fact. One of the earliest of these was written in 1835 by Judge James Hall and was published in a book entitled, *Tales of the Border*. In one story a traveler wandering through the prairies of northern Illinois "halted once upon the 'Starved Rock,' a spot rendered memorable by a most tragic legend which has been handed down in tradition." Hall described Starved Rock "like the ramparts of a tall castle, frowning over the still surface of that beautiful stream, and commanding an extensive prospect of low, but richly adorned, and quiet, and lovely shores." It was there, Hall wrote, that a band of Indians fled their enemies and took shelter on the summit of the Rock. Unlike the "pomp, or pride, or circumstance" engendered in the marshalling of the "plumed troops" who fought in "big wars, which often deceive us into an admiration of deeds of violence," Hall opined, how differently the "deliberate murder, was that savage act of starving to death a whole tribe,—the warriors, the aged, the females, and the children!" Hall's *Tales of the Border* would help to perpetuate period oral traditions concerning the destruction of an Indian tribe at the site. His reference to the name "Starved Rock" is significant as it has the distinction of being one of the very first to apply this now well-known moniker to the famous bluff.[25]

About the time Hall's *Tales of the Border* was published, the writer, poet, and traveler Charles Fenno Hoffman toured the West. In a horse-drawn sleigh, Hoffman and his traveling companion left Ottawa and headed west along the old stagecoach-road, what is now the Deer Park Blacktop, arriving at a log inn located somewhere between today's towns of Lowell and Tonica.[26] There Hoffman heard someone "speaking in terms of enthusiasm of the fine view" from "Starved Rock." The intriguing name caught Hoffman's attention—he must see this place. Hoffman arranged to borrow a pair of horses, "two miserable nags," as he referred to them, for himself and his companion to ride to Starved Rock.

Leaving the inn, the two riders braved a "chill north-easter." They traversed the "bleak prairie" on an old Indian trail until they reached a cliff high above the frozen Vermilion River. The two riders negotiated a steep, rocky ravine, coated by a sheet of ice, to get to the frozen stream below. So treacherous was their descent that Hoffman and his horse slid down the precipice together, the horse at one point sliding over the top of Hoffman. The two travelers next crossed the Vermilion, climbing another steep and icy ravine to reach the rich prairie above. Successfully overcoming their first obstacle, the riders continued their quest and eventually entered the timber high above the south bluff of the Illinois River flood-plain, part of today's Starved Rock Nature Preserve. Leading their mounts on foot into the ravines and through the timber, Hoffman and his friend arrived at present-day Joliet Canyon, where they beheld a double cascade. Having spent the better part of the day searching in vain for the famous rock, and noting that their two "nags" were exhausted, the travelers returned to the inn.[27]

Hoffman's *Winter in the West* provides a peek at life in the Starved Rock area in 1834. Before automobiles and paved roads, travel was difficult: our modern-day highways had not yet been built. Although Starved Rock was known in literary circles, the site itself remained hidden from public view, serving no practical military or strategic purpose. Hoffman's account reveals to us the rough and unsophisticated character of frontier life, of Indian trails, log inns, and haggard horses.

Between 1823 and 1837, a steady flow of settlers moved into LaSalle County and the Starved Rock area, many of whom were rugged souls from southern Illinois, Kentucky, Virginia, and Ohio. These new arrivals first staked their claims along the county's rivers and watercourses. Later, after the debut of John Deere's plow, settlers moved inland and away from these wooded corridors to build farms in the open prairie. Land purchased from the US government at this time sold for $1.25 per acre, rising to $2.25 per acre by 1851 if the property was located within six miles of the Illinois Central railroad survey.[28]

At about this same time, engineers associated with the Illinois and Michigan Canal platted towns along the channel's course between La Salle and Chicago. One of these men was Daniel Fletcher Hitt, a Black Hawk War veteran who would later serve as colonel of the 53rd Illinois Volunteer Infantry during the Civil War. He was also the first private owner of Starved Rock, having purchased the famous site and sixty-eight acres on June 23, 1835, for $85.00. In subsequent years, Hitt would buy more property around Starved Rock, land that would eventually become part of Starved Rock State Park. It is remarkable that this place called Starved Rock, the beacon of the Illinois prairies—a place where Native Americans camped, fought, and lived for 10,000 years—the site of a French fort that had once anchored Louis XIV and France's westernmost claim in North America, and land that became part of King George III's British Empire, now belonged to one American settler.

John Wallace, a relative of Hitt by marriage, was an early settler who had purchased property west of Starved Rock—not far from where Hoffman and his companion had observed the double waterfall. In 1835 Wallace built a log cabin on the site. There he and his wife and eleven children lived for the next six years. Because there were few educational opportunities in the Starved Rock area at that time, Wallace moved his family to Mount Morris, in Ogle County. One of his sons is best known to students of the Civil War as William Hervey Lamme Wallace (W. H. L. Wallace), who commanded one of Grant's six divisions at the Battle of Pittsburgh Landing, also known as Shiloh, during the Civil War. As a youngster Will reportedly roamed "through the neighboring cañons and over the far-famed Starved Rock, where he gathered arrows and beads left by the vanquished Illini."[29]

Settlers like the Wallaces and Hitts continued to migrate to the Starved Rock area until the financial Panic of 1837, a crisis that had many aspects but at its root was land speculation. According to one writer, "When the Government offered the lands in the center of a county for sale in 1835, the settlers took but a small proportion, and the balance was taken by speculators."[30] Even Starved Rock was targeted by land speculators, who proposed to build "The City of Gibraltar," unaware that although the Rock may have been at one time a suitable location for a fort, it was certainly no place to build a city.[31] Before the Panic, land bought from the US government for $1.25 an acre was selling for $5 to $10 an acre in the East, and in some places even higher. Speculation had artificially inflated prices, which gave people who had purchased the land a false sense of wealth and financial security. Adding to the area's economic crisis were the inverse supply and demand hardships created by exceptionally bountiful harvests—yields that exceeded consumer demand. As a consequence, grain prices plummeted, deepening the debt of farmers who now owned land that at least for the immediate future had lost value, as had the crops it yielded.

During this same period governments also faced financial problems. States that had been building canals and other expensive infrastructure projects had gone deeply into debt, both to build the projects and to compensate irate counties and towns that had been by-passed, as in the case of new railroad lines.[32] Additionally, local jurisdictions had borrowed heavily to build courthouses, jails, and other public buildings. When the crash occurred in 1837, the consequences were profound. Migration to the Starved Rock area essentially ceased. Work on the new Illinois and Michigan Canal slowed to a crawl and by 1839 had halted. The price of pork dropped from twenty-five dollars per barrel to one dollar per one hundred barrels. The only items of value were "hides, tallow, deer skins, and furs." According to Illinois state legislator and historian Elmer Baldwin, the "breaking down of all business relations, the disappearance of a circulating medium, and the impossibility of selling produce for cash" created an economy that few area residents had ever experienced or would ever experience again.[33]

Public unease over state debt also increased, and this anxiety spread to other states. Some prominent southern Illinois citizens described the situation as "beyond the ability of redemption." This fueled a debate between the State of Illinois and holders of Illinois bonds in the State of New York. Some condescending New Yorkers portrayed Illinois citizens as "deeply" deploring the "low state of her credit." Defenders of Illinois fiscal policy insisted that these "fabricated" statements by the "enemies of Illinois" were driving away immigrants such as farmers and canal workers. Eventually an open letter to the "Holders of Illinois Bonds," which spoke directly to the debt issue, was published statewide in newspapers that included Ottawa's *Illinois Free Trader*. This dispatch focused on Illinois' potential wealth—a reality that would come to fruition when its unfinished canals and railroads were completed and when its fertile farmland was again under cultivation.[34] Whether grounded in fact or belief, and in the case of the Panic of 1837 probably a measure of both, financial repercussions of the Panic spread nationwide, even reaching the White House, leading in 1840 to the defeat of incumbent president Martin Van Buren.

While the Americans dealt with bank failures, unemployment, and financial loss, the Indians continued their emigration out of Illinois. According to an 1840 report, between five and six hundred Potawatomi and Odawa Indians had already passed through the Starved Rock area on their way west, and more were expected soon. One group was reported "in good health" and was said to have "made quite a display."[35] These downtrodden and broken tribesmen so impressed one local poet, that he wrote a few tearful lines:

They are passing away, they are passing away,
As dew disappears in the morning's sun's ray;
Or the light fleecy clouds that are hurrying by,
And leave not a trace on the bright summer sky.
They are passing away from the land of their birth,
From the scenes they have loved both in sorrow and mirth,
From the spot where the bones of their fathers are laid,
To sleep in the forest trees' whispering shade.
They are passing away from the prairie and grove:
There the light hearted hunter no longer may rove.
On the flow'r-cover'd prairie no warrior may rest;
For the plough of the white man has furrow'd its breast."

Continuing his sad refrain, the poet concludes:

"When the broad Mississippi's dark waters are crossed,
Their homes and their country to them will be lost.
And the march of improvement will soon leave no trace
In the land of their birth of a once noble race:
But their *name* will remain far on forest and flood—
From mountain to sea it is written in blood![36]

The poet laments the passing of an epoch, the sad fate of Native Americans who were forced by treaty to move west of the Mississippi. As if the writer were paying his respects to a noble foe that tenaciously fought to keep the lands where for millennia they had lived, died, and were buried, he recognizes the beginning of a new period, when the newly arrived Americans could claim the spoils of conquest. Although this reflective tribute to the passing of Indian life east of the Great River was written with respect, it serves as a prime example of the disconnect between the aims of Manifest Destiny and the devastating cultural realities brought about by the American conquistadors. The victors could now boast of their long-sought extirpation of many tribes east of the Mississippi, and could now safely view their vanquished foe with a bit of pity-driven honor and respect.

Treaties and land cession agreements written by representatives of the US government were intended to swindle the tribes; they denied basic due process rights to the Indians. But it didn't end in 1840. This policy would continue for the next half-century. In their final display of cultural pride in the lands where they had once lived, the tribes exhibited their swan song, a last hurrah as they passed through the Starved Rock area, performing a show that captivated the newcomers.

These Indians were only a very small part of the many that were required to leave their Michigan, Indiana, and Illinois camps. Between 1836 and 1840, the United State government purchased and extinguished the title to 45,600,960 acres of Indian land, purchases that reportedly had cost $14,078,634.00.[37] The Americans were in Starved Rock country to stay and the days of old were gone.

10

1841–1885:
WAIT! ITS HEART IS STILL BEATING

(Eeskwa perakiiwi ateehi)

Privately owned starting in 1835, Starved Rock was the domain of Daniel
Hitt. He could exploit it, preserve it, or utilize it in any way. To supplement his income, Hitt rented the tillable farmland to the west of the Rock,
as well as some of his island property, to local farmers. He allowed visitors to enjoy the view of the valley from atop Starved Rock and he even
allowed them to probe its summit to search for relics. In 1840 one guest
wrote his "Reflections on a Visit to Starved Rock." In it the writer admitted that "a visit to this [summit of Starved Rock] is indeed calculated to
set the imagination busily to work, to bring into action all the poetry, and
give full scope to what little imaginative genius we may possess."[1]

A story published on New Year's Eve in 1841 tells the tale of a visitor
to Starved Rock who alone with his thoughts watched the sun set from
its heights. Around him he wrote, "The smiling flowers exhaled their fra-
grant odor, offering sweet incense to the retiring monarch of the skies. The
tranquil Illinois rolled majestically along beneath the wild and towering
bluff, gently winding among the green and lovely islands, reflecting from

its bright bosom the crimson folds of the floating clouds." The writer then mentions that he was aroused from his meditations by the sound of someone approaching. From his hiding place behind some evergreens, the writer observed an old Indian who slowly approached an earthen mound located in the center of the summit. There the Indian knelt down and began a "mournful dirge," slowly at first, then a chant and then "loud shrieks that echoed through the glens below." When he had finished his ceremony, the old Indian "erected a white flag over the mound, in accordance with their custom, to show the Great Spirit where he may find his warriors when he makes the great hunt." Fascinated by what he had just witnessed, the chronicler was determined to understand the meaning of this ritual. Leaving his concealment, he approached the aged Indian and asked, "Did you belong to that unhappy tribe who perished here?" "Alas! Young man," the Indian replied, and with that he began to recount his sad tale.

The Indian told the man that "After famine had destroyed most of our numbers, and finding longer residence would be in vain, I resolved to make my escape." One night, the Indian had fashioned a rope from his blanket and had quietly lowered himself down the bluff to the river. There he silently slipped into a canoe and, availing himself of the downstream current, drifted into the darkness and escaped. A few moments later, the chronicler relates that the Indian heard "the wild, demonic yell of victory, mingled with the suffering cries of the victims." The old Indian, it is said, saw by moonlight his enemies "butchering and torturing the small remainder of my tribe, who were unable to offer any resistance," finishing with "I am the only remnant of the once powerful Illini."[2]

The idealized image and romantic appeal of Starved Rock was growing as was public interest in it. An 1857 article in the *Chicago Daily Tribune* referred to Starved Rock as an "Indian Mausoleum" from which one could gaze "for miles around upon the most beautiful and enchanting scene." The article concluded, "The scene is gorgeous, magnificent, sublime, and should be visited by every lover of the beautiful."[3]

The following year, Professor W. P. Jones, "the efficient head of the Female College at Evanston," composed a poem entitled *The Fate of the Illini, the Legend of Starved Rock.* So popular was the poem that Jones recited his work at a distinguished and acclaimed affair held at

Chicago's prestigious Metropolitan Hall on December 13. In part, the poem reads:

Bereft of hope the wretched sufferers lie,
Racked by such pangs as make it bliss to die.
Beneath the trees grim skeletons they sit,
Or round the rock like horrid goblins flit."
As the last fading breath of life left their bodies;
"Aha' he cries, "my father's ghost,
I hear you and obey.
I come; I come ye spirit hosts!
And thou poor lump of clay.
Go rest thee now—the vigor spent—
Beneath thy nation's monument."
A plunge far down from that terrific height,
A gurgling roar of waters midst the night.
High over all a war-whoop's wild "aw-oy,"
And hushed forever are the Illinois.[4]

In addition to descriptions appearing in the press and poetry, public fascination with Starved Rock was also revealed in images. In 1860, Princeton, Illinois, artist Julian E. Bryant painted a series of scenes depicting the "Geology of the Mississippi Valley," three of which were displayed in the State Natural History Hall during the 1860 Illinois State Fair. According to one report, Bryant was "a careful observer, and long possessed an intimate acquaintance and sympathy with Nature." Bryant's series included a painting of Starved Rock: "a place deriving its name from the Indian legend." Not only were the paintings reported to have been accurate reflections of their respective regions, they were also "a source of lingering pleasure to every lover of art."[5]

In time private development of the Starved Rock region grew. The adjacent property south and east of Starved Rock was purchased by private individuals, mainly farmers, industrious people whose labor brought forth the promise of the underdeveloped lands of Illinois that had years before been reclaimed by nature. In addition to tillable land, the farmers utilized erodible land for pasture to feed domestic livestock. The upper canyons and bluffs around Starved Rock acted as natural barriers that kept livestock from wandering away. For the first time ever, domestic animals were grazing in the uplands around Starved Rock.[6] Like the French and Indians who had lived before them, the farmers had to fend for themselves. They grew their own crops, raised their own livestock, made many of their own mechanical parts, and repaired their own equipment. Lacking other options, they were often their own leather workers, blacksmiths, veterinarians, carpenters, ropers, and teamsters. Small shops were eventually established, owned and operated by blacksmiths, coopers, weavers, and harness makers. Stores built during the construction of the Illinois and Michigan Canal offered a variety of goods for sale. Clay pipes sold for three-cents each, tobacco was thirty-five-cents per pound, a pound of beef sold for five cents, a wooden casket sold for between two and a half dollars to four dollars and transport to the cemetery was extra, usually around seven dollars.[7]

Like the French and Indians, settlers needed wood for a multitude of purposes such as fuel, building and vehicle construction, and fences. Recognizing the importance of this natural resource, farmers at the time often set aside ten-acre woodlots from which to acquire wood. Even the lowlands around Starved Rock were used by farmers. Hitt's tenant, Charles Rundle, farmed where the parking lot and picnic areas are located in today's Starved Rock State Park. It appears that Rundle also farmed Plum Island, another Hitt-owned property.[8]

In 1867 the US Army Corps of Engineers dispatched a party of cartographers to map the Illinois River. Although a rough map of the river's course had been drawn by Armstrong's men in 1790, this new chart contained much more detail including latitudinal and longitudinal notations, town and township plats, and even noted places of interest such "Old Fort St. Louis." It is interesting that this new, rough hand-drawn map not only mentions "Starved Rock" by name, it also indicates a site located a short distance south of the Rock, a place the cartographer called "Old Fort Saint Louis." This differentiation between Starved Rock and the site of Fort St. Louis is one of the earliest references to a place known as the "Newell site," a series of earthen anomalies where French colonial period artifacts were said to have been uncovered by Utica residents "Jack" and John Newell during the Great Depression.[9] Next to Starved Rock on the map can be seen two "store rooms," buildings that were once used by Hitt or his tenant farmer. The map indicates that in 1867, Plum Island was called "Big School Island" and Leopold Island Number 2 was known as "Simonson's Island."[10]

While the Corps was studying the river and its nearby landforms, historian Francis Parkman was researching his book, *The Discovery of the Great West*, the story of La Salle that included the explorer's exploits in the Starved Rock area during the 1680s. Stopping at the village of Utica, located about a mile north of the Rock, Parkman met James Clark, a man he described as the town's "principal inhabitant." During their conversation, Clark told Parkman that his hired-hands had often plowed up teeth, bones, and other assorted Indian relics in a field along the north side of the river. To Parkman this could only mean one thing: Clark's property was located at the site of old Kaskaskia, the Illinois village from the time of La Salle. This assumption led Parkman to wrongly conclude that Kaskaskia was *downstream* from Starved Rock, not *upstream* from it. This mistake was perpetuated for the next eighty years until the village site's correct location was confirmed by archaeology in the 1940s.[11]

Parkman also questioned Clark about locales that were mentioned in seventeenth-century French documents, including the Vermilion River (*Aramoni*) and Starved Rock (*Le Rocher*). Rather than talk about them, Clark and his friend Daniel Hitt showed Parkman the sites so that Parkman could make his own examination. Parkman, who was knowledgeable about the region, amazed his two guides when he revealed that he knew more about the sites than many of the locals. In fact, Hitt noted that Parkman "told us what we should see every time before we got there."[12]

Both the face and the culture of the region had changed dramatically since Jolliet and Marquette had paddled past the Rock in 1673. That significant event in the nation's history was so unremarkable at the time that Marquette had not mentioned Starved Rock in his journal. Two hundred years later, the citizens of LaSalle County marked that historic bicentennial with an elaborate gala.

Planning and organizing the celebration were a virtual "who's who" of LaSalle County dignitaries who met at the Ottawa Opera House to form committees for arrangements, invitations, fundraising, and entertainment. Emcees and speakers were recruited, including Illinois State Senator and State Attorney General Washington Bushnell ("President of the day") and historian and Chief Justice of the Illinois Supreme Court Sidney Breese.[13] Many "distinguished persons throughout the State" were also invited to join the celebration as was the public. The Bicentennial promised to be a prestigious and well-attended affair.

On September 16 thousands of people came to Starved Rock, arriving in horse-drawn carriages, hacks, and wagons, on horseback and on foot. Visitors reportedly "filled up the woods," climbed to "Camp Rock," what is now Eagle Cliff, or "clambered up the rocky cliffs of Starved Rock."[14] Some of the more affluent attendees ate "sumptuous dinners" while others cooked their meals over a campfire or enjoyed a simple basket lunch. Ottawa photographer W. E. Bowman, with the help of two assistants, hauled their bulky camera gear up the bluff where at 2:00 p.m. Denhard's band trumpeted people to their seats.[15]

On the summit of Starved Rock were assembled many local dignitaries including Hitt, a group of early county settlers, and assorted politicians. All was proceeding as planned with one exception—the event's key-note speaker, Judge Breese, was not present and did not appear even after a delay in the festivities. Bushnell, unable to defer the commencement of the gala any longer, walked to the podium and addressed the crowd:

> Here, upon this hallowed ground, we meet to-day, not to celebrate the religious opinions of any people or sect, but to unite in commemorating the day when the first white man set foot upon this soil—irrespective of discordant sentiments, we meet to celebrate this event—and with religion we have nothing to do. This is an event long to be remembered and treasured.[16]

Reverend J. L. Steele of Christ Church in Ottawa next recited the opening prayer. Bushnell then returned to the podium and apologized for Judge Breese's absence. Fortunately, in the audience was an individual who was seemingly eminently qualified to speak about Starved Rock, one Perry Armstrong, early county resident, historian, attorney, and state legislator. Speaking to the crowd, Armstrong told them that he would "relate something of the history of Starved Rock, as it was imparted" to him in 1831, when he was a young boy, by the "Indian chief Shick-Shack."

Shick-Shack, according to Armstrong, was an aged Odawa chief, 104 years old, six feet tall, dressed in buckskins with a few feathers and beads. The chief reportedly told Armstrong that the Illinois Indians had had a series of disputes with the Miami, Potawatomi, and Kickapoo over hunting ground boundaries. The quarrels had evolved into a series of battles that began along the Wabash River in southern Illinois and Indiana and spread to northern Illinois, reaching today's Morris where an Illinois warrior killed the enemy allied war commander, Moquet. Shick-Shack then became the commander of the enemy forces. From Morris, Shick-Shack and his allied warriors pursued the Illinois to the summit of Starved Rock. There the Illinois were surrounded and besieged. One dark night, the Illinois escaped from the enemy by climbing down the side of the Rock. Once on the ground below, they were discovered by enemy sentries. A tremendous battle ensued wherein nearly all of the Illinois men were killed, with seven escaping. The Illinois women and children who survived the carnage were kept as spoils of war by the Miami, Potawatomi, and Kickapoo. According to Shick-Shack as related by Armstrong, the Illinois Indians ceased to exist.

Ultimately, the alliance of the Miami, Potawatomi, and Kickapoo fractured as the victors fought among themselves, the Miami versus the Potawatomi and Kickapoo. For four long years, the three tribes battled back and forth across Illinois at many locations including Peoria and Kaskaskia. Finally at Sugar Creek near Terre Haute, Indiana, the two sides selected three hundred of their best warriors to fight their opponents to the death. After twelve hours of combat, only twelve of the original six hundred remained; one of these was Shick-Shack. In the end, the two groups, the Miami and the combined group of the Potawatomi and Kickapoo, divided the land between them and lived in peace.

After Armstrong finished relaying Shick-Shack's story and had concluded his own remarks, the band played songs and local celebrities addressed the crowd. These were followed by a reading from Father Marquette's journal about the beauty of the Illinois Valley. Finally, the band played "the national air" and the gala was concluded.

Armstrong's tale of Shick-Shack's destruction of the Illinois at Starved Rock and the eventual disintegration of the Miami, Potawatomi, and Kickapoo alliance that ended near Terre Haute, Indiana, is unadulterated fiction. Although an Indian named Shick-Shack did exist, the stories that Armstrong claimed were from the chief are not only improbable, they contradict the well-know and verifiable historical record. There is no evidence, written or physical, that corroborates the claim that the Illinois Indians waged war with the combined Miami, Potawatomi, and Kickapoo and fought pitched battles across the state of Illinois; that Shick-Shack ever led a Miami, Potawatomi, and Kickapoo alliance against the Illinois; or that the Illinois were destroyed at Starved Rock by Shick-Shack and his warriors. We do know, however, that the Illinois Indians sold land to a British firm, allied with George Rogers Clark, and signed treaties with the US government, including ones at Vincennes, Edwardsville, and Castor Hill long after they were allegedly defeated at Starved Rock by Shick-Shack's forces. We know that the remaining Illinois subtribes merged with the larger Peoria group in 1832 and moved to Kansas where they merged in 1854 with the Wea and Piankashaw, Miami subtribes. We also know that the Peoria group relocated to what is now northeastern Oklahoma in 1868. Today the Peoria maintain tribal headquarters in Miami, Oklahoma.

While thousands of people attended the 1873 pageant, the unadorned Starved Rock had been attracting large numbers of visitors for many years. One account boasts that it "swarms with 10,000 visitors every summer."[17] Another report detailed that "thousands of visitors" climb Starved Rock, which made the path to the summit "more accessible." On the summit, visitors often searched for Indian relics. W. W. Calkins, a long-time resident of LaSalle County, wrote that in addition to "disintegrating remains of thousands of clam-shells on the summit," some people had found hatchets, arrowheads, and, remarkably, swords.[18] In 1877 members of Chicago's Academy of Sciences probed the Rock's summit and found what Dr. Andrews, a member of the Academy, believed were buffalo bones.[19] More curious were the quests to find buried treasure on Starved Rock. In the mid—nineteenth century, rumors spread throughout the Starved Rock region that Tonti, La Salle's second-in-command, had buried a hoard of gold at Fort St. Louis, proceeds from his fur trading business. The exciting rumors spurred local fortune seekers who came with picks and shovels in hand. Although they effectively disrupted the Rock's summit, they never found the reported cache.[20] The physical scar on the landscape that the fortune hunters left behind was one of the topics, in addition to his Shick-Shack account, that Armstrong had incorporated into his 1873 speech at the Jolliet-Marquette celebration. While his motivation was not clear—perhaps more of the colorful and enthralling storytelling of the day—Armstrong, rather than attributing the relatively recently dug holes to gold-diggers, instead claimed that smallpox-infected feverish Indians had dug the holes to cool themselves and treat the disease during the siege. Good storytelling survives generations. Even today, the tale is very much alive. In May 2011, the online *Ottawa Daily Times* published an article entitled "Go for the Gold? Forget it," in which two retired Illinois Department of Natural Resources employees, including this author, refuted the claims.[21] The facts are that Tonti never had any gold because he was penniless. He had never been able to recoup all of the money he had spent fighting the Iroquois, settling intertribal disputes, and investing in the Illinois fur trade. He wrote about this just a few years before his death: "All the voyages I made for the success of this country have ruined me."[22]

In August 1875 heavy rains and high water raised river levels that allowed the *Grey Eagle* steamboat to pass over the rapids and land at Starved Rock. Arriving there, most of the 290 passengers climbed the steep path to the summit to hunt for arrowheads, pick flowers, or read the names carved in the soft sandstone. There they also listened to "impromptu speeches" by the Reverend P. S. Perley of Henry, and Allen Ford, "ex-editor of the Lacon Gazette," both of whom expressed their pleasure of now "standing upon one of the most renowned, valued, and important spots in the state of Illinois."[23]

Steamboats were more than mere vehicles used by visitors anxious to see Starved Rock. Some steamboats that could navigate the shallow Illinois as far as the docks at Utica were also a source of entertainment. One local resident reported, "One of the big events of our young lives was to drive to the Illinois River at Utica and see the steamboats arrive. They usually had two or more deckhands who would play a fiddle and that music sounded grand from the shore. Father did not think that it was heavenly music."[24]

In September and October of 1883, another group of Army engineers under the supervision of W. H. H. Benyaurd surveyed the Illinois River. This survey, the most accurate yet undertaken up to that time, mapped not only the river's shoreline and islands, it also illustrated timber and farm ground located adjacent to the river. The survey also depicted proposed sites for dams including one near today's Starved Rock Boat ramp. It is interesting to speculate just how Starved Rock State Park would appear had this dam been constructed. The dam would certainly have flooded the entire park Lower Area including the Visitor Center, main parking lot, and picnic area, as well as roads, residences, and buildings. The dam was never built, perhaps because a platted but undeveloped town named Science was located adjacent to the proposed dam site. The property had been surveyed by Daniel Hitt sometime after nearby Utica, originally located on the north bank of the river, was relocated a mile north along the newly constructed Illinois and Michigan Canal.[25] Hitt's survey incorporated part of the old village of Utica on the north bank of the river as well as land along the south shore of the river. The site remained undeveloped, the southern portion becoming part of Starved Rock State Park in 1911. Another group of Army engineers led by Captain W. L. Marshall returned to the Illinois River and Starved Rock in August 1889 to sound the river and document the composition of the river bottom. The information gathered by Marshall and his party was added to Benyaurd's 1883 survey which was published twenty years later as *The Woermann Maps*.

By the close of the nineteenth century, mining and industry were becoming an important part of the Starved Rock area's economy. Coal mines, limestone quarries, and silica sand pits provided area residents with steady employment. Agricultural technology—for example, tractors, combines, and planters—later transformed more acres into tillable land. Technology in the first two decades of the twentieth century contributed to improvement in the daily lives of ordinary Americans—and the advent of leisure time. With the new paved highways and affordable mass-produced automobiles, many Americans would use their leisure time to travel and to sightsee captivating places that were previously only visited in print. Starved Rock, the place of romance and Indian legendry, was destined to be one of those get-away places.

11

1886–1911:
IT WILL ALWAYS
BE SITTING HERE, BEAUTIFUL

(Peehkisita moonšaki apiwa kata)

The burgeoning populations and the industrial growth in America's cities in the second half of the nineteenth century stirred a longing for open spaces and natural surroundings. One of the most noteworthy public projects born of this interest was New York's Central Park, 843 acres of naturalistic landscape designs which opened to the public in 1857. During this same period, as more towns dotted the heartland and as farmers transformed prairie and woodlands into cultivated fields, people began to recognize the need for and benefits of land use more in concert with nature, with safeguards to keep some lands wild. Influential writers like Henry David Thoreau, in *Walden* (1854) wrote of his observations of nature and his appreciation of it. John Muir traveled the American West and wrote about natural treasures in a series of articles in the very successful *Century* magazine. Muir joined forces with others to preserve the wilderness, and became a cofounder of the Sierra Club. Popular artists such as Albert Bierstadt and Frederic Edwin Church painted works that accurately depicted the beauty of untamed America. From the mid-1800s through the first two decades of the twentieth century, a growing public sentiment, sometimes called the "Conservation Movement" gained support. In response, both state and federal governments purchased some of the last representative examples of untamed America, forever preserving these places for the public. By 1912 the federal government had reportedly purchased "four million acres in thirteen different localities" including Yosemite, Crater Lake, Sequoia, and Glacier National Parks. On the state level, New York, Michigan, Ohio, California, Massachusetts, and other states bought local treasures such as Niagara Falls Park, Serpent Mounds, and Mackinac Island.

With new highways and automobiles, the twentieth century gave birth to the idea of traveling to public lands and natural wonders. Americans were leaving home to see the sights, enjoy nature, and breathe the fresh country air. For residents of Chicago the Starved Rock area, just about a hundred miles away, offered the best that Illinois nature had to offer—cliffs, hills, rivers, pine trees, and wildlife. The Starved Rock area was an ideal locale for the new tourism industry. A large park, be it public or private, with a resort as its centerpiece, would make related tourism services—from lodging to restaurants and transportation to souvenirs—a profitable industry and a boon to the local economy. Local residents suggested two locations for such an important park.

One of these was Buffalo Rock, the steep sandstone bluff located on the north side of the Illinois River between Ottawa and Utica. Buffalo Rock had been where some Miami Indians settled between 1683 and 1689, and it also had been the site of La Chapelle's Fort Ottawa during the winter of 1760 and 1761. It was well-known to area residents, many of whom boasted that "No finer site for a summer hotel exists in the Illinois Valley." To promote selection of this site, prominent Ottawa businessmen pursued a plan to run an electric railway between Buffalo Rock and Ottawa. The press also endorsed the site. According to the *Ottawa Free Trader*, "Unlike Starved Rock, which is rather ornamental than useful, being but a half acre in area, Buffalo Rock could afford to thousands an elevation certain to catch every breath of air stirring." Curiously, the support for Buffalo Rock as the site for a park that would welcome tourists was later revealed as a "scheme." "The scheme" as reported by the *Free Trader*, "is to make Buffalo Rock a resort for the people of Ottawa somewhat upon the plan of the parks of Chicago" where pavilions, tennis courts, walks, and drives "would be a blessing to the tired matrons and husbands." In essence, Buffalo Rock would be a park for Ottawa residents, not for tourists.[1] Once the deception had been revealed, the site was instead put to use by the First Brigade of the Illinois National Guard for drills and maneuvers. In 1900 Duke Farson, a Chicago banker known for his "leadership and work in the Methodist church," purchased Buffalo Rock, where the "great national camp-meeting of the Methodists" was held in that year.[2] Farson hired civil engineers whose work included "locating roads and doing the necessary preliminary work to improve the spot and make it a delightful resort."[3] Although Farson's work added to the site's allure, there was little public support beyond Ottawa to purchase Buffalo Rock as the site for the public park space. Eventually, the site was purchased by the Crane Company. In addition to using some of the land for construction of a tuberculosis sanitarium, the site was also used by the Crane Company as a vacation spot for "thousands of employees and their families."[4] In 1928, the company donated the land to the State of Illinois.

In early 1890, Chicago businessman Ferdinand Walther saw an opportunity to prosper from the enthusiasm of tourism and the renown of Starved Rock. Walther purchased the site and an additional one hundred acres. His plan was to make Starved Rock a private park that included a "first class health and summer resort."[5]

Although it is not known for certain when Walther and Hitt first met to discuss the sale of Starved Rock, it appears that negotiations may have taken place in late 1889. In January 1890, Harris Huehl, one of Walther's business partners, wrote to Hitt advising him that one their colleagues, E. W. Huncke, had fallen ill. Because of this Huehl would have to postpone their Chicago meeting to discuss the land sale.[6] In early February, Huehl wrote to Hitt again. This time he explained that it would be "almost impossible for all the parties who are interested in this matter to get the time to go down to Ottawa." Huehl requested again that Hitt come to Chicago, assuring him that their meeting would take no more than "a half day at the utmost."[7] Hitt had no interest in traveling a hundred miles to sell *his* land. If the group of investors wanted to make the purchase, they would all have to join Hitt in Ottawa. The partners realized that they had to meet with Hitt on his terms. On February 11 they sent Hitt a telegraph message requesting that he meet with them at the Harrison in La Salle. While La Salle was much closer than Chicago, it was still a considerable fourteen miles from Hitt's home; Hitt declined. Finally recognizing that the only way the purchase would come to fruition would be to meet on Hitt's terms, the partners accepted. They met with Hitt at his attorney's office in Ottawa on February 15.[8] A tentative deal was struck between the two parties; it read:

> This certifies that D.F. Hitt has this day sold to Ferdinand Walther, one hundred acres of land including Starved Rock in La Salle County, Illinois, the same being shown by plat furnished to said Walther, for the sum of fourteen thousand dollars—one hundred dollars cash, and six thousand nine hundred dollars on or before sixty days from this date, and balance to be secured by first mortgage on same on or before five years from date.[9]

The five-year $13,900.00 loan to Walther was at six-percent interest annually. Walther and the other investors also had an option to purchase the "land adjoining said tract—265 acres more at $45.00 per acre within one year."

While the investors were bargaining with Hitt, Walther's attorney, Joseph Mulke, was carefully searching the title of the property to ensure that there were no liens or other encumbrances on it. On March 21 Mulke wrote to the partners, "I find the title as to the premises first above described substantially good in Daniel Hitt."[10] Supporting the future success of his purchase, Walther and his Starved Rock Improvement Company of Chicago had been working behind the scenes. They had persuaded the Rock Island Railroad to sell "cheap round-trip tickets" and "excursions to the Rock" from Chicago at regular intervals. They had also negotiated with local transportation heads for expansion of the electric "interurban" line to get visitors from the railway station in Utica to the future hotel.

With a plan for the infrastructure of a successful resort firmly in place, Walther faced the challenge of transforming the neglected site into a popular tourist attraction. Walther recognized that building a first-class resort from cornfields and a few decrepit shacks would take a great deal of work and money. He would have to get electricity to the site, drill a well, clear the underbrush, and build roads and parking lots. With the growing public interest in nature, many people felt that the future park's real attraction was its brooks and canyons, not the rock itself; they hoped that Walther would build a road that would connect these natural features to the location of the future hotel. To accomplish this, and to invest in the needed site development, the Starved Rock Improvement Company allocated $50,000.00 of a $100,000.00 capital investment fund for improvements. The other half of the fund was allocated for construction of the hotel and adjacent complex, including cabins and a dining hall. In March the Illinois Secretary of State's Office issued a license for Walther's company to "conduct a pleasure resort in LaSalle county."[11]

Walther's plan proceeded. The railroad was agreeable, the state license was secured, and the interurban was extending its line. It appears that the formal contract between Hitt and Walther was signed on Friday, April 25, 1890. From the Indians to the French to the British to the Americans to Daniel Hitt, Starved Rock's ownership was now held by a group of investors.

Hitt must have savored the fact that he had purchased the property for only $1.25 per acre and had thus made a huge profit on the sale. So pleased was he with the sale that local residents reported an uplifted change in his demeanor. In fact, it was reported that he "puts on more style than half the young men in Ottawa. A reporter saw him walking around town yesterday with a cane about five feet in length, and if cut into cordwood, would not have run a cook-stove over two hours."[12]

The locals eagerly anticipated the financial benefits that the hotel would bring to the area. One prediction proclaimed, "The Starved Rock Hotel, all say, will be a vast improvement to the business interests in Utica."[13] Word of the new park and resort spread well beyond the immediate vicinity. Two days before the hotel opening scheduled for June 1, 1891, five of the park's cottages had already been reserved by Chicagoans at a rate of fifty dollars per month. Because of demand, Walther planned to build six more of them; in the end, though, they were never constructed. Hotel guests paid three-dollars per day on the American plan (all meals included).[14] Travel to the new resort by train between Utica and Chicago cost $4.90.

While the hotel was under construction, someone at the site had a good laugh when the report of an unearthed grave was telegraphed to the *Chicago Herald* newspaper. According to the account, the grave belonged to Henri Tonti—an obvious hoax since the French explorer had died and been buried in 1704 near Mobile Bay, Alabama, not at Starved Rock. The report alleged that the remains had a mechanical hand (Tonti was

Figure 11.1 A postcard of the Starved Rock Hotel. The hotel was built in 1891 by Ferdinand Walther. It fell into disrepair and was demolished after the opening of the current Starved Rock Lodge in 1939. Photo: Starved Rock State Park archives.

reportedly fitted with an artificial one). The *Herald* checked the information and found that "The people at the Rock know nothing about any such find and laugh at the story as a good joke."[15]

Interest in the park brought visitors to Starved Rock even before the hotel had been opened. Some came to watch the construction, some to see the site's transformation from farm to park, and others came in hopes of finding a profit-making niche for themselves. On May 30, 1891, a steamboat left Peru, Illinois, for Starved Rock, five miles downstream. Its mission was to find a navigable channel that was deep enough for passenger vessels, ones that could transport visitors and guests to the hotel from places downstream. It was not to be, however, for as in times past, it was only during periods of high water, when heavy rains doused the valley, that larger boats could skirt the rapids between Utica and Peru.[16] The Illinois River was permanently altered in 1900 with the opening of the Sanitary and Ship Canal, an engineering feat that reversed the flow of the Chicago River, sending Chicago River water south and into the Illinois River rather than into Lake Michigan where it had previously flowed.

In June 1891 Walther's hotel at last opened. Starved Rock, just a few yards away, was touted as "The Mecca of Romance and Indian Legendry" and "The most beautiful spot between the Allegheny and Rocky Mountains." It was also reportedly the "Finest Summer Resort in Illinois," having "all modern improvements." There were fifty guest rooms, five cottages, "where the cool shade during the day affords rest and a night of sleep that is foreign to many summer hotels." It also had a dining room capable of seating 150 guests.

Once at Starved Rock, in 1891, visitors reportedly participated in a host of activities set in the natural environment. One advertisement for the park and hotel suggested "rambles over the prairies, scaling the bluffs and precipices, exploring the canyons and glens, and searching out new and unexplored beauty spots." People gathered mosses and picked ferns and wildflowers. They enjoyed horseback riding or a drive in a rented carriage in the countryside or along the bluffs overlooking the valley. The site was described as "something of a paradise for the angler." Skies were epitomized as "a peculiar Italian blue." On bright moonlit nights the canyons "gave a picture not readily forgotten." Starved Rock was promoted as the place to relax, have fun, and enjoy the best that nature could offer, and admission to the park was only ten cents.[17]

In April 1888 archaeologist T. H. Lewis, working under the auspices of the Northwestern Archaeological Survey, an endeavor sponsored by Alfred J. Hill (1881–1895), conducted a cursory archaeological survey on the summits of both Lover's Leap and Starved Rock. Concerning his observations on the summit of Starved Rock, Lewis noted that from first appearance, the summit of the site held little archaeological value as a portion of it was reportedly "more or less mutilated." Lewis left the Illinois Valley that year and returned to Starved Rock in late August 1894 to obtain more detailed information about the site. To get permission to survey Starved Rock's summit, it appears that Lewis won favor with Walther by staying at and patronizing the Starved Rock Hotel. Although Lewis did not believe that La Salle's Fort St. Louis had been built on the summit of Starved Rock when he first visited the site in 1888, he later changed his mind after studying La Salle period documents, noting that the place matched the description of the location of La Salle's fort. Although an accurate map of his survey work was never published as Lewis died in 1895, his brief survey work is important because it is the first and only archaeological survey to have been completed before work on the summit was completed by the Civilian Conservation Corps in the 1930s.[18]

The hotel became part of the area's social fabric and society. Dancing was popular at Walther's hotel; the dining room doubled as a dance hall when the Clover Club reportedly "gave one of their mid-summer parties at Starved Rock." When the group arrived, the hotel's "genial landlord," Harris Huell, one of Walther's business partners, "took them in tow and informed them that the hotel was theirs for the night." With music provided by Professor Willis and his orchestra, seventy-five partygoers danced from 9:00 p.m. until midnight, when a late dinner was served. After the meal, the tables were cleared again and the party continued until 2:30 a.m.[19] The following Friday a local LaSalle County hero, Colonel Douglas Hapeman, and his wife met forty of their friends for dinner at the Starved Rock Hotel. During the Civil War, Hapeman had been the regimental commander of the 104th Volunteer Illinois Infantry Regiment, a unit comprised nearly exclusively of LaSalle County men. He was also a Medal of Honor winner, having earned the prestigious award for meritorious services at the Battle of Peachtree Creek near Atlanta. The group included some of the regiment's officers and soldiers and a few high-ranking public officials and their wives. The event reportedly inaugurated the Starved Rock Hotel's "Summer's Brilliant Social Season."[20]

During Walther's tenure, not only did vacationers, politicians, and local celebrities come to the see the sights, so did academics and scientists. Between 1891 and 1936, a group of American botanists traveled throughout the United States to photograph an array of habitats, from swamps, bogs, and prairies to woodlands and dunes, as a method of recording America's many unique plants and ecosystems. They also recorded long-term changes on these systems, both natural and man-made, to evaluate and document the impact of development. During these years, a collection of about 4,500 photographs were taken and are now accessible at the Library of Congress under the title of *American Environmental Photographs, 1891–1936: Images from the University of Chicago*. During some of these expeditions, researchers photographed the park's unique flora and beautiful canyons as well as the unequalled view from the summit of Starved Rock.

The astonishing beauty to be seen from the summit included the canyons and rock formations. The first French to visit the Illinois Country had named certain sites including *Le Rocher*, what is now Starved Rock. When the Americans arrived, they called Starved Rock "the Rock" and the adjacent bluffs "Small Rocks" and "Little Rock." In the late 1800s, Lover's Leap had become known as "Maiden Rock" or "Maiden Bluff" while adjacent Eagle Cliff had become known as "Camp Rock."[21] As noted above, Plum Island was once called "Big School Island" while "Delbridge Island," named after its owner John Delbridge, now submerged above the Starved Rock Dam, was once called "Grass Island" as well as "Goose Island." Like "Delbridge Island," area canyons were originally named after the people who owned them. Today's Saint Louis Canyon was once called "Clayton Canyon" after landowner William Clayton, who owned the canyon and 293 acres of adjacent property. The creek that flows through Saint Louis Canyon was called "Clayton Run." Hennepin Canyon was once called "Atwood Canyon," after its owner H. Atwood: in the same fashion, Kaskaskia Canyon was once known as "Fishburn Canyon," after its owner, Benjamin Fishburn. These straight-forward designations for the local sites changed in 1890 when Walther bought the property. Interested in attracting visitors to *his* place of legendry and romance, it appears that Walther renamed the canyons and glens, using names of famous Frenchmen, Indians, and Indian tribes. The new names gave the park's natural features historic reference and ambiance. French Canyon, the chasm closest to the old Starved Rock Hotel, became known by that name shortly after Walther purchased the site. At about the same time, the small bluff to the south of Starved Rock became Devil's Nose. There were some exceptions: Ottawa Canyon, located on private property several miles east of the hotel complex, remained unnamed until 1912.[22] Illinois Canyon, a site that was inaccessible to tourists prior to state ownership, possessed the unromantic name of "Salt Well Canyon," after the nearby salt well.

Accessibility was essential to the success of Walther's investment, and part of that transport involved crossing the Illinois River. Between 1890 and 1911, tourists arriving at the Rock Island Railroad station in Utica on the north side of the river reached the hotel south of the river by first boarding the interurban rail line. From there, the interurban transported passengers to a ferry owned by Walther that was located near the Army

Corps of Engineers Visitor's Center along Dee Bennett Road. From there, visitors could cross the river and walk to the hotel. According to one report, in 1904, the ferry carried about 22,000 people; in 1905 about 31,000; in 1906 about 41,000; in 1907 about 41,000; and in 1908 about 36,000.[23] Because these numbers included round-trip ticket holders who would have been counted twice, along with hotel employees, it is difficult to determine the exact number of people who visited Walther's park. The best estimates ascribe the number at 25,000 visitors every year.[24] Walther's investment appears to have been very profitable. His financial records indicate that between 1905 and 1911, his net profit from room, meals, the bar, souvenirs, and other concessions had increased by nearly one hundred percent, from $6,456.17 to $12,291.50.

Despite the success of the venture, the improvement of the site, the satisfaction of the guests and the positive impact on the local economy, the clamor for land to be set aside for public use continued to grow. Citizens of Illinois wanted public ownership of the site.[25] Further, with an interest in safeguarding the natural beauty of the Rock, the public wanted to eliminate the risk of destruction that was inherent in private ownership of the land. Of specific concern was the sandstone of the Rock itself. In private hands, the Rock could be demolished, and the sandstone of the Rock itself could be sold as a valuable commodity to the local glass works. According to one source, "The increasing commercial exploitation of the Starved Rock vicinity and the danger of the glass industry, especially to the upper canyons, led to an agitation for the acquisition, by the people of Starved Rock and the canyons immediately about it."[26]

Citizens with political clout and politicians across the state and even across the nation, such as Jessie Palmer Weber, secretary of the Illinois State Historical Society: landscape architect Jens Jensen: attorney and LaSalle County Circuit Clerk Horace Hull: Dr. Wallace W. Atwood of the University of Chicago, and Reverend Theodore Jessup of Boonville, New York, appealed to well-established and respectable organizations such as the Geographic Society of Chicago, the Daughters of the American Revolution, the Chicago Historical Society, and even the Catholic Church, to join the effort for state purchase of Starved Rock. In his presentation to the Chicago Historical Society, Eaton Osman, a local author and amateur historian, proclaimed Fort St. Louis to be the "keystone" of the empire of

New France. Osman's presentation included exciting details about Tonti and the Illinois Indians, as well as the enthralling legend of Starved Rock. Osman also used his celebrity to influence the vote in favor of state purchase of the site by presenting to Illinois legislators complimentary copies of his book, *Starved Rock: A Chapter of Colonial History.* From 1905 until the state's purchase of the site in 1911, people and organizations with influence gave speeches, published articles, and wrote letters, hoping to ensure the natural integrity of the site through the purchase of Walther's property by the State of Illinois.[27]

In 1909, the Illinois General Assembly created a commission to look at the "feasibility of acquiring Starved Rock and other sites." The commission was legally required to investigate the park world to examine and scrutinize the benefits and liabilities of park ownership and maintenance, and to compare parks in Illinois with those in other states. When their investigation was completed, they were to submit a report of their findings to Governor Charles Deneen.

There were two immediate hurdles in evaluating the site as a purchase for a state park. First, although Walther owned most of the land (360 acres), much of the adjacent property was owned by other private individuals and companies. If purchase of the site was to proceed, the state would be required to reach purchase agreements with several different entities, not just one. Moreover, before the state could consider the purchase of any property, the land's "fair market value" had to be calculated as the state was prohibited by law from paying more than fair market value unless the purchased land had unique archaeological, historical, or geological significance.

Walther's agent, E. H. Heilbron, gave the commission first option to purchase the land at an unrealistic $300,000.00.[28] The state geologist assessed the property's value at only $125,000.00.[29] This seemingly unbridgeable financial chasm was only one issue for the commission. Complicating matters further was the fact that at this same time the state was also evaluating two other sites for purchase: what is now White Pines Forest State Park in Ogle County and Monk's Mound at today's Cahokia Mounds State Historic Site. Both of these places were indeed valuable in their own way—one as the last old growth white pine timber site in Illinois, the other an archaeological site so unique that today it is recognized as a UNESCO World Heritage Site. The Starved Rock site had the distinction of unique indigenous and rare canyon flora as well as the historical importance of the Rock.[30]

Having completed its investigation in 1911, the commission recommended that not only should the state purchase Walther's property, it should also purchase additional acreage, a total of 1,155 acres of land. They proposed buying a tract from the Utica Road, today's Illinois Route 178, east to the South Ottawa Township line. The purchase included only about 285 of Walther's 360 acres since the remaining land was farm ground that "cannot be used for park purposes." This plan looked good on paper, but in reality the state still had the onerous challenge of negotiating the purchase of 870 acres from 18 different landowners at a price of between $40 and $100 per acre. The governor was reportedly "favorable to the proposition" but added that "it was up to the friends of the state park proposition to prevail." Some of these friends were members of a committee created by the "commercial associations of Ottawa, La Salle, and Streator," whose mission was to "cooperate in securing the passage of the bills necessary to acquire and establish a State Park in this county." State Representative William Scanlan of Peru introduced House Bill 390 that created a new park commission, appropriated $225,000.00 for the purchase and improvement of the property, and outlined the legal boundaries of the proposed park.[31] Scanlan's bill reportedly received a favorable recommendation by the House Committee on Parks and Boulevards, which sent the bill to the appropriations committee. Although the appropriations committee attempted to reduce the $225,000.00 expenditure by $75,000.00, the original bill eventually passed and was sent to the state senate. There it was reduced to the appropriations committee's $150,000.00. To get final passage of this lesser amount through the senate, an amendment that prohibited sale, possession, or consumption of any alcohol in state parks was added to the bill.[32] The bill was returned to the House for a vote on the new alcohol prohibition amendment and it passed the next day.[33]

On June 31, 1911, Governor Deneen appointed James Alton James, Alexander Richards, and Reverend D. L. Crowe to the new Illinois Park Commission. They were authorized to purchase and manage state parks.[34] On September 20, the commission began negotiations with Walther. Two days later, he agreed to accept the entire $150,000.00 appropriation for his land and buildings. Before the deal could be completed, the state insisted that an audit of Walther's books be conducted by "prominent bankers, bond brokers, and hotel owners." According to the bankers, the property was worth $146,428.00. The bond brokers believed that the price should be somewhat less while the hotel owners believed that the price should be considerably higher. An agreement was eventually reached between the two parties for the 280 acres of land that had initially been in the agreement and for an additional ten acres of woodland "lying outside of the reservation." The price tag was $146,000.000. The state also purchased 6.04 acres from the Hitt/Russell estate located in the platted town of Science, adjacent to the present-day Starved Rock boat ramp, for $875.00 and an additional 18.59 acres for $2,665.00.

On December 20, 1911, the property was officially transferred to the State of Illinois. The State of Illinois used the next five months preparing to open the new state park. Park staff was hired, roads were repaired, and concessions were awarded. Starved Rock State Park was first opened under state management on May 1, 1912.[35]

For ten thousand years the Rock had been claimed by Native Americans, for about eighty-three by the French, for twenty by the British, for fifty-two by the United States, for fifty-five by one private individual, for twenty-one years by a group of investors, and finally today, by the State of Illinois.

CONCLUDING THOUGHTS

Under state management, the new park grew in popularity. In 1912, the park boasted 75,000 visitors, a three-fold increase in attendance when compared to the 25,000 people who annually visited the site when it was under private management. During that same year the American Film Company directed movie location scenes at the park. In 1918 more than 20,000 people attended Illinois' centennial celebration there. On Labor Day weekend 1923, the park hosted an estimated 50,000 people, many of whom camped at one of the most modern campgrounds in the country, the Starved Rock Campground. The Starved Rock Hotel guests were entertained by such music greats as Louis Armstrong, Duke Ellington, and Guy Lombardo. During the Great Depression, the park was home to Company 1609 of the Civilian Conservation Corps who, along with three other CCC companies, built bridges, shelters, and parts of the Starved Rock Lodge, all while rebuilding their own lives and America. The park provided specialists from the US Army Corps of Engineers with a training area to master the military art of pontoon bridge assembly in preparation for the Allied invasion of Germany in World War II. Equally important, the park was where locals came to work and to relax in the 1950s and 1960s, and it is where today over two million people come to hike, camp, picnic, fish, hunt, and enjoy nature every year.

The park's splendor as well as its legendary notoriety make it part of the area's economic foundation. To keep tourists and travelers in area motels, restaurants, gift shops and other retail establishments, towns such as Utica, Oglesby, and Ottawa have a vested interest in preserving the park and its environs.

Within the park itself, a conflict that began more than a century ago continues to this day. It is the controversy over park concessions versus nature. There are several private concessions at Starved Rock State Park that, in the view of some people, have little place in a public park. Nonetheless, the reality is that park visitors want a place to feed their families, take a boat ride, and purchase a T-shirt, preferably one that sports some recognition of the place, Starved Rock. Arguably, these concessionaires compete with merchants in nearby towns for these same customers. Striking a balance between nature and commerce, and between in-park merchants and local business owners, will continue to be an important matter for state stewardship of the site.

The very geologic composition of Starved Rock and its environs has created a new challenge for the twenty-first century. Sand companies now mine silica sand near the park. The challenge is one of balance between protection of the park's fragile natural resources—coupled with the beauty and serenity of the park experience—versus the competing interests of local governments and residents desiring new employment opportunities. This balance of conflicting goals is as delicate as it is formidable.

In addition, the Starved Rock Dam, completed in 1933, raised the level of the Illinois River above the dam about ten feet. The newer and wider river continues to erode the shoreline of the park and a very significant archaeological site on the other side of it, the old Kaskaskia village, known to archaeologists as 11-LS-13 or the Zimmerman Site, and to the public as the Grand Village of the Illinois Historical Site. The dam is also responsible for submerging Delbridge, Gypsy, and many other islands, losing them to the river.

Pedestrian traffic throughout the park has also accelerated the erosion process, a problem that was addressed in the early 1980s and 1990s when wooden walkways were constructed. Still, park visitors illegally climb the cliffs, enter restricted areas, and stray from marked trails. These activities tear away at the site's fragile environment. Although signs and brochures warn park visitors that it is against the law to leave marked trails, the problem continues, and couldn't be solved if a thousand park employees were detailed in every canyon and along every trail. While the huge bluffs appear solid and impervious, "fortress-like," as Charlevoix described them, they are fragile, very fragile sandstone, a mineral that easily disintegrates with the slightest bit of pressure. Not only is climbing and off-trail activity illegal, it's also dangerous, as every year this risky behavior leads to critical injuries and deaths at the park. Maintaining the park's trail system is a continuous process, requiring a great deal of energy and resources.

In terms of the State of Illinois and its spending resources, parks and public lands are and typically have been very low, falling well beneath most other state budget items. While this might seem sensible and understandable because state budget expenditures related to people, justice, and commerce seemingly should have priority over those used for maintenance of trees and riverbanks, a few lesser known facts compel further consideration. For example, the entire Illinois Department of Natural Resources (IDNR), when fully staffed, is about one-third of one percent of the total state budget, and continues to shrink at an alarming rate. Even if the agency were eliminated, it would have an almost unnoticed financial impact on the state's budget. Additionally, this tiny agency has more positive contact and interaction with the public than many other state agencies combined. IDNR employees maintain and protect all state parks for the enjoyment of hikers, photographers, bird watchers, geologists, picnickers, wildflower and butterfly enthusiasts, fishermen, hunters, boaters, historians, and a host of other people who find enjoyment there. This very small financial investment in the preservation and upkeep of Starved Rock is money well spent.

The Illinois Department of Natural Resources employees at Starved Rock State Park are dedicated to preserving and maintaining the park and to serving park visitors. In the face of increased visitor demand, park maintenance, and decreased budgets, their efforts are supported by the Starved Rock Foundation, which sells books, conducts guided hikes, serves the public at the information desk located in the Visitor Center, and contributes in other ways to running the site. The Foundation also donates all of its sales income to Starved Rock State Park.

The purpose of this narrative has been to provide insight into the true history of Starved Rock and its strategic importance over the centuries. The enduring nature of the rock itself, made of fragile sandstone that survived prehistoric glacial meltwater torrents, and the excellence of the site as a park today, provide more allure for visitors than any legend. When set against all that truly is Starved Rock, the legend pales in significance. While the legend remains part of the fabric of this place, it is not the history. Yet the Rock's history encompasses both the legend and the unraveling of the legend. Today Starved Rock is a beautiful park enjoyed by millions of people from all over the world. Their experiences too, recounted at some point in the future, will become part of the history of this special place. Starved Rock is the historical, archaeological, geological, and recreational jewel of Illinois.

Timeline of Starved
Rock 1673–1911

1673

- Louis Jolliet and Jacques Marquette pass Starved Rock while returning north during their voyage of discovery. They stop at Kaskaskia, an Illinois Indian village located a mile upstream and on the opposite shore from Starved Rock.

1674

- Marquette and two traveling companions, Jacques Largillier and Pierre Porteret, leave the Jesuit mission near Green Bay, Wisconsin, and begin the return trek to the Kaskaskia village.

1675

- Marquette arrives at Kaskaskia. He establishes the Mission of the Immaculate Conception at Kaskaskia, the first Christian mission in present-day Illinois.
- Marquette dies in May, near Ludington, Michigan.

1677

- Jesuit missionary Claude-Jean Allouez arrives at Kaskaskia to continue Marquette's work.

1678

- French explorer René-Robert Cavelier Sieur de La Salle in France obtains a five-year patent to explore the wilderness in New France.

1679

- Above Niagara Falls, La Salle's men build the first bark to sail the Great Lakes, a vessel whose name history records as the Griffon.
- The Griffon is lost somewhere on Green Bay.

1680

- The La Salle expedition arrives at Kaskaskia on January 1. Four days later, the expedition arrives at Lake Peoria where they encounter a large winter village of Illinois Indians.
- La Salle's men build Fort de Crèvecoeur.
- La Salle leaves Fort de Crèvecoeur for his post on the Saint Joseph River in southwest Michigan. La Salle instructs Tonti to examine Starved Rock and to build a strong fort on it. This is the first historical reference to the famous bluff.
- Most of the Frenchmen at Fort de Crèvecoeur desert. Tonti and the remaining French are forced to impose on the Illinois at Kaskaskia to wait for La Salle to return to Illinois.
- In September, a large Iroquois war party invades the Illinois Country. They drive the Illinois from their claimed homeland.
- In November, La Salle returns to the Illinois Country. He sees that Kaskaskia has been destroyed by the Iroquois. There is no sign of Tonti or any of his men.
- La Salle leaves the Illinois Country and travels to his post on the St. Joseph River.

1681

- La Salle returns to the Illinois Country and encounters some Illinois hunting near Kaskaskia.

- La Salle meets with the Miami in northwestern Indiana and asks them to live peacefully with the Illinois.
- La Salle reunites with Tonti at Michilimackinac.
- La Salle spends the rest of the year organizing an expedition to locate the mouth of the Mississippi River.

1682

- La Salle's expedition reaches the mouth of the Mississippi River in April. He claims the entire Mississippi basin for France.
- La Salle heads back north and eventually arrives at Michilimackinac. He learns that Governor Frontenac has been recalled to France and that a new governor, Le Fèbvre de La Barre, is Canada's governor.
- In late December, a group of Frenchmen arrive at Starved Rock and begin construction of Fort St. Louis on the bluff's summit.

1683

- Construction of La Salle's fort is completed in March.
- Thousands of Miami, Illinois, Shawnee, and other tribes relocate to the Starved Rock region.
- In April, La Salle awards Jacques Bourdon d'Autray a grant of land near Starved Rock. The grant is the first of its kind in Illinois.
- In August La Salle also awards a grant of land to Pierre Prudhomme. Part of Prudhomme's grant is in the present-day city of La Salle, Illinois.
- With his royal license to operate in the West expired, La Salle leaves Starved Rock for Quebec, and eventually sails to France.
- Lieutenant Louis-Henri Baugy, an officer appointed by Governor La Barre, takes command at Fort St. Louis.
- While in France, La Salle receives permission to sail to the Gulf of Mexico to establish a post at the mouth of the Mississippi River.

1684

- La Salle sails to the Gulf with settlers, soldiers, and supplies under a battleship escort.
- In March, two hundred Iroquois besiege Fort St. Louis on Starved Rock. After six days, the local Indians, returning to the Starved Rock area from their winter hunts, drive the Iroquois away.

- Tonti is in Quebec where he learns that Fort St. Louis has been returned to La Salle. Tonti and François Dauphin, Sieur de la Forest, are in charge of La Salle's operations.
- Tonti writes contracts and hires French traders to conduct trade at Starved Rock.

1685

- La Salle's colonists disembark at Matagorda Bay, Texas, and begin construction of another Fort St. Louis.
- Tonti arrives at Fort St. Louis in the north and assumes command of the fort.

1686

- Tonti travels to the Gulf to find La Salle. He returns without locating La Salle.
- Calamity plagues La Salle's Texas colony.

1687

- La Salle is murdered by one of his own men while attempting to return to Starved Rock.
- Tonti leaves Starved Rock to fight Iroquois in the East in Governor Denonville's campaign.
- While Tonti is away, several survivors of La Salle's Texas expedition arrive at Starved Rock. The chronicler of the group, Henri Joutel, writes an account of his observations of the fort and the surrounding area during the winter of 1687. The group keeps La Salle's death a secret.
- Tonti arrives back at the fort in October.

1688

- The Texas survivors leave Starved Rock for Canada and then France.
- Some months later, Tonti learns that La Salle had been murdered in Texas. Tonti journeys south again to find what remains of La Salle's colony. His attempt is unsuccessful as flood waters prevent him from reaching the gulf.
- In December the few French that remain at Fort St. Louis in Texas are either killed by Karankawa Indians or carried away as captives.

- Jesuit Jacques Gravier and Jesuit *donné* Jacques Largillier arrive at Kaskaskia.

1689

- Most of the non-Illinois tribes are gone the Starved Rock area. Only some Illinois Indians remain at Kaskaskia.
- Father Allouez, the pioneering Jesuit missionary, dies at a Miami village on the Saint Joseph River.

1690

- La Forest leaves Canada for France and petitions the court successfully for La Salle's Illinois trade concession.

1691

- Pierre-Charles Delliette, Tonti's cousin, is in command at Fort St. Louis while Tonti travels to Michilimackinac.
- With natural resources dwindling in the Starved Rock area and with the possibility of an Iroquois attack, the Illinois leave Kaskaskia and establish a new village at Lake Peoria.

1693

- La Forest sells half of his Illinois trade interest to Michael Accault.

1696

- Tonti and La Forest are exempt from the general trade prohibition; they are allowed two canoes of furs per year.

1698

- Alphonse Tonti becomes a partner in the Illinois trade concession when his brother Henri cedes him one-half of his share.

1699

- Tonti escorts three missionaries of the *Société des Missions Étrangères* to the Arkansas River. One of the three missionaries, Jean-François Buisson de St. Cosme, leaves an account of the group's travels that includes his observations at Kaskaskia and at Starved Rock.
- Pierre Le Moyne d'Iberville establishes a French post on the Gulf of Mexico at today's Ocean Springs, Mississippi.

1700

- The Kaskaskia Indians and their Jesuit associates leave Lake Peoria for the Mississippi Valley. They establish a village at De Pères Creek near modern-day St. Louis.

1701

- Antoine de la Mothe Cadillac establishes a French post at Detroit. Sauk, Miami, Wendat, Potawatomi, and other northern tribes resettle in Michigan's Lower Peninsula.

1702

- The King abolishes the Illinois trade concession and orders Tonti to report to D'Iberville's colony on the Gulf. La Forest is ordered to report to Canada.

1703

- French missionaries and the Indians leave De Pères Creek and establish a new village at the Kaskaskia River, in today's Randolph County, Illinois. The second Kaskaskia becomes Illinois' first state capital.

1704

- Tonti dies of yellow fever at Mobile Bay, Alabama.

1705

- Father Gravier is seriously wounded in the arm by an arrow shot by a Peoria Indian. The Peoria mission closes until Jesuit missionary Pierre-Gabriel Marest reopens it in 1712.

1708

- Unable to have the stone arrow tip removed from his arm in Canada or in France, Gravier sails to D'Iberville's colony and dies at Mobile Bay from complications from his wound.

1710

- Nineteen-year-old Joseph Kellogg, an Englishman, passes Starved Rock in the company of French voyageurs.

1712

- One band of the Peoria Indians establishes a village at Starved Rock.
- Jesuit Father Pierre-Gabriel Marest visits the Peoria at Starved Rock while passing through the Illinois Valley. He notes that Frenchmen were living among the Peoria at the Rock.
- One Mesquakie band relocates to Detroit. There they are besieged by the French and their Indian allies. The Peoria Indians from Starved Rock participate in the hostilities against the Mesquakie.
- The episode at Detroit commences the "Fox Wars," a period of intertribal attacks and skirmishes in Michigan, Wisconsin, and Illinois.

1713–1722

- Mesquakie war parties intermittently raid the Illinois Valley, killing Peoria Indians.

1715

- Frenchmen Maunoir and Bisaillon arrive at the Starved Rock Peoria village to recruit men to attack the Mesquakie in Wisconsin.

1716

- French and Indians led by Louis de la Porte de Louvigny besiege a fortified Mesquakie village at Wisconsin's Big Lake Butte des Morts.
- The Mesquakie capitulate to the French and their Indian allies and agree to stop attacks on the Illinois and other tribes. They also agree to return prisoners they hold captive.

1717

- The Illinois Country becomes part of the new French colony of Louisiana.

1718

- New Orleans is founded.
- An anonymous memoir reports that the Illinois (Peoria) Indians live along the shore of the Illinois River next to Starved Rock while some French traders live on the Rock's summit.
- Approximately 2,000 Peoria Indians live at Starved Rock.

1719

- Construction on the first Fort de Chartres in southern Illinois begins. The fort is completed in 1721. French colonial government in the Illinois Country establishes headquarters at the new fort.

1721

- Several Mesquakie prisoners including the nephew of a Mesquakie chief are burned to death by the Peoria, possibly at Starved Rock.
- Jesuit Pierre-François Xavier de Charlevoix arrives at Starved Rock. He notes that the Peoria live on an island at the foot of the Rock. He also reports that some remains of old Fort St. Louis can still be seen on the Rock's summit.

1722

- François Philippe Renault, French superintendent of mines, arrives at Starved Rock in search of copper mines.
- The two Peoria bands (from Lake Peoria and Starved Rock) are living together at Starved Rock but reportedly were "not agreeing well together."
- Mesquakie chief Ouashala leads a large war party against the Peoria village at Starved Rock. The Peoria are besieged on Starved Rock. A negotiated settlement between the two sides is reached. The Peoria Indians abandon the Starved Rock area for the next eight years.

1725

- Construction of the second Fort de Chartres begins.

1730

- Some Peoria and Cahokia Indians are again living at Starved Rock.
- Mesquakie Indians abandon Wisconsin and begin the trek to the Seneca Indian homelands of western New York State. They follow the Fox River into Illinois, arriving somewhere near today's city of Ottawa.
- The Mesquakie are discovered by the Illinois and, after a brief skirmish, seventeen Illinois are taken prisoner. The Mesquakie burn their Illinois captives to death.

- The Illinois pursue the Mesquakie south into the Illinois prairies. Eventually, the Mesquakie are surrounded by the French, Illinois, and other Indian allies, presumably near Arrowsmith, Illinois. Another Fox Fort siege occurs. Many Mesquakie are killed.

1732

- Approximately 1,200 Peoria Indians live at Starved Rock.
- Peoria Indians from Starved Rock join an intertribal war party that attacks a fortified Mesquakie village at "Lake Marameg," likely today's Pistakee Lake in Lake County, Illinois.

1736

- Only about 250 Peoria Indians live at Starved Rock.

1741

- Last reference to the Peoria living near Starved Rock in semi-permanent summer villages.

1751

- Members of an Ojibwe war party kill a Frenchman at Starved Rock. The group continues to Lake Peoria where they are ambushed and driven away

1753

- Construction on the third Fort de Chartres begins. The fort is completed three years later.

1754

- The opening volleys of the French and Indian Wars are fired as George Washington's troops skirmish with French and Indians in Pennsylvania.

1755

- Most Peoria Indians abandon their semi-permanent summer villages at Lake Peoria and move to the lower Illinois Valley and the Mississippi Valley in southern Illinois.

1758

- Of the approximately fourteen Illinois subtribes that existed in 1673, only four remain: the Kaskaskia, Peoria, Cahokia, and Michigamea.

1760

- British traders hope to trade with the tribes at Starved Rock.
- Captain Sieur Passerat de la Chapelle establishes winter quarters on Buffalo Rock, a temporary post called Fort Ottawa.
- La Chapelle meets a group of Peoria Indians wintering near Starved Rock. This is the last known reference to the Illinois Indians in the Upper Illinois Valley.

1763

- Treaty of Paris signed. The British assume formal possession of Canada and lands east of the Mississippi River, except for New Orleans.
- The Jesuits are banished by royal decree and are expelled from the Illinois Country.
- The land between the Des Plaines River and Starved Rock is claimed by the Potawatomi Indians as hunting grounds.

1764

- Although British troops do not yet occupy the Illinois Country, Upper Louisiana is technically under British authority.

1765

- British occupy the Illinois Country when the 42nd Royal Highland Regiment takes possession of Fort de Chartres.

1766–1767

- British authorities consider building forts in Illinois to prevent French traders from trading with regional tribes.

1769

- Odawa war chief Pontiac is murdered by an Illinois Indian at Cahokia.
- Fearing reprisals for the murder, the Illinois establish camps next to British Fort de Chartres for protection. Illinois scouting parties scour the Illinois and Mississippi Rivers in search of enemy war parties. They encounter none.

1773

- Led by Patrick Kennedy, a British expedition in search of copper mines in the Illinois Valley stops at Starved Rock. Kennedy encounters Frenchmen living near the confluence of the Des Plaines and Kankakee Rivers.
- An English land company buys land in southern Illinois from the Illinois Indians.

1776

- The United States declares its independence from Great Britain.

1777

- Many Potawatomi, Odawa, and Ojibwe Indians (the Three Fires) are living in the Illinois Country in villages located along the streams and rivers of northeastern and northern Illinois.

1778

- The Kaskaskia, Peoria, and Michigamea, along with the Miami and Kickapoo, ally with George Rogers Clark during the American Revolution.
- Clark's force takes Kaskaskia from the British.

1783

- American Revolution ends.

1787

- Starved Rock becomes part of the Northwest Territory.

1788

- Arthur Saint Clair becomes first governor of the Northwest Territory.

1790

- Armstrong expedition passes Starved Rock while mapping the Illinois River.
- French voyageurs and an Englishman, Hugh Heward, pass Starved Rock while descending the Illinois River.

1795

- Treaty of Greenville is signed.

1800

- Indiana Territory is carved from the Northwest Territory.

1803

- The Kaskaskia sign the Treaty of Vincennes, ceding most of their land in Illinois for two reserves.
- The United States purchases over 800,000 square miles of land west of the Mississippi River from France, a deal known as the Louisiana Purchase.

1804

- A Sauk Indian delegation is tricked into signing the Treaty of 1804, a document that cedes Sauk Indian land in Illinois, Wisconsin, and Missouri. This treaty will become one of the causes of the Black Hawk War of 1832.

1809

- The Illinois Territory is established.

1811

- Indian Superintendent William Clark fears that the Indians, especially those who live along the Illinois River, will incite an uprising against the United States.

1812

- The War of 1812 begins.
- Fifty-three people are killed and many others are wounded while evacuating Fort Dearborn at Chicago.

1814

- Indians attack two US Army flotillas on the Mississippi River near Rock Island, Illinois.

1817

- Illinois Territorial Governor Ninian Edwards is ordered to begin proceedings to extinguish Indian lands east of the Illinois River.

1818

- Illinois becomes the twenty-first state.
- The Peoria sign the Treaty of Edwardsville, which gives them 640 acres in Missouri in exchange for much of their land in Illinois.
- Gurdon Hubbard joins American Fur Co. He visits Starved Rock.

1821

- Henry Schoolcraft is at Starved Rock with the Governor of Michigan Territory, Lewis Cass.

1823

- The first American settlers arrive in Starved Rock area.

1827

- Starved Rock area settlers build a temporary fort to protect themselves during the Winnebago War.

1831

- LaSalle County, Illinois is organized. Starved Rock is now in a county of the State of Illinois.

1832

- Illinois bands sign the Treaty of Castor Hill, relinquishing all of their lands in Illinois and Missouri.
- The four remaining Illinois subtribes merge and become the Peoria Indian tribe. They later settle on their "western reserve on the Osage River in what would become the state of Kansas."
- Black Hawk War is fought in Illinois and Wisconsin. Two forts are built near Starved Rock, Forts Wilbourn and Fort Johnson.

1833

- Treaty at Chicago is signed between the US government and the Potawatomi Indians. The Potawatomi sell their remaining land east of the Mississippi to the US government. The tribe must leave Illinois and resettle west of the Mississippi.

1834

- Charles Fenno Hoffman is in the Starved Rock area. Hoffman's account of his time in the area is written in a book entitled, *A Winter in the West*. Hoffman's book is one of the first written references to the name "Starved Rock."

1835

- Daniel Fletcher Hitt purchases sixty-eight acres of land, including Starved Rock, along the Illinois River for $85.

1836

- Construction of the Illinois and Michigan Canal begins. The canal connects the Illinois River at LaSalle, Illinois, with Chicago. Construction is completed in 1848.

1837

- The Panic of 1837 befalls the United States.

1840

- Potawatomi Indians heading west of the Mississippi are still seen passing through the Starved Rock area.

1854

- The Wea and Piankashaw, Miami subtribes, are incorporated into the Peoria Indian tribe.

1867

- US Army Corps of Engineers makes the first detailed map of the Illinois River.
- Historian Francis Parkman is at Starved Rock while researching his book, *The Discovery of the Great West*.

1868

- The Peoria Indians leave Kansas and move to northeastern Oklahoma where they remain the Peoria Indian tribe of Oklahoma.

1873

- Several thousand visitors attend the two hundred-year celebration of the Jolliet-Marquette expedition at Starved Rock.

- It is at this pageant that Perry Armstrong relays the legend of Starved Rock, a fanciful tale that he allegedly heard from Shick-Shack, a 104-year-old Indian chief in 1831.

1883

- US Army Corps of engineers map the Illinois River, a compilation later called the Woermann Maps.

1888

- The LaSalle County Board of Supervisors proposes that Starved Rock become a state park. The idea is "turned down."
- T. H. Lewis visits Starved Rock and conducts a cursory archaeological survey of the summit.

1890

- Chicago businessman Ferdinand Walther purchases Starved Rock from Daniel Hitt.
- Walther plans to turn the property into a private park.

1891

- The Starved Rock Hotel is built next to Starved Rock. The building hosted visitors and guests until the present-day Starved Rock lodge opens in 1939.
- Ferry service opens to transport park visitors across the Illinois River and to Walther's Starved Rock Park.

1894

- T. H. Lewis returns to Starved Rock and concludes that Fort St. Louis had been built on the summit of Starved Rock.

1905

- Public support for state purchase of Starved Rock begins in earnest.

1909

- Illinois General Assembly creates commission to look at the "feasibility of acquiring Starved Rock and other sites."

1910

- Walther offers to sell Starved Rock and adjacent property to the State of Illinois for $300,000, considered an outrageous sum at the time.

1911

- May 4: Illinois House of Representatives recommends $225,000.00 for the purchase of Starved Rock and adjacent lands.
- May 19: Illinois Senate votes to cut the suggested amount to $150,000.00.
- June 31: the Illinois Park Commission is established by Governor Deneen.
- September 20: Commission members begin negotiations with Walther for state purchase of Starved Rock.
- November 29: The Commission and Walther agree upon the sum of $146,000.00 for Starved Rock and adjacent land.
- December 15: LaSalle County Board proposes county purchase of Buffalo Rock as a county park.
- December 20: Walther's property officially transferred to State of Illinois.

1912

- Starved Rock State Park officially opens under state management in May.

NOTES

Introduction

1. A full account of his time at Starved Rock and his exploits in Illinois can be found in *Inquietus, La Salle in the Illinois Country*, by Mark Walczynski, published by the Center for French Colonial Studies, 2019.

2. Mark Walczynski, *Massacre 1769, The Search for the Origin of the Legend of Starved Rock* (Plano, TX: Center for French Colonial Studies, 2013).

1. 1673–1679: The Black Robe Arrives at Kaskaskia

1. Michael McCafferty, "Illinois Voices, Observations on the Miami-Illinois Language," in *Protohistory at the Grand Village of the Kaskaskia, The Illinois Country on the Eve of Colony*, ed. Robert F. Mazrim, *Studies in Archaeology* 10, Illinois State Archaeological Survey (Urbana: University of Illinois, 2015), 122.

2. According to Michael McCafferty, linguist at Indiana University in Bloomington, in the Illinois language, č represents the sound written "ch" in English and š represents the sound written "sh" in English. All other vowels and consonants have "continental values." Geminate, or double, vowels represent vowel sounds with additional length.

3. Father Pierre-François Pinet, a French Jesuit missionary in the Illinois Country who created the first French-Miami-Illinois dictionary, got the name for the Illinois River in the form "In8ca asipi8mi," meaning "Inoca-his-river." Moreover, the exact pronunciation of the term *Inoca* is unknown. However, the nature of this ethnonymic hydronym indicates

that Pinet got the name from a non-Inoca, presumably from the Wea at Chicago. In addition, according to McCafferty the term *Illiniwek* is foreign to the Illinois language. Michael McCafferty, email message to author, November 1, 2006. See also David J. Costa, "Illinois: A Place Name," *Society for the Study of the Indigenous Languages of the Americas* 25, no. 4 (January 2007): 9.

4. Pierre Deliette in "De Gannes Memoir," *The French Foundations, 1680–1693*, Collections of the Illinois State Historical Library 23, French series 1, ed. Theodore Calvin Pease and Raymond C. Werner (Springfield: Trustees of the Illinois State Historical Library, 1934), 340.

5. Claude-Jean Allouez in Jacques Marquette, *Jesuit Relations and Allied Documents, 1610–1791*, ed. Reuben Gold Thwaites (Cleveland: Burrows, 1901), 60: 161.

6. Marquette, *Jesuit Relations*, 59:161.

7. Marquette, *Jesuit Relations*, 59:163; 58:108. Jolliet lost Marquette's map and journal when his canoe wrecked near Montreal the following year. Fortunately, Marquette kept a copy of it at the Des Pères mission, which reached Dablon in 1675.

8. Thomas E. Emerson, ed., *The Archaeology of the Grand Village of the Illinois, Report of the Grand Village Research Project, 1991–1996: Grand Village of the Illinois State Historic Site (11-LS-13), LaSalle County, Illinois* (Urbana, Champaign: Board of Trustees of the University of Illinois, 1998), 22.

9. Michael McCafferty, email message to author, February 4, 2012.

10. Marquette, *Jesuit Relations*, 59:187.

11. Allouez had been baptizing dying children and adults, victims of an epidemic that struck the Green Bay area, when he was ordered to go to Kaskaskia.

12. Allouez, *Jesuit Relations*, 60:161.

13. Ibid., 159.

14. Ibid., 161.

15. Gilbert J. Garraghan, S.J., "La Salle's Jesuit Days," *Mid-America* 19 (1937): 101–3.

16. The Sulpician Order was founded in Paris in 1642 by Father Jean-Jacques Olier. The order first arrived in New France in 1659.

17. Historians disagree on the year of La Salle's arrival in Canada. Dates range from 1666 to 1668.

18. The French administration in Canada in 1750 claimed that La Salle had discovered the Ohio River (in 1669). See "Memoir on the French Colonies in North America," *Documents Relating to the Colonial History of New York*, ed. Edmund Bailey O'Callaghan, 15 vols. on CD (Saugerties, NY: Hope Farm Press, 2001 edition), 9:229 [hereafter cited as O'Callaghan, *Colonial History of New York*].

19. O'Callaghan, *Colonial History of New York*, "Journal of Count de Frontenac's Voyage to Lake Ontario in 1673," 9:95–114.

20. René-Robert Cavelier de La Salle, *Relation of the Discoveries and Voyages of Cavelier de La Salle from 1679 to 1681, The Official Narrative*, trans. Melville B. Anderson (Chicago: Caxton Club, 1901), 15.

21. "Letters Patent, Granted by the King of France to the Sieur de La Salle, on the 12th May 1678," in *Historical Collections of Louisiana*, part 1, ed. Benjamin Franklin French (New York: Wiley and Putnam, 1846), 35–36.

22. Henry Tonti (1650–1704) was an Italian by birth. Tonti joined the French army and lost his right hand. The missing hand was replaced with an artificial one. His name was Henri Tonti, not "de" Tonti, as he was not a nobleman. As an Italian, Tonti's name was likely Gallicized to "Tonty" when he became a subject of France. See Jean Delanglez, "The Voyages of Tonti in North America, 1678–1704," in *Mid-America* 26 (October 1944): 257; and Louise

Phelps Kellogg, ed., *Early Narratives of the Northwest, 1634–1699* (New York: Scribner's Sons, 1917; Heritage Books, 2001), 286.

23. In a 1680 letter to Governor Frontenac, La Salle lambasted deceptive information that Jolliet provided to Dablon about the lands and waterways of the Great Lakes and Illinois Country. For example, La Salle wrote that, contrary to Jolliet's claims, the route through the Great Lakes was full of navigational hazards, Jolliet's proposed canal between the Chicago and Des Plaines Rivers would quickly fill-in, that the Illinois River was not navigable for barks between the Des Plaines River and Kaskaskia, that Illinois Country lands were either too dry to cultivate or were swampy and needed to be drained, and that bison were becoming scarce. He also criticized information depicted on Franquelin's 1675 *La Frontenacie* map including notations that show Europeans living at the mouth of the Mississippi and that the Mosopela Indians noted on the map, no longer existed. See "La Salle on the Illinois Country," in Pease and Werner, *French Foundations*, 1–10.

24. Anderson, *Relation of La Salle*, 41.

25. The Griffon reportedly picked up 12,000 *livres* worth of hides. Anderson, *Relation of La Salle*, 43.

2. 1680–1682: Everything Is Difficult

1. Marquette, *Jesuit Relations*, 59:159. Marquette wrote that Kaskaskia was located at a portage on the Illinois River.

2. It is highly unlikely that La Salle knew how to speak the Miami-Illinois language the way he is portrayed in the historical record. It appears that La Salle's first encounter with Miami-Illinois speakers occurred during his first expedition to the Illinois Country in 1680. He likely relied on one of the Indians in his group to translate for him, possibly an Indian named Ouiouilamet who had been in La Salle's employ for two years, might have been able to speak Miami-Illinois, and also knew some French. La Salle's *Relation* reveals that there was at least one Indian in his entourage while the explorer and his group were in the Illinois Country at this time. For a detailed discussion on La Salle and the Miami-Illinois language see *Inquietus, La Salle in the Illinois Country*, by Mark Walczynski, published by the Center for French Colonial Studies, 2019.

3. For example, "La Salle to a Friend," in Pierre Margry, *Découvertes et établissements des Français dans l'ouest et dans le sud de l'Amérique septentrionale, 1614–1754*, 6 vols. (Paris: Maisonneuve, 1875), 2:295–99; and Anderson, *Relation of La Salle*, 289.

4. Anderson, *Relation of La Salle*, 269; and Pease and Werner, *French Foundations*, 11.

5. The first Jesuits to arrive in New France were Énemond Massé and Pierre Biard, who arrived at Port-Royal in 1611. Their service ended in 1613 when they were captured by the British under Samuel Argall. Both missionaries eventually arrived back in France. In 1625 Massé, in the company of Jesuits Charles Lalemant, Jean de Brébeuf, and two lay brothers returned to the colony to continue their missionary work. See Canadian Encyclopedia, accessed on June 30, 2018, https://www.thecanadianencyclopedia.ca/en/article/jesuits/.

6. Marquette, *Jesuit Relations*, 54:183.

7. Kellogg, *Early Narratives*, 142.

8. For more about Allouez's admission and Jesuit collusion to destroy La Salle, see 5.

9. R. David Edmunds and Joseph L. Peyser, *The Fox Wars, The Mesquakie Challenge to New France* (Norman and London: University of Oklahoma Press, 1993), 23–24.

10. An Indian La Salle had encountered in the forest near the fort drew the explorer a map with charcoal that showed free and unobstructed access by water to the Gulf. See Anderson, *Relation of La Salle*, 139. Hennepin also makes reference to this chance meeting with

the Illinois and to the charcoal map in Louis Hennepin, *A New Discovery of a Vast Country in America*, ed. Reuben Gold Thwaites, 2 vols. (Toronto: Coles Publishing, 1903), 1:175.

11. The Accault/Hennepin party were captured by Sioux Indians on the Mississippi and taken to a Sioux village likely located in Minnesota, but were released later that September.

12. The fifteen men included François Boisrondel, three shipwrights, one blacksmith, two joiners, two sawyers, four soldiers, and also two Franciscan missionaries, Gabriel de Ribourde and Zénobe Membré. La Salle and his group left Fort de Crèvecoeur on March 1, 1680. Anderson, *Relation of La Salle*, 147, 183.

13. This formula is based on the following ratio: four non-warriors to every one warrior. See Joseph Zitomersky, *French Americans: Native Americans in Eighteenth Century French Colonial Louisiana* (Lund, Sweden: Lund University Press, 1995), 219.

14. "Memoir of the Sieur de La Tonty," *Historical Collections of Louisiana*, 1:55; and Anderson, *Relation of Tonty*, 33.

15. Anderson, *Relation of La Salle*, 169–79.

16. Ibid., 201.

17. Anderson, *Relation of Tonty*, 35, 37.

18. The number 2,000 is based on Tonti's Memoir that states that four hundred Illinois warriors left the village to confront the Iroquois. French missionaries used the following formula to estimate the number of Illinois Indians who lived in a village: for every one warrior there were four noncombatants, or a four-to-one ratio. Each family consisted of about five people. There were two families per fire, and two fires for cabin. Therefore each cabin consisted of twenty people. Joseph Zitomersky, *French Americans: Native Americans in Eighteenth Century French Colonial Louisiana* (Lund University Press, 1995), 179.

19. Anderson, *Relation of Tonty*, 41. Tonti told the Iroquois that his force consisted of eleven hundred Illinois and fifty French, whereas Tonti's memoir in Kellogg, *Early Narratives*, states that he led "1,200" Illinois and "sixty" French.

20. Tracy Neal Leavelle, *The Catholic Calumet* (Philadelphia: University of Pennsylvania Press, 2012), 27–29.

21. As early as 1665, some Iroquois sought reconciliation with the French. It appears that news of a possible cessation of hostilities spread to the Great Lakes. Some western tribes, believing it was safe to do so, traveled to Montreal to trade with the French. When they left Montreal to return to their homelands, Frenchmen, such as Allouez and Nicolas Perrot, accompanied the Indians.

22. William J. Eccles, *The Canadian Frontier 1534–1760* (Albuquerque: University of New Mexico Press, 1969), revised edition, 113; and Eccles, *The French in North America:1500–1783*, rev. ed. (East Lansing: Michigan State University Press, 1998), 49, 50.

23. Anderson, *Relation of La Salle*, 227, 229.

24. Where Jolliet and Marquette visited the Peoria in 1673.

25. Period maps indicate that the Tamaroa likely lived in villages along the Mississippi in southern Illinois during this time. They may have had no idea that the Illinois who lived in the Upper Illinois Valley had been attacked and pursued by the Iroquois.

26. Anderson, *Relation of La Salle*, 239.

27. Ibid., 243. Isle à la Cache was known by that name as early as 1698, referenced by the French missionary Jean-François Buisson de St. Cosme. See Kellogg, *Early Narratives*, 349.

28. While La Salle was sidelined with snow blindness, two of his men left the explorer and encountered a winter camp of Mesquakie (Fox) Indians. The Mesquakie told the men that Tonti was alive and living with the Potawatomi in Wisconsin.

29. "Remonstrance of Sieur de la Salle against M. de la Barre's Seizure of Fort Frontenac," in O'Callaghan, *Colonial History of New York*, 9:215.

30. William J. Eccles, "Buade de Frontenac et de Palluau, Louis de," in *Dictionary of Canadian Biography*, 1:133–42.

31. Ibid.

32. "Letter from M. de La Barre to Colbert," Ministries des Colonies, Amerique de Nord, *Enterprises de Cav. De La Salle*, c. 13, vol. 3, fol. 37, reel 1, sec. 2, pp. 303–5, found in *Miami Tribal History Document Series, Great Lakes—Ohio Valley Ethnohistory Collection*, Erminie Wheeler-Voegelin Archives, Indiana University, Bloomington.

33. M. Du Chesneau, "Memoir on the Western Indians, &c," in O'Callaghan, *Colonial History of New York*, 9:163.

34. Kellogg, *Early Narratives*, 304–5.

3. 1683: The French Build a Fort

1. La Salle in Margry, *Découvertes*, 2:175–76. Translation from *Miami Tribal History Document Series, Great Lakes—Ohio Valley Ethnohistory Collection, Erminie Wheeler-Voegelin Archives*, Indiana University, Bloomington.

2. Ibid. The perimeter of the Lover's Leap bluff measures about 1,575 feet, whereas nearby Eagle Cliff measures about 350 feet.

3. La Salle in Margry, *Découvertes*, 2:175–76. Translation from *Miami Tribal History Document Series, Great Lakes—Ohio Valley Ethnohistory Collection*, Erminie Wheeler-Voegelin Archives, Indiana University, Bloomington.

4. Work and progress report of archaeologist Richard Hagen to Joseph F. Booton, Chief of Design, Illinois Department of Public Works and Buildings, dated July 23, 1950.

5. It was reported by Frenchman Henri Joutel, who spent the 1687–1688 winter at Fort St. Louis, that the chief "received M. de la Salle and made a kind donation of the entire country that they [the Illinois Indians] occupied, recognizing him as their father." Joutel in *Margry, Découvertes*, 1:493.

6. Henri Joutel, "Joutel's Historic Journal of Monsieur de La Salle's Last Voyage to Discover the River Mississippi," in *The Journeys of Rene Robert Cavelier Sieur de La Salle*, 2 vols., ed. Isaac Joslin Cox (New York: Allerton Book Co., 1906), 2:213, 217; and "Grant of La Salle to D'Autray, 1683," in *Cavelier de La Salle to Jacques Bourdon d'Autray*, deed in French America Collection, Chicago History Museum Research Center.

7. Anderson, *Relation of La Salle*, 287.

8. Besides the Tohatchaking "Miamy," Oiatenon, Kilatica, and Pepikokia, La Salle also wrote that other Miami subtribes, including the Piankeshaw, Megancockia, and Melomelinoia had also relocated to northern Illinois during this time. The Parkman map accounts for all of these tribes with the exception of the Megancockia and Melomelinoia. Where these two Miami subtribes established camps is unknown, although the 1688 Franquelin map shows the Megancockia living in what is today, Bureau County.

9. Benjamin Franklin French, ed., *Historical Collections of Louisiana*, part 1 (New York: Wiley and Putnam, 1846), 66. Tonti wrote that the "Illinois established themselves, to the number of 300 cabins [6,000 people] near the Fort Illinois, as well as Miamis and Chawanons [Shawnee]."

10. For La Salle's claim that these tribes returned to Kaskaskia, see Margry, Découvertes, 2:201.

11. For an in-depth discussion on the problems associated with determining the Indian population of northern Illinois during this time see *Inquietus, La Salle in the Illinois Country*, by Mark Walczynski, published by the Center for French Colonial Studies, 2019.

12. Pease and Werner, *French Foundations*, 19. Jacques Burdon, Sieur d'Autray, was a Canadian nobleman and son of the first *Procureur Général* of Quebec. He joined La Salle in

1675 and accompanied the explorer between 1679 and 1683. In 1687 d'Autray and Tonti joined Denonville's Iroquois campaign. D'Autray was killed by Iroquois Indians in 1688 while en route to Montreal from Fort Frontenac.

13. *Cavelier de La Salle to Jacques Bourdon d'Autray*, deed in the French America Collection, Chicago History Museum Research Center; and Pease and Werner, *French Foundations*, 20.

14. "La Salle to the People of Fort St. Louis, September 1, 1683," Pease and Werner, *French Foundations*, 41.

15. "Remonstrance of Sieur de la Salle against M. de la Barre's Seizure of Fort Frontenac," in O'Callaghan, *Colonial History of New York*, 9:215.

16. Ibid.

17. See "Letter of Father Enjalran to Le Febvre de la Barre," 1683, in Thwaites, *The French Regime in Wisconsin I: 1634–1727*, Collections of the State Historical Society of Wisconsin, vol. 16 (Madison: State Historical Society of Wisconsin, 1902), 110–11 [hereafter cited as *WHC French Regime I*]; and "Remonstrance of Sieur de la Salle against M. de la Barre's Seizure of Fort Frontenac," in O'Callaghan, Colonial History of New York, 9:213–16.

4. 1684: The Iroquois Lay Siege to the Fort

1. Tonti, *Relation of Tonty*, 115. We know that there were seventeen men, as La Salle wrote that there were twenty men at the fort. La Salle left for Canada with three of them.

2. Jean Hamelin, "Louis-Henri de Baugy," *Dictionary of Canadian Biography*, 2:48–49.

3. For scholarly information on the name "Teakiky," see Michael McCafferty's 'Kankakee': An Old Etymological Puzzle," in *Names, Journal of Onomastics* 62, no. 2 (June 2014): 107–14.

4. "Instructions from Monsieur de La Barre to Monsieur de Salvaye," in O'Callaghan, *Colonial History of New York*, 3:450–51; and "Account of a Journey in the Country of the Islinois by M. M. Beauvais, Provost, des Rosiers 1683–1684," in Margry, Découvertes, 2:338–44. Margry translation found in *Miami Tribal History Document Series, Great Lakes—Ohio Valley Ethnohistory Collection*, Erminie Wheeler-Voegelin Archives, Indiana University, Bloomington.

5. The Mesquakie (Fox) were allies of the Mascouten during this time. "Baugy to La Durantaye," dated March 24, 1684. National Archives of Canada, Source RC 6515, call number MG1-Series C11A. Translation from a copy of the original by Michael McCafferty of Indiana University.

6. Baugy to La Durantaye, March 24, 1684.

7. About beards, Allouez wrote, "It is said of them [the Mesquakie Indians] and of the Ousaki [Sauk] that, when they find a man alone and at a disadvantage, they kill him, especially if he is a Frenchman; for they cannot endure the beards of the latter people." Kellogg, *Early Narratives*, 129.

8. Tonti, *Relation of Tonty*,115.

9. Nouvel collation in Baugy to La Durantaye, March 24, 1684.

10. For example, Charles J. Balesi, *The Time of the French in the Heart of North America, 1673–1818* (Chicago: Paginae Publications, 2014), 71.

11. According to Tonti, La Durantaye was in command at the Chicago post in early 1686. Kellogg, *Early Narratives*, 308.

12. "Louis XIV to La Barre," in Pease and Werner, *French Foundations*, 47–48.

13. "Presents of the Onondagas to Onontio at La Famine," in O'Callaghan, *Colonial History of New York*, 9:236–38.

14. Ibid., "Louis XIV to Intendant M. de Meulles," 269.

15. It appears that Tonti never met with La Barre at this time.

16. Kellogg, *Early Narratives*, 306.

17. "Engagement of Pacquereau to Tonti," in Pease and Werner, *French Foundations*, 53–54.

18. "Engagement to Beauvais to Tonti," ibid., 56–58.

5. 1685–1691: Trade and the Beaver

1. "Tonty to M. Cabart de Villermont," in Margry, *Découvertes*, 3:544–47.

2. Kellogg, *Early Narratives*, 306.

3. Ibid.

4. Ibid. Tonti says that he left the Rock with thirty Frenchmen, whereas Delanglez, using other period French sources, concludes that Tonti left with twenty-five French. Jean Delanglez, "Voyages of Tonti in North America 1678–1704," *Mid-America, An Historical Review* 26, no. 4 (October 1944): 274.

5. Ibid., 308.

6. Ibid., 308. Tonti arrived at Montreal in late July.

7. "Abstract of M. de Denonville's Letters and of the Minister's Answers Thereto," in O'Callaghan, *Colonial History of New York*, 9:316. In June 1687 Denonville wrote to the Minister, "You may rely on it, My Lord, that I shall study M. de la Salle's interest in whatever depends on me. Chevalier de Tonty intended to have gone to France last year, but I dissuaded him from so doing in order to prevail on him to proceed again in search of news of said Sieur de la Salle." O'Callaghan, *Colonial History of New York*, 9:329.

8. Kellogg, *Early Narratives*, 308.

9. William J. Eccles, "Brisay de Denonville, Jacques-Rene de, Marquis de Denonville," *Dictionary of Canadian Biography*, 2:98–105.

10. Although the Texas survivors didn't know it at the time, the people who remained at Fort St. Louis in Texas were killed by Karankawa Indians in December 1688. Several of them were taken captive and survived the ordeal.

11. The Texan's journey began on January 12 and ended on September 14, 1687.

12. "Journal of Henri Joutel," in Margry, *Découvertes*, 3:478. Translation of Joutel's journal found in Margry, *Découvertes*, vol. 3, by Michael McCafferty of Indiana University.

13. Ibid., 479.

14. Ibid.

15. Allouez arrived at the fort as a member of La Durantaye's relief party, in May 1684.

16. "Journal of Henri Joutel," in Margry, *Découvertes*, 3:480.

17. Ibid.

18. Ibid., 3:483.

19. Ibid.

20. Ibid., 3:484.

21. Ibid., 3:485.

22. Ibid., 3:484.

23. Ibid., 3:487.

24. Ibid., 3:489.

25. Ibid., 3:490.

26. Ibid.

27. Ibid., 3:491–92.

28. Ibid., 3:493.

29. Ibid., 3:494.

30. Footnote 1, in Pease and Werner, *French Foundations*, 19.

31. "Journal of Henri Joutel," in Margry, *Découvertes*, 3:497.

32. Ibid., 3:498.

33. Ibid., 3:500.

34. Ibid.

35. Ibid., 3:505.

36. Ibid.

37. Jean Delanglez, ed., "Jean Cavelier, The Journal of Jean Cavelier" (Chicago: Institute of Jesuit History, 1938), 127.

38. "Journal of Henri Joutel," in Margry, *Découvertes*, 3:502.

39. Margry, *Découvertes*, 2:175. La Salle reported "the rapid at the end of these nine leagues [from the Forks to what is now Marseilles] makes it [navigation] very difficult."

40. "Journal of Henri Joutel," in Margry, *Découvertes*, 3:508.

41. A Parisian boy named Bartholomew. Joutel, "Journal of Monsieur de La Salle's Last Voyage," in Cox, *Journeys of Rene Robert Cavelier*, 2:199.

42. Kellogg, *Early Narratives*, 311–12.

43. It is unknown for certain when Tonti left Starved Rock for the Gulf. Balesi, *Time of the French*, p. 94, says that it was in 1688, while Jean Delanglez wrote that Tonti left the fort in 1689. Delanglez, "Voyages of Tonti," 280–81.

44. "Engagement of De Broyeux to La Forest," in Pease and Werner, *French Foundations*, 123–25.

45. "Engagement of Du May to La Forest," in Pease and Werner, *French Foundations*, 126–28.

46. "Engagements of Dumais Brothers, Filastreau, Maillou, Cardinal, and Farfart to La Forest," in Pease and Werner, *French Foundations*, 181–86, 199.

47. "Engagement of Dumais Brothers to Boisrondel," in Pease and Werner, *French Foundations, French Foundations*, 200–201.

48. "Engagement of Morin to La Forest," in Pease and Werner, *French Foundations*, 150–52.

49. "Engagement of Tardiff to La Forest," in Pease and Werner, *French Foundations*, 159–61.

50. "Engagements to La Forest," in Pease and Werner, *French Foundations*, 147–49, 157–59.

51. "Engagements with La Forest," in Pease and Werner, *French Foundations*, 249–50.

52. "M. de Denonville to M. de Seignelay, and the latter's Answer," in O'Callaghan, *Colonial History of New York*, 9:276.

53. "The King to Denonville to Champigny," in Pease and Werner, *French Foundations*, 90.

54. "Instructions from Monsieur de La Barre to Monsieur de Salvaye," in O'Callaghan, *Colonial History of New York*, 3:450–51; and "Account of a Journey in the Country of the Islinois by M. M. Beauvais, Provost, des Rosiers 1683–1684," in Margry, *Découvertes*, 2:338–44. Margry translation found in *Miami Tribal History Document Series, Great Lakes—Ohio Valley Ethnohistory Collection*, Erminie Wheeler-Voegelin Archives, Indiana University, Bloomington.

55. Engagements in Pease and Werner, *French Foundations*, 126–27, 129, 151, 154, 199, 202–3.

56. Anderson, *Relation of La Salle*, 73.

57. "LaSalle on the Illinois Country," in Pease and Werner, *French Foundations*, 3.

58. Anderson, *Relation of La Salle*, 221, 229, 243.

59. Balesi, *Time of the French*, 71.

60. For example, engagements to Dumay, Barette, Rouillard and Froment, Morin, Beaujean. Pease and Werner, *French Foundations*, 126–27, 148, 151, 154.

61. Engagements to Filastreau, Maillou, Cardinal, Farfart, Morin, Dumais, de Villeneuve, Carignan, in Pease and Werner, *French Foundations*, 181–85, 195, 202, 207, 210.

62. Although some pre-contact Native American technology may have been in use well into the eighteenth century by some tribes living east of the Mississippi River, as a general rule Native Americans preferred many items of European manufacture to their own. For example, one reason for the formidability of the Iroquois during the 1680s was their use of European-made muskets that they acquired from Dutch traders. See Leavelle, *Catholic Calumet*, 27–29. Likewise, according to archaeologist John Walthall, the Illinois "abandoned the production of their own pottery between 1680 and 1719," preferring instead items made of "metal and, later, ceramic vessels, obtained through French trade." See John Walthall, "Aboriginal Pottery and the Eighteenth-century Illini," in John A. Walthall and Thomas E. Emerson, eds., *Calumet and Fleur-De-Lys* (Washington and London: Smithsonian Institution Press, 1992), 168.

63. "M. de Denonville to M. de Seignelay," in O'Callaghan, *Colonial History of New York*, 9:344–45.

64. "Abstract of Letters from Canada and the Minister's Remarks thereupon," in O'Callaghan, *Colonial History of New York*, 9:398.

65. Lindsay, Lionel, "Jacques Gravier," The Catholic Encyclopedia, vol. 6 (New York: Robert Appleton Company, 1909), accessed January 17, 2019, http://www.newadvent.org/cathen/06732b.htm.

66. Michael McCafferty, "Jacques Largillier, French Trader, Jesuit Brother, and Jesuit Scribe Par Excellence," *Journal of the Illinois State Historical Society* 104, no. 3 (Fall 2011): 188–97.

67. McCafferty, "Jacques Largillier, French Trader, Jesuit Brother, and Jesuit Scribe Par Excellence," 191.

68. La Forest gave Boisrondel power of attorney. See "Authorization to Boisrondel," in Pease and Werner, *French Foundations*, 192.

69. One contract that acknowledged this obligation was signed on May 16, 1690, between Boisrondel and Jean Nafrechoux, wherein payment for the debt was to be made in "good beaver at the price and as the bureau of Quebec will receive it for letters of exchange in France." See "Obligation of Boisrondel to Nafrechoux," in Pease and Werner, *French Foundations*, 225–27.

70. "The King to Frontenac and Champigny," in Pease and Werner, *French Foundations*, 263.

71. William J. Eccles, "Buade de Frontenac et de Palluau, Louis de," *Dictionary of Canadian Biography*, 1:133–42.

72. "Observations on the State of Affairs in Canada, November 18, 1689," in O'Callaghan, *Colonial History of New York*, 9:434.

73. "M. de Champigny to the Minister," in O'Callaghan, *Colonial History of New York*, 9:501.

74. "Louis XIV to Count de Frontenac and M. de Champigny," in O'Callaghan, *Colonial History of New York*, 9:494.

75. Delliette, "De Gannes Memoir," *French Foundations*, 324.

76. John T. Penman in *The Archaeology of the Grand Village of the Illinois, Report of the Grand Village Research Project, 1991–1996: Grand Village of the Illinois State Historic Site (11-LS-13), LaSalle County, Illinois*, ed. Thomas E. Emerson (Urbana, Champaign: Board of Trustees of the University of Illinois, 1998), 207.

77. Pierre Delliette in "De Gannes Memoir," in Pease and Werner, *French Foundations*, 327.
78. Ibid.
79. Marest, *Jesuit Relations*, 65:81.

6. 1692–1712: The Rock Is Abandoned

1. Jean Mermet, *Jesuit Relations*, 66:49.
2. Michael McCafferty, "Peoria," *Le journal*, Center for French Colonial Studies (Fall 2011): 11.
3. Richard Hagen excavated portions of the Starved Rock summit during the summers of 1949 and 1950. Richard Hagan to Joseph F. Booton, Chief of Design, Division of Architecture and Engineering, Illinois Department of Public Works and Buildings, dated June 1, 1950, from a series of correspondences from excavations at Starved Rock during the summer of 1950, Starved Rock State Park Archives.
4. Hagan to Booton, September 11, 1949, Starved Rock State Park Archives.
5. Kellogg, *Early Narratives*, 343.
6. Henri Tonti, "Extract From A Letter of M. Tonti to His Brother Dated From the Quinipissa Village in Mississippi, 60 Leagues From The Sea, February 28, 1700," in A Jean Delanglez, S.J., Anthology, ed. Mildred Mott Wedel (New York and London: Garland Publishing, 1985), 218.
7. Kellogg, *Early Narratives*, 350.
8. Allouez wrote, "Canoes they [the Mesquakie] do not use, but commonly make their journeys by land, bearing their packages and their game on their shoulders." Kellogg, *Early Narratives*, 129.
9. See map of Meskwaki and Sauk Migration: Cartography by R. Vanderwerff and J. Artz, Earthview Environmental Inc., Coralville, Iowa, based on historical research by Jonathan L. Buffalo, Meskwaki Tribal Historian, June 2013.
10. According to Edmunds and Peyser, the Jesuits used Catholic symbols and practices that the tribesmen might associate with their own spiritual conceptions to make headway into the Mesquakie psyche. Christian symbols, such as crosses, were at first, taken for charms for good luck in battle after a Mesquakie war party who wore articles of clothing and bore weapons adorned with crosses, successfully attacked and defeated a Sioux war party. However, a later war party that employed crosses was unsuccessful and the crosses were no longer valued as good luck medicine. In addition, several people who the priest baptized died. Allouez, a hardline Jesuit, also alienated himself from the tribe by railing against what the missionary viewed as superstition. See Edmunds and Peyser, *The Fox Wars*, 14–16. See also Leavelle, *The Catholic Calumet*, 31.
11. Edmunds and Peyser, *The Fox Wars*, 51.
12. Edmunds and Peyser, *The Fox Wars*, 51.
13. Kellogg, *Early Narratives*, 344.
14. Raymond Phineas Stearns, "Joseph Kellogg, Observations on Senex's Map of North America (1710)," *Mississippi Valley Historical Review* 23, no. 3 (December 1936): 353. Accessed June 10, 2018, http://www.jstor.org/stable/1886369.
15. Kellogg, *Early Narratives*, 350.
16. Binneteau, *Jesuit Relations*, 65:67–69.
17. Maud M. Hutchieson, "Pierre-Gabriel Marest," *Dictionary of Canadian Biography*, 2:454–55.
18. Marest, *Jesuit Relations*, 66:287.
19. "Official Report, made by the commanding officer, Mr. Dubuisson to the Governor of Canada of the war which took place at Detroit in 1712," in Thwaites, *WHC French Regime I*, 16:285.

20. Raymond E. Hauser, *Ethnohistory of the Illinois Indian Tribe 1673–1832* (PhD diss., Northern Illinois University, 1973), 284–85.

21. Marest, *Jesuit Relations*, 66:287.

22. Zitomersky, *French Americans–Native Americans*, 257.

23. Marest, *Jesuit Relations*, 66:289.

24. Pierre Delliette, for example.

7. 1712–1730: Starved Rock and the Fox Wars

1. Edmunds and Peyser, *The Fox Wars*, 60–62.

2. Joseph Jablow, *Indians of Illinois and Indiana* (New York and London: Garland Publishing, 1974), 144–45.

3. "Official Report, made by the commanding officer, Mr. Dubuisson to the Governor of Canada of the war which took place at Detroit in 1712," in Thwaites, *WHC French Regime I*, 16:277.

4. Ibid., 16:277–78.

5. Ibid., 16: 277–78.

6. Ibid., 16:284.

7. Ibid.

8. "Vaudreuil and Begon to the Minister," dated November 15, 1713, in Thwaites, *WHC French Regime I*, 16:298.

9. Edmunds and Peyser, *The Fox Wars*, 78.

10. Ramezay replaced Louvigny with Constant Marchand de Lignery.

11. "Letter from Ramazay to the French minister," dated November 3, 1715, in Thwaites, *WHC French Regime I*, 16:322–26.

12. It appears that the Illinois group included warriors from other Illinois villages as there were only an estimated four hundred Peoria warriors living at Starved Rock during this time. See Jablow, *Indians of Illinois and Indiana*, 150.

13. "Governor de Vaudreuil to Council of Marine," dated October 14, 1716, in Thwaites, *WHC French Regime I*, 16:341.

14. Ibid. See also Edmunds and Peyser, *The Fox Wars*, 81.

15. Sometime after the battle, the Indians who had attacked the Kickapoo and Mascouten were themselves attacked by a large Mesquakie contingent. Thwaites, *WHC French Regime I*, 16:341.

16. Louise Phelps Kellogg, *Fox Indians During the WHC French Regime* (Madison: State Historical Society of Wisconsin, 1907), 164.

17. Edmunds and Peyser, *The Fox Wars*, 83.

18. "Governor de Vaudreuil to Council of Marine," dated October 14, 1716, in Thwaites, *WHC French Regime I*, 16:342.

19. Carl J. Ekberg, *Stealing Indian Women, Native Slavery in the Illinois Country* (Urbana and Chicago: University of Illinois Press, 2007), 11; and Hauser, *Ethnohistory*, 328.

20. Ekberg, *Stealing Indian Women*, 10.

21. Ibid. See Brett Rushforth quotation.

22. "Governor de Vaudreuil to Council of Marine," dated October 14, 1716, in Thwaites, *WHC French Regime I*, 16:343.

23. "Conference of Western Indians with Governor Vaudreuil, at Montreal, part of a letter from Vaudreuil to Council," dated October 30, 1718, in Thwaites, *WHC French Regime I*, 16:377.

24. Edmunds and Peyser, *The Fox Wars*, 93.

25. Ibid.

26. Anonymous, "Memoir on the Savages of Canada as far as the Mississippi River, Describing Their Customs and Trade," in Thwaites, *WHC French Regime I*, 16:373.

27. Zitomersky, *French Americans–Native Americans*, 225.

28. Michael McCafferty, "The Illinois Place Name 'Pimiteoui,' " in *The Journal of the Illinois State Historical Society* (Summer 2009), 182.

29. "Letters to Du Tisné from missionaries at Kaskaskia," dated January 10, 1725, *in Thwaites WHC French Regime I*, 16:459.

30. Edmunds and Peyser, *The Fox Wars*, 96; see also "Opinions of the Illinois Missionaries Regarding Fox War," in Thwaites, *WHC French Regime I*, 16:454.

31. Edmunds and Peyser, *The Fox Wars*, 96.

32. According to Charlevoix, the Iroquois River takes its name from an ambush, wherein the Illinois attacked and "killed a great many Iroquois." Pierre-Francis Xavier de Charlevoix, *Journal of a Voyage to North America*, 2 vols, ed. Louise Phelps Kellogg (Ann Arbor: University Microfilms, 1966), 2:202–03.

33. Charlevoix, *Journal*, 2:199.

34. *Ottawa Daily Times*, December 7, 2003.

35. Charlevoix, *Journal*, 2:200.

36. Ibid., 200–201.

37. Ibid.

38. Ibid., 202–03.

39. Adam Stueck, *A Place Under Heaven: Amerindian Torture and Cultural Violence in Colonial New France, 1609–1729* (PhD diss., Marquette University, 2012), 57–58, accessed July 26, 2018, http://epublications.marquette.edu/dissertations_mu/174.

40. Stueck, *A Place Under Heaven*, 61.

41. Ibid., 65.

42. Kellogg, *Early Narratives*, 130. According to the Catholic Encyclopedia, Allouez met the Peoria Indians in 1667 at La Pointe. See James Mooney, "Peoria Indians," *The Catholic Encyclopedia* (New York: Robert Appleton Co.), accessed March 22, 2013, http://www.newadvent.org/cathen/11662a.htm.

43. Legardeur Delisle, "The Journal of Legardeur Delisle, 1722," *Journal of the Illinois State Historical Society*, ed. Stanley Faye (March 1945), 55–56.

44. Ibid., 56.

45. "Speeches of the Foxes at a Council Held at the House of Monsieur De Montigny, in the presence of the missionary, September 6, 1722," in Thwaites, *WHC French Regime I*, 16:418.

46. According to Louise Phelps Kellogg, the Mesquakie war party included "Mascouten, Kickapoo, Winnebago, Sauk, Sioux, and Abenaki Indians." See "Fox Indians during the French Regime," 169. Inspector General of Louisiana, Diron d'Artaguette, wrote that the Foxes "had come 'en village,' that is to say, with their women and children," Diron d'Artaguette, "The Journal of Diron D'Artaguette," entry for October 23, 1722, *Travels in the American Colonies*, ed. Newton D. Mereness (New York: Macmillan, 1916), 32. See also "Letter from Governor Vaudreuil to the Minister," dated October 11, 1723, in Thwaites, *WHC French Regime I*, 16:434.

47. The adult captives were reportedly tortured to death later. Thwaites, *WHC French Regime I*, 16:460.

48. Ibid., 16:429.

49. "Speeches of the Foxes," in Thwaites, *WHC French Regime I*, 16:418–19.

50. Ibid., 16:419. Ouashala reportedly told his warriors that he "represented to them at once that their father Onontio [Vaudreuil, Governor of Canada] was a good model, and that

they ought to imitate him in following the example he had set for us, when, in a similar case, our lives were spared by Monsieur de Louvigny."

51. "Speeches of the Foxes," in Thwaites, *WHC French Regime I*, 16:429. Vaudreuil probably received his information from Montigny, who heard it from Ouashala.

52. Ibid., 16:418.

53. Mereness, "The Journal of Diron D'Artaguette," in *Travels in the American Colonies*, 32.

54. "Speeches of the Foxes," in Thwaites, *WHC French Regime I*, 16:419–20.

55. According to Tecumseh's biographer John Sugden, "The United States army lost only 948 men killed by Indians in all the country's wars between 1866 and 1890." John Sugden, *Tecumseh, A Life* (New York: Henry Holt, 1997), 398.

56. "Speeches of the Foxes," in Thwaites, *WHC French Regime I*, 16:421.

57. Ibid., 16:421–22.

58. "Speeches of the Foxes," in Thwaites, *WHC French Regime I*, 16:502–3.

59. D'Artaguette prepared the fort for battle and readied the men in case the reports were true. D'Artaguette, *Journal*, 70, accessed February 26, 2013, http://www.archive.org/stream/travelsinamerica00mereuoft/travelsinamerica00mereuoft_djvu.txt. See also Wayne Temple, *Indian Villages of the Illinois Country*, Illinois State Museum Scientific Papers, vol. 2, part 2 (Springfield: Illinois State Museum, 1966), 40–41.

60. D'Artaguette, *Journal*, entry May 10, 1723, accessed February 26, 2013, http://www.archive.org/stream/travelsinamerica00mereuoft/travelsinamerica00mereuoft_djvu.txt.

61. "Vaudreuil to Boisbriant," dated August 17, 1724, in Thwaites, *WHC, French Regime I*, 16:442.

62. Ibid., 16:451.

63. "Letter to Du Tisné from the missionaries at Kaskaskia," dated January 10, 1725, in Thwaites, *WHC, French Regime I*, 16:454.

64. "De Lignery makes a temporary peace with the Foxes; policy of the French toward that tribe," in Thwaites, *WHC French Regime I*, 16:464–65.

65. Ibid., 16:466.

66. Joseph Peyser, "The Fate of the Fox Survivors, A Dark Chapter in the History of the French in the Upper Country 1726–1737," *Wisconsin Magazine of History* (Madison: Wisconsin Historical Society, 1989–1990), 91.

67. Edmunds and Peyser, *The Fox Wars*, 129.

68. Ibid., 135.

69. Ibid., 137.

70. "Letter of De Villiers," *The French Regime in Wisconsin, II—1727–1748*, Collections of the State Historical Society of Wisconsin (Madison: State Historical Society of Wisconsin, 1906), 17:114–15. It is probable that the Illinois sent messengers to Fort de Chartres first, as Saint Ange, commandant of the fort, had arrived at the Fox Fort before De Villiers' group. See also *History and Archaeology: New Evidence of the 1730 Mesquakie (Renard, Fox) Fort*, Lenville J. Stelle Center for Social Research, Parkland College (1992), accessed March 24, 2013, http://virtual.parkland.edu/lstelle1/len/center_for_social_research/Fox_Fort/idotfx.htm.

71. "Letter of commandant of Detroit (Deschaillons) to Beauharnois," dated August 22, 1730, in *The French Regime in Wisconsin, II*, 17:100.

72. According to De Villiers, the Mesquakie had also attacked the Potawatomi, Kickapoo, and Mascouten tribes. These tribes appear to have been with the Illinois from Starved Rock when Mesquakie advancement was halted in the Illinois prairies. It is unknown where these battles occurred. See "Letter of De Villiers," in *The French Regime in Wisconsin, II*, 17:114.

73. D'Auteuil de Monceaux in Peyser, "The Fate of the Fox Survivors," 106.

74. Edmunds and Peyser, *The Fox Wars*, 150–51.

75. D'Auteuil de Monceaux in Peyser, "The Fate of the Fox Survivors," 107, states that five hundred—two hundred men and three hundred women and children—were killed. "Périer to Maurepas," dated March 25, 1731, states that eleven to twelve hundred Mesquakie were killed. *Mississippi Provincial Archives, 1729–1748*, vol. 4, French Dominion, ed. Rowland Dunbar, A.G. Sanders, and Patricia Kay Galloway (Baton Rouge: Louisiana State University Press, 1984), 72, accessed February 23, 2013, http://books.google.com/books?id=4c566jr4-DgC &printsec=frontcover&dq=Mississippi+Provincial+Archives,+vol.+4&hl=en&sa=X&ei= QOUoUd-ML-bf2QXKpoGoBw&ved=0CDMQ6AEwAA#v=onepage&q=Mississippi%20 Provincial%20Archives%2C%20vol.%204&f=false.

8. 1730–1776: We Leave, Never to Return

1. "Letter of commandant of Detroit (Deschaillons) to Beauharnois," dated August 22, 1730, in *WHC French Regime II*, 17:100.

2. "Hocquart to the French Minister," in *WHC French Regime II*, 17:129.

3. "Resumé of French relations with the Foxes from 1715 to 1726," dated April 27, 1727, *WHC French Regime II*, 17:3.

4. Jablow, *Indians of Illinois and Indiana*, 183.

5. Jesuit missionary, Jean-Antoine-Robert Le Boullenger, in Judith A. Franke, *French Peoria and the Illinois Country, 1673–1846*, Illinois State Museum Popular Science Series, vol. 12 (Springfield, Illinois State Museum, 1995), 89.

6. Zitomersky, *French Americans–Native Americans*, 273. He wrote, "Here we may note that they collectively show a rather important decline among the Illinois from an estimated total warrior population of 760 in 1723 to one of something over or about 600 by the early 1730s—that is about a 21% decline—no small amount—in only a decade or so

7. Zitomersky, *French Americans–Native Americans*, 258.

8. "Beauharnois to French Minister of the Marine Jean-Frédéric Phélypeaux, count de Maurepas," dated October 1, 1731, in Joseph Peyser, "The Fate of the Fox Survivors: A Dark Chapter in the History of the French in the Upper Country, 1726–1737," *Wisconsin Magazine of History* 73 (Madison: Wisconsin Historical Society, 1989–1990), 96.

9. Edmunds and Peyser, *The Fox Wars*, 164; and *WHC French Regime II*, 17:148–52.

10. Peyser, "The Fate of the Fox Survivors," 97.

11. "Beauharnois to the French Minister," dated May 1, 1733, in *WHC French Regime II*, 17:174. Researcher Joseph Jablow suggests a different location for the 1732 Fox fort. Jablow wrote, "Having weighed the possible alternatives with regard to their location, it may be suggested that the likelihood is greater that the Fox fort was west of the Mississippi in 1732." See Jablow, *Indians of Illinois and Indiana*, 183.

12. Edmunds and Peyser, *The Fox Wars*, 172–73.

13. Ibid., 175; see also "Letter of Beauharnois to the French Minister," dated July 1733, in *WHC French Regime II*, 17:182–83.

14. Peyser, "The Fate of the Fox Survivors," 99.

15. Edmunds and Peyser, *The Fox Wars*, 184–85.

16. Peyser, "The Fate of the Fox Survivors," 99.

17. Ibid., 99.

18. Edmunds and Peyser, *The Fox Wars*, 187–88.

19. Ibid.; see also "Letter of Beauharnois to the French Minister," dated October 9, 1735, in *WHC French Regime II*, 17:216–21.

20. "Letter from Beauharnois to the French Minister," dated October 1, 1733, in *WHC French Regime II*, 17:183.

21. "Beauharnois to the French Minister," dated July 1, 1733, in *WHC French Regime II*, 17:183–84.

22. "Enumeration of the Indian Tribes Connected with the Government of Canada; The Warriors and Armorial bearing of each nation," in *WHC French Regime II*, 17:245–51.

23. Ibid.

24. "Beauharnois and Hocquart to the French Minister," dated October 16, 1736, in *WHC French Regime II*, 17:259–60.

25. Ibid., 318–20. Words of the Puants to the Sieur Morin and Words of Mekaga, a Renard chief, in "Letter of Beauharnois to the French Minister," dated June 30 and October 12, 1739.

26. Ibid., 366. "Extract from a letter from Beauharnois to the French Minister," dated September 26, 1741.

27. Ibid.

28. R. David Edmunds. *Potawatomis, Keepers of the Fire* (Norman and London: University of Oklahoma Press, 1978), 48–49; "La Jonquière to the French minister," dated September 25, 1751, *The French Regime in Wisconsin—1743–1760*, Collections of the State Historical Society of Wisconsin, ed. Reuben Gold Thwaites, 18:89, accessed February 23, 2013, http://content.wisconsinhistory.org/cdm4/document.php?CISOROOT=/whc&CISOPTR=14910&CISOSHOW=14458.

29. Ibid., 677.

30. Zitomersky, *French Americans–Native Americans*, 285. In 1712, there were approximately 3,750 Peoria Indians, but by 1758 their population had shrunk to only 1,250.

31. "Macarty to Vaudreil," dated September 2, 1752, in *Illinois on the Eve of the Seven Years' War*, Collections of the Illinois State Historical Library, vol. III, ed. Theodore Calvin Pease and Ernestine Jenison (Springfield: Trustees of the Illinois State Historic Library, 1940), 667.

32. Zitomersky, *French Americans–Native Americans*, 279.

33. Temple, *Indian Villages of the Illinois Country*, 47.

34. "Vaudreuil to the French Minister," June 24, 1760, in O'Callaghan, *Colonial History of New York*, 10:1092.

35. Passerat de La Chapelle, "La Chapelle's Remarkable Retreat Through the Mississippi Valley, 1760–1761," ed. Louise P. Kellogg, *The Mississippi Valley Historical Review* (June 1935), 66.

36. Ibid., 67.

37. Ibid., 68.

38. The British wielded trade power as they controlled the Illinois trade. They also provided security to the Illinois tribe. For example, after a Peoria killed the famous war chief Pontiac at Cahokia in 1769, the panicked Illinois left their villages and fled to Fort de Chartres to beseech the British commandant under Major Wilkins, for British protection against Pontiac's allies, who the Illinois believed would exact revenge for Pontiac's killing.

39. Archives de la Société de Jésus Canada Français, Montreal. Ms. Pierre Potier, Gazettes, p. 171, "Chemin de S. joseph aux illinois par Le tiatiki."

40. Anonymous, "Minutes of Mr. Hamburgh's Journal, 1763," in *Travels in the American Colonies*, ed. Newton D. Mereness (New York: Macmillan, 1916), 359–64.

41. Patrick Kennedy, "Mr. Patrick Kennedy's Journal up the Illinois River," in *A Topographical Description of the Western Territory of North America*, ed. Gilbert Imlay (London: printed for J. Debrett, 1797), 510.

42. Jablow, *Indians of Illinois and Indiana*, 282.

43. Thomas G. Conway. "Potawatomi Politics," *Journal of the Illinois State Historical Society* 65, no. 4 (Winter 1972): 398. This is the model that the Potawatomi practiced in northern Illinois during the first thirty years of the nineteenth century.

9. 1777–1840: The Big Knives Will Be in Control

1. Coulton Storm, "Lieutenant John Armstrong's Map of the Illinois River, 1790," *Journal of the Illinois State Historical Society* 37 (March 1944): 48–53.

2. Hugh Heward, *Hugh Heward's Journal from Detroit to the Illinois: 1790*, accessed February 23, 2013, http://archive.lib.msu.edu/MMM/JA/09/a/JA09a001p008.pdf.

3. Tribes included in the treaty were the Wendat as well as the Delaware, Odawa, Ojibwe, Potawatomi, and Miami. See the Treaty of Greenville, accessed February 23, 2013, http://www.earlyamerica.com/earlyamerica/milestones/greenville/text.html.

4. Gary Clayton Anderson, *Kinsmen of Another Kind, Dakota-White Relations in the Upper Mississippi Valley, 1650–1862* (St. Paul: Minnesota Historical Society Press, 1984), 156, 230.

5. Sauk Indian Quash-ma-quilly (Jumping Fish) in "Memorandum of Talks between Edmund P. Gaines and the Sauk," held at Rock Island, Mississippi River, June 4, 5, 7, 1831, in *The Black Hawk War 1831–1832*, Collections of the Illinois State Historical Library, vol. 2, Letters and Papers part I, ed. Ellen M. Whitney (Springfield: Illinois State Historical Library, 1973), 28–29.

6. William T. Hagan, *The Sac and Fox Indians* (Norman and London: University of Oklahoma Press, 1958), 16–22; and Temple, *Indian Villages*, 98–99.

7. *Black Hawk War 1831–1832*, vol. 2, part 1, 29.

8. Black Partridge quoted in Jablow, *Indians of Illinois and Indiana*, 402.

9. The Treaty of St. Louis in 1816 finalized this agreement.

10. Jablow, *Indians of Illinois and Indiana*, 377.

11. Edmunds, *Potawatomis*, 186–87.

12. Hagan, *The Sac and Fox Indians*, 62–66.

13. Jablow, *Indians of Illinois and Indiana*, 416.

14. Henry Rowe Schoolcraft, "Travels in the Central Portions of the Mississippi Valley: Comprising Observations on its Mineral Geography, Internal Resources, and Aboriginal Population," *Pictures of Illinois, One Hundred Years Ago*, in Milo Milton Quaife (Chicago: Lakeside Press, 1918), 108.

15. 250 feet high is an exaggeration. The Rock rises about 125 feet above the river. He later corrected this error by writing: "Of the height of this cliff, the estimate which we have given is merely conjectural. The effect upon the observer is striking and imposing." Later writers who used Schoolcraft as a source kept Starved Rock's height at 250 feet.

16. The stones were possibly slag left from the blacksmith's forge during the time of La Salle's Starved Rock fort.

17. "Travels," 106. Biological sense: for example, the black bear was extirpated from Illinois in 1810. However, there were other black bear populations in Wisconsin, Michigan, and Minnesota.

18. Schoolcraft, "Travels in the Central Portions of the Mississippi Valley," 106.

19. Elmer Baldwin, *History of La Salle County, Illinois* (Chicago: Rand, McNally, 1877), 80.

20. Ibid., 80–81.

21. Jesse White, Secretary of State, *Origin and Evolution of Illinois Counties* (printed by the authority of the State of Illinois, June 2005), 9.

22. Anonymous, "Rock Fort on the Illinois River," *The Monthly Repository and Library of Entertaining Knowledge* 1, no. 11 (New York: Francis S. Wiggins Publisher, April 1831), 340–42.

23. Timothy Flint, *The History and Geography of the Mississippi Valley*, 2nd ed., 2 vols. (Cincinnati: E.H. Flint and L.R. Lincoln, 1832), 331.

24. Fort Johnson was built to shelter local residents who had fled to Ottawa after the attack on the Davis settlement by the Potawatomi that occurred on May 21, 1832.

25. James Hall, *Tales of the Border* (Saddle River, N.J: Literature House, 1970), 15–19.

26. Ray Richardson, *Ray Richardson's History of Tonica, the First 100 Years* (1990; reprint, LaSalle County Historical Society, Utica, 1953), 31.

27. Charles Fenno Hoffman, *A Winter in the West*, 2 vols. (New York: Harper and Brothers, 1835), 1:273–79.

28. Richardson, *History of Tonica*, 21–22.

29. General W.H.L. Wallace commanded one of U.S. Grant's six divisions at the Battle of Pittsburgh Landing (Shiloh) in April 1862. His determined stand at the "Hornet's Nest," where he was mortally wounded, helped save Grant's army. Isabel Wallace, *The Life and Letters of General W.H.L. Wallace* (Chicago: R.R. Donnelly and Sons, 1909), 2. Isabel was the general's adopted daughter.

30. Baldwin, *History of La Salle County*, 174.

31. Carl O. Sauer, Gilbert H. Cady, and Henry Cowles, *Starved Rock State Park and its Environs* (Chicago: University of Chicago Press, 1918), 71.

32. The Northern Cross Railroad, funded by the 1837 Illinois Internal Improvement Act, was the first railroad in Illinois. See Illinois State Museum, accessed April 28, 2015, http://www.museum.state.il.us/RiverWeb/harvesting/transportation/trains/northern_cross.html.

33. Baldwin, *History of La Salle County*, 175–76.

34. *Illinois Free Trader*, October 15, 1841.

35. *Illinois Free Trader*, August 28, 1840.

36. *Illinois Free Trader*, September 4, 1840.

37. *Illinois Free Trader*, September 4, 1840.

10. 1841–1885: Wait! Its Heart Is Still Beating

1. *Illinois Free Trader*, August 14, 1840.

2. *Illinois Free Trader*, December 31, 1841.

3. *Chicago Daily Tribune*, December 3, 1857.

4. *Chicago Daily Tribune*, November 24, 1858. W.P. Jones and J. Wesley Jones founded the "Female College at Evanston" in 1855.

5. *Chicago Press and Tribune*, September 20, 1860.

6. Sauer, Cady, and Cowles, *Starved Rock and Environs*, 81.

7. Charlotte Gardner Garside, *A Short History of the Illinois and Michigan Canal* (LaSalle County Historical Society, 1971), 6.

8. See Woermann Maps, slide 21.

9. It is uncertain exactly what the Newell Site was. Unfortunately, nothing of it remains today because it was destroyed by people digging for artifacts during the 1930s. Some items that allegedly came from the site such as gun parts, glass beads, and other artifacts of European origin are on display at the Starved Rock Visitor Center located at Starved Rock State Park.

10. Copies of the hand-sketched maps were given to the author by US Army Corps of Engineers personnel from the Starved Rock Lock and Dam.

11. The site was confirmed to have been the Grand Illinois Village during the period of La Salle in the 1940s by Dr. Sara Tucker of the University of Chicago.

12. Daniel Hitt, quoted in Robert L. Hall, *Archaeology of the Soul, North American Indian Belief and Ritual* (Urbana and Chicago: University of Illinois Press, 1997), 17, accessed February 23, 2013, http://books.google.com/books?id=yUvbvgFakkwC&printsec=frontco ver&source=gbs_ge_summary_r&cad=0#v=snippet&q=told%20us%20what%20we%20 should%20see%20every%20time%20before%20we%20got%20there&f=false.

13. *Ottawa Weekly Republican Times*, September 11, 1873. Bushnell was state senator and state attorney general and had been LaSalle County prosecutor.

14. The event is covered in the *Ottawa Free Trader*, September 20, 1873. The *Free Trader* states there were between five and six thousand people in attendance while the *Ottawa Weekly Republican*, September 18, 1873, says that there were between three and four thousand.

15. According to the *Ottawa Daily Republican*, Bowman "made a series of twenty elegant, large and stereoscopic views, which, for excellence and beauty, have never been equaled." *Ottawa Daily Republican*, September 20, 1873.

16. Washington Bushnell, *Ottawa Free Trader*, September 20, 1873.

17. *Ottawa Free Trader*, February 15, 1890.

18. W.W. Calkins, *Chicago Tribune*, January 2, 1875. Archaeologists Edward B. Jelks and Preston A. Hawks reported, "As at most places in the site [summit of Starved Rock], Area 2 had been repeatedly disturbed by the Indians, French, the Civilian Conservation Corps of the 1930s, and treasure hunters, confounding the stratigraphy." See Edward B. Jelks and Preston A. Hawks, *Archaeological Explorations at Starved Rock, Illinois (11-Ls-12)*, Midwestern Archaeological Research Center (Illinois State University, Normal, Illinois, 1982), 11.

19. *Chicago Daily Tribune*, November 14, 1877.

20. Nehemiah Matson, *French and Indians of the Illinois River* (Carbondale and Edwardsville: Southern Illinois University Press, 2001), 183.

21. Dan Churney, *Ottawa Daily Times*, May 25, 2011, accessed February 23, 2013, http://mywebtimes.com/archives/ottawa/display.php?id=432685.

22. Tonti, "Henri Tonty Letters," in Wedel, *A Jean Delanglez Anthology*, 235. Tonti also wrote: "It cost me 800 *pistoles* to equip them [the 300 Indians he led in Denonville's Iroquois campaign] and I have never been reimbursed anything."

23. Anonymous, "Excursion to Starved Rock," in the *Henry Republican*, August 12, 1875, found at the Genealogy Trails History Group, accessed February 23, 2013, http:// genealogytrails.com/ill/lasalle/history/StarvedRock.html.

24. Richardson, *History of Tonica*, 32.

25. Sauer, Cady, and Cowles, *Starved Rock and Environs*, 74.

11. 1886–1911: It Will Always Be Sitting Here, Beautiful

1. *Ottawa Free Trader*, February 20, 1890.

2. The Methodist National Camp Meeting was held between August 24 and September 9, 1900, at Buffalo Rock.

3. Anonymous, *Nattinger's Souvenir of Ottawa, Illinois in Nineteen Hundred, Complete Review* (Ottawa, 1995; repr., La Salle County Genealogy Guild, 1900), 101.

4. Buffalo Rock State Park, Illinois Department of Natural Resources, accessed February 26, 2013, http://dnr.state.il.us/lands/landmgt/PARKS/i&m/east/buffalo/home.htm.

5. *Ottawa Free Trader*, February 16, 1890.

6. Harris W. Huehl to Daniel Hitt, January 7, 1890, Starved Rock State Park Archives.

7. Huehl to Hitt, February 3, 1890, Starved Rock State Park Archives.

8. Hitt's attorney was R. F. Lincoln.

9. Contract drawn up and signed between Ferdinand Walther and Daniel Hitt, dated February 15, 1890, in Ottawa, Illinois, Starved Rock State Park Archives.

10. Joseph Mulke to Huncke, Harris, Huehl, and Walther, dated March 21, 1890, Starved Rock State Park Archives.

11. The other members of the company were Harris Huehl, E. W. Hencke, and Ed Reinke.

12. *Ottawa Free Trader*, December 14, 1889.

13. *Ottawa Free Trader*, February 14, 1891.

14. *Ottawa Free Trader*, May 30, 1891.

15. *Ottawa Free Trader*, February 21, 1891.

16. *Ottawa Free Trader*, May 30, 1891.

17. John D. Hammond, "The Cliffs, Glens, and Canyons of the Illinois Valley in LaSalle County, Ill.," in *Souvenir Starved Rock* (Ottawa: Free Trader Publishing House, 1894), and *La Salle Daily Tribune*, July 14, 1910.

18. Fred A. Finney, "Starved Rock Fort," *Illinois Archaeology* 22, no. 1 (2010): 240–55, accessed April 22, 2013, http://www.academia.edu/1910188/The_Starved_Rock_Fort.

19. *Ottawa Free Trader*, July 4, 1891.

20. *Ottawa Free Trader*, July 11, 1891.

21. *Ottawa Free Trader*, September 19, 1902.

22. It is probable that the locals had a name for Ottawa canyon, but whatever it was, it was unknown to the publishers of the 1912 LaSalle County plat book.

23. Sauer, Cady, and Cowles, *Starved Rock and Environs*, 81.

24. *Report of the Illinois State Park Commission of the State of Illinois* (Springfield: Illinois State Journal Co. State Printers, 1913), 25.

25. According to one Starved Rock area newspaper, public interest in purchasing Starved Rock as a state park first arose in 1888. *La Salle Daily Tribune*, December 15, 1911.

26. Sauer, Cady, and Cowles, *Starved Rock and Environs*, 82.

27. William Steinbacher-Kemp, "The Establishment of Starved Rock State Park," in the *Journal of Illinois History* 2 (Summer 1999): 127–29.

28. Ibid., 134.

29. *La Salle Daily Tribune*, February 16, 1911.

30. Steinbacher-Kemp, "Establishment of Starved Rock State Park," 135.

31. *La Salle Daily Tribune*, February 20, 1911.

32. The penalties for sale, distribution, drinking, or giving away alcoholic beverages on park property were severe. The first offense carried a fine of no less than $25 and no more than $100. A second conviction carried a fine of no less than $50 and no more than $200, and confinement in the La Salle County Jail for no less than ten days. *La Salle Daily Tribune*, June 2, 1911.

33. Steinbacher-Kemp, "Establishment of Starved Rock State Park," 137–38; also *La Salle Daily Tribune*, March 16, 1911.

34. James was from Evanston, Richards from Ottawa, and Crowe from Kewaunee.

35. Renovations on the hotel complex had not been completed by opening day.

BIBLIOGRAPHY

Primary Sources

Anderson, Melville B., trans. *Relation of Henri de Tonty Concerning the Explorations of La Salle from 1678 to 1683*. Chicago: Caxton Club, 1898.

——. *Relation of the Discoveries and Voyages of Cavelier de La Salle from 1679 to 1681, The Official Narrative*. Chicago: Caxton Club, 1901.

Anonymous. "Chemin de S. joseph aux illinois par Le tiatiki." Archives de la Société de Jésus Canada Français, Montreal. Ms. Pierre Potier, *Gazettes*.

Anonymous. "Minutes of Mr. Hamburgh's Journal, 1763." In *Travels in the American Colonies*, edited by Newton D. Mereness. New York: Macmillan, 1916.

Anonymous. "Rock Fort on the Illinois River." *The Monthly Repository and Library of Entertaining Knowledge* 1, no. 11. New York: Francis S. Wiggins Publisher, April 1831.

"Baugy to La Durantaye," dated March 24, 1684. National Archives of Canada, Source RC 6515, call number MG1-Series C11A.

Cavelier de La Salle to Jacques Bourdon d'Autray. Deed in the French America Collection, Chicago History Museum Research Center.

Charlevoix, Pierre-Francis Xavier de. *Journal of a Voyage to North America*. Edited by Louise Phelps Kellogg. 2 vols. Ann Arbor: University Microfilms, 1966.

Cox, Isaac Joslin, ed. *The Journeys of Rene Robert Cavelier Sieur de La Salle*. 2 vols. New York: Allerton Book Co. 1906.

Delanglez, Jean, ed. "Cavelier, Jean, The Journal of Jean Cavelier." Chicago: Institute of Jesuit History, 1938.

Deslisle, Legardeur. "The Journal of Legardeur Delisle, 1722. Edited by Stanley Faye. *Journal of the Illinois State Historical Society* 38 (March 1945).

Dunbar, Roland, A. G. Sanders, and Patricia Kay Galloway, eds. French Dominion, Mississippi Provincial Archives. vol. 4, 1729–1748, Baton Rouge: Louisiana State University Press, 1984, in Google Books, https://books.google.com/books?id=4c566jr4-DgC&pg=PA11&dq=mississippi+provincial+archives+volume+4&hl=en&sa=X&ved=0ahUKEwjXhvrYhYDgAhUFIVAKHWgMDhQQ6AEIKjAA#v=onepage&q=mississippi%20provincial%20archives%20volume%204&f=false.

French, Benjamin Franklin, ed. *Historical Collections of Louisiana*, part 1. New York: Wiley and Putnam, 1846.

The French Regime in Wisconsin, I—1634–1727. Collections of the State Historical Society of Wisconsin. Vol. 16. Madison: State Historical Society of Wisconsin, 1902.

The French Regime in Wisconsin, II—1727–1748. Collections of the State Historical Society of Wisconsin. Vol. 17. Madison: State Historical Society of Wisconsin, 1906.

"Grant of La Salle to D'Autray, 1683." *Cavelier de La Salle to Jacques Bourdon d'Autray*. Deed in French America Collection, Chicago History Museum Research Center.

Hennepin, Louis. *A New Discovery of a Vast Country in America*. Edited by Reuben Gold Thwaites. 2 vols. Toronto: Coles Publishing, 1974.

Heward, Hugh. *Hugh Heward's Journal from Detroit to the Illinois: 1790*. Accessed February 23, 2013, http://archive.lib.msu.edu/MMM/JA/09/a/JA09a001p008.pdf.

Hubbard, Gurdon Saltonstall. *The Autobiography of Gurdon Saltonstall Hubbard*. New York: Citadel Press, 1969.

Kellogg, Louise Phelps, ed. *Early Narratives of the Northwest, 1634–1699*. New York: Scribner's Sons, 1917, reprinted by Heritage Books, 2001.

Kennedy, Patrick. "Mr. Patrick Kennedy's Journal up the Illinois River." In *A Topographical Description of the Western Territory of North America*. Edited by Gilbert Imlay. London: printed for J. Debrett, 1797.

Margry, Pierre, ed. *Découvertes et établissements des Français dans l'ouest et dans le sud de l'Amérique septentrionale, 1614–1754*. 6 vols. Paris: Maisonneuve, 1875–1891.

Mereness, Newton D. "The Journal of Diron D'Artaguette." In *Travels in the American Colonies*. New York: Macmillan, 1916.

Miami Tribal History Document Series, Great Lakes—Ohio Valley Ethnohistory Collection, Erminie Wheeler-Voegelin Archives. Indiana University, Bloomington.

O'Callaghan, Edmund Bailey, ed. *Documents Relating to the Colonial History of New York*. 15 vols. on CD. Saugerties, NY: Hope Farm Press, 2001.

Pease, Theodore Calvin, and Ernestine Jenison, eds. *Illinois on the Eve of the Seven Years's War*, Collections of the Illinois State Historical Library. Vol. 3. Springfield: Trustees of the Illinois State Historic Library, 1940.

Pease, Theodore Calvin, and Raymond C. Werner, eds. *The French Foundations, 1680–1693*. Collections of the Illinois State Historical Library 23, French series 1. Springfield: Trustees of the Illinois State Historical Library, 1934.

Schoolcraft, Henry Rowe. "Travels in the Central Portions of the Mississippi Valley: Comprising Observations on its Mineral Geography, Internal Resources, and Aboriginal Population." In *Pictures of Illinois, One Hundred Years Ago*. Edited by Milo Milton Quaife. Chicago: Lakeside Press, 1918.

Thwaites, Reuben Gold, ed. *Jesuit Relations and Allied Documents, 1610–1791*. Cleveland: Burrows, 1901.

Whitney, Ellen M., ed. *The Black Hawk War 1831–1832*. Collections of the Illinois State Historical Library. Vol. 2, Letters and Papers, part 1. Springfield: Illinois State Historical Library, 1973.

Secondary Sources

Anderson, Gary Clayton. *Kinsmen of Another Kind, Dakota-White Relations in the Upper Mississippi Valley, 1650–1862*. St. Paul: Minnesota Historical Society Press, 1984.

Anonymous. "Excursion to Starved Rock." In *The Henry Republican*, Aug. 12, 1875. Genealogy Trails History Group. Accessed February 23, 2013, http://genealogytrails.com/ill/lasalle/history/StarvedRock.html.

Baldwin, Elmer. *History of La Salle County, Illinois*. Chicago: Rand, McNally, 1877.

Balesi, Charles J. *The Time of the French in the Heart of North America, 1673–1818*. Chicago: Paginae Publications, 2014.

Buffalo Rock State Park from the Illinois Department of Natural Resources. Accessed February 26, 2013, http://dnr.state.il.us/lands/landmgt/PARKS/i&m/east/buffalo/home.htm.

Cleland, Charles E. *Rites of Conquest*. Ann Arbor: University of Michigan Press, 1992.

Delanglez, Jean. "The Voyages of Tonti in North America 1678–1704." *Mid-America: An Historical Review* 26 (October 1944).

Eccles, William, J. *The Canadian Frontier 1534–1760*. Revised edition. Albuquerque: University of New Mexico Press, 1983.

The French in North America: 1500–1783. Revised edition. East Lansing: Michigan State University Press, 1998.

Edmunds, R. David. *Potawatomis, Keepers of the Fire*. Norman and London: University of Oklahoma Press, 1978.

Edmunds, R. David, and Joseph L. Peyser. *The Fox Wars, The Mesquakie Challenge to New France*. Norman and London: University of Oklahoma Press, 1993.

Ekberg, Carl J. *Stealing Indian Women, Native Slavery in the Illinois Country*. Urbana and Chicago: University of Illinois Press, 2007.

Flint, Timothy. *The History and Geography of the Mississippi Valley*. 2nd edition. 2 vols. Cincinnati: E. H. Flint and L. R. Lincoln, 1832.

Franke, Judith A. *French Peoria and the Illinois Country, 1673–1846*. Illinois State Museum Popular Science Series. Vol. 12. Springfield, Illinois State Museum, 1995.

Garside, Charlotte Gardner. *A Short History of the Illinois and Michigan Canal*. LaSalle County Historical Society, 1971.

Hagan, William T. *The Sac and Fox Indians*. Norman and London: University of Oklahoma Press, 1958.

Hagen, Richard. Richard Hagen to Joseph F. Booton, Chief of Design, Division of Architecture and Engineering, Illinois Department of Public Works and Buildings, dated June 1, 1950. Series of correspondences from excavations at Starved Rock during the summer of 1950.

Hall, James. *Tales of the Border*. Saddle River, NJ: 1835, reprinted by Literature House, 1970.

Hammond, John D. "The Cliffs, Glens, and Canyons of the Illinois Valley in LaSalle County, Ill." In *Souvenir Starved Rock*. Ottawa (Free Trader Publishing House, 1894), and *La Salle Daily Tribune*, July 14, 1910.

Hoffman, Charles Fenno. *A Winter in the West*. 2 vols. New York: Harper and Brothers, 1835.

Jablow, Joseph. *Indians of Illinois and Indiana*. New York and London: Garland Publishing, 1974.

Kellogg, Louise Phelps, *Fox Indians During the French Regime*. Madison: State Historical Society of Wisconsin, 1907.

Leavelle, Tracy Neal. *The Catholic Calumet*. Philadelphia: University of Pennsylvania Press, 2012.

Matson, Nehemiah. *French and Indians of the Illinois River*. Carbondale and Edwardsville: Southern Illinois University Press, 2001 reprint of 1874 edition.

Nattinger's Souvenir of Ottawa, Illinois in Nineteen Hundred, Complete Review. Ottawa: 1995, reprint of 1900 work published by the LaSalle County Genealogy Guild.

Parkman, Francis. *La Salle and the Discovery of the Great West*. Edited by Jon Krakauer. New York: Modern Library, 1999.

Richardson, Ray. *History of Tonica, the First 100 Years*. Tonica, IL: 1953, reprinted by LaSalle County Historical Society, 1990.

Sugden, John. *Tecumseh, A Life*. New York: Henry Holt. 1997.

Temple, Wayne. *Indian Villages of the Illinois Country*. Illinois State Museum Scientific Papers, vol. 2, part 2. Springfield: Illinois State Museum, 1966.

Wedel, Mildred Mott, ed. *A Jean Delanglez, S.J., Anthology*. New York and London: Garland Publishing, 1985.

Wallace, Isabel. *The Life and Letters of General WHL. Wallace*. Chicago: R. R. Donnelly and Sons, 1909.

White, Jesse. *Origin and Evolution of Illinois Counties*. Printed by the authority of the State of Illinois, June 2005.

Zitomersky, Joseph. *French Americans—Native Americans in Eighteenth Century French Colonial Louisiana*. Lund, Sweden: Lund University Press, 1995.

Journals and Reference Material

Conway, Thomas G. "Potawatomi Politics." *Journal of the Illinois State Historical Society* 65, no. 4 (Winter 1972).

Costa, David J. "Illinois." *Society for the Study of the Indigenous Languages of the Americas* 25, no. 4 (January 2007).

Eccles, William J. "Brisay de Denonville, Jacques-Rene de, Marquis de Denonville." *Dictionary of Canadian Biography*. Vol. 2. University of Toronto/Université Laval: 1969, revised 1982. Accessed June 22, 2018, http://www.biographi.ca/en/bio/brisay_de_denonville_jacques_rene_de_2E.html.

Finney, Fred A. "Starved Rock Fort." *Illinois Archaeology* 22, no. 1 (2010): 240–55. Accessed April 22, 2013, http://www.academia.edu/1910188/The_Starved_Rock_Fort.

Garraghan, Gilbert J., S.J. "La Salle's Jesuit Days." *Mid-America Magazine* 19 (1937).

Hall, Robert L. *Archaeology of the Soul, North American Indian Belief and Ritual*. Urbana and Chicago: University of Illinois Press, 1997. Accessed February 23, 2013, http://books.google.com/books?id=yUvbvgFakkwC&printsec=frontcover&source=gbs_ge_summary_r&cad=0#v=snippet&q=told%20us%20what%20we%20should%20see%20every%20time%20before%20we%20got%20there&f=false.

Hamelin, Jean. *Baugy, Louis-Henri de, Chevalier de Baugy*. Dictionary of Canadian Biography, vol. 2. University of Toronto/Université Laval, 1969, revised 1982. Accessed June 22, 2018, http://www.biographi.ca/en/bio/baugy_louis_henri_de_2E.html.

Hauser, Raymond E. *Ethnohistory of the Illinois Indian Tribe 1673–1832*. PhD diss., Northern Illinois University, 1973.

Kellogg, Louie Phelps. "La Chapelle's Remarkable Retreat Through the Mississippi Valley, 1760–1761." *Mississippi Valley Historical Review* 22, no. 1 (June 1935).

Lee, David, and Terry Smyth. "Ouachala." *Dictionary of Canadian Biography*. Vol. 2. University of Toronto/Université Laval, 1969, revised 1982. Accessed June 22, 2018, http://www.biographi.ca/en/bio/ouachala_2E.html.

Hutchieson, Maud M. "Pierre-Gabriel Marest." *Dictionary of Canadian Biography*. Vol. 2. University of Toronto/Université Laval, 1969, revised 1982. Accessed June 22, 2018, http://www.biographi.ca/en/bio/marest_pierre_gabriel_2E.html.

McCafferty, Michael. "French Trader, Jesuit Brother, and Jesuit Scribe Par Exellence." *Journal of the Illinois State Historical Society* 104, no. 3 (Fall 2011).

——. "Illinois Voices, Observations on the Miami-Illinois Language." Chapter 8 in *Protohistory at the Grand Village of the Kaskaskia: The Illinois Country on the Eve of Colony*. Edited by Robert F. Mazrim. Studies in Archaeology, no. 10, Illinois State Archaeological Survey. Urbana: University of Illinois, 2015.

——. "The Illinois Place Name 'Pimiteoui.'" *Journal of the Illinois State Historical Society* 102, no. 2 (Summer 2009).

——. Kankakee, An Old Etymological Puzzle." *Names, Journal of Onomastics* 62, no. 2 (June 2014).

Peyser, Joseph. "The Fate of the Fox Survivors, A Dark Chapter in the History of the French in the Upper Country 1726–1737." *Wisconsin Magazine of History*. Wisconsin Historical Society, Madison, 1989–1990.

Report of the Illinois State Park Commission of the State of Illinois. Springfield: Illinois State Journal Co. State Printers, 1913.

Sauer, Carl O., Gilbert H. Cady, and Henry Cowles. *Starved Rock State Park and its Environs*. Chicago: University of Chicago Press, 1918.

Spillane, Edward. "François Xavier Charlevoix." *The Catholic Encyclopedia*. Vol. 3. New York: Robert Appleton Co. 1908. Accessed February 22, 2013, http://www.newadvent.org/cathen/03631a.htm.

Stearns, Raymond Phineas. "Joseph Kellogg, Observations on Senex's Map of North America (1710)." *Mississippi Valley Historical Review* 23, no. 3 (December 1936): 353. Accessed June 10, 2018, http://www.jstor.org/stable/1886369.

Steinbacher-Kemp, William. "The Establishment of Starved Rock State Park." *Journal of Illinois History* 2 (Summer 1999): 127–29.

Storm, Coulton. "Lieutenant John Armstrong's Map of the Illinois River, 1790." *Journal of the Illinois State Historical Society* 37 (March 1944).

Stueck, Adam. *A Place Under Heaven: Amerindian Torture and Cultural Violence in Colonial New France, 1609–1729*. PhD diss., Marquette University, 2012. http://epublications.marquette.edu/dissertations_mu/174.

Walthall, John A., and Thomas E. Emerson, eds. *Calumet and Fleur-De-Lys*. Washington and London: Smithsonian Institution Press, 1992.

Archaeological Reports

Brown, James A., ed. *The Zimmerman Site*. Report of Excavations at the Grand Village of Kaskaskia No. 9. Springfield: Illinois State Museum, 1961.

Emerson, Thomas E., ed. *The Archaeology of the Grand Village of the Illinois, Report of the Grand Village Research Project, 1991–1996: Grand Village of the Illinois State Historic Site (11-LS-13), LaSalle County, Illinois*. Urbana, Champaign: Board of Trustees of the University of Illinois, 1998.

Ferguson, Jacqueline A., ed. *Upper Illinois Valley Archaeology: The Cultural Resources of Starved Rock State Park*. Illinois State Museum Quaternary Studies Program Technical Report No. 94–866–14. Springfield, Illinois, May 1995.

Jelks, Edward B., and Preston A. Hawks. *Archaeological Explorations at Starved Rock, Illinois (11-Ls-12)*. Midwestern Archaeological Research Center, Illinois State University, Normal, Illinois, 1982.

Mazrim, Robert, ed. *Protohistory at the Grand Village of the Kaskaskia, the Illinois Country on the Eve of Colony*. Studies in Archaeology 10. Illinois State Archaeological Survey. Urbana: University of Illinois, 2015.

Stelle, Lenville J. *History and Archaeology: New Evidence of the 1730 Mesquakie (Renard, Fox) Fort*. Center for Social Research, Parkland College, 1992. Accessed March 24, 2013, http://virtual.parkland.edu/lstelle1/len/center_for_social_research/Fox_Fort/idotfx.htm.

Starved Rock State Park Archival Material

Richard Hagan to Joseph F. Booton, Chief of Design, Division of Architecture and Engineering, Illinois Department of Public Works and Buildings, dated June 1, 1950, from a series of correspondences from excavations at Starved Rock during the summer of 1950.

Harris W. Huehl to Daniel Hitt, January 7, 1890.
Harris W. Huehl to Daniel Hitt, February 3, 1890.
Joseph Mulke to E. W. Huncke, Harris Huehl, and Ferdinand Walther, dated March 21, 1890.

Newspapers

Chicago Daily Tribune
Illinois Free Trader, Ottawa, IL
Ottawa Daily Times, Ottawa, IL
Ottawa Weekly Republican Times, Ottawa, IL

Maps

A.C.E. maps of the Illinois River, 1867.
Franquelin, Jean-Baptiste. *La Colbertie*, 1674 map drawn for Louis Jolliet.
——. *La Frontenacie*, 1675 map drawn for Louis Jolliet.
Meskwaki and Sauk Migration. Cartography by R. Vanderwerff and J. Artz. Earthview Environmental Inc., Coralville, Iowa.
Woermann Maps. Army Corps of Engineers, 1883–1889.

CPSIA information can be obtained
at www.ICGtesting.com
Printed in the USA
BVHW030021101019
560731BV00001B/3/P